PRAISE FOR *OP*
DIGITAL STRATE

'*Optimizing Digital Strategy* successfully challenges the perception that more and more technology is the always answer – the organization is often the biggest barrier to online success and this book explores why and what to do about it. It's a commercial and engaging book that shows leaders how to improve performance. Full of useful frameworks and case examples, it sets out a structure with which leaders can assess their business and then focus on what needs to change to drive growth online.' **Anna Rawling, Managing Director, Product and Portfolio Strategy,** *The Economist*

'Every retail leader should read this book. What the authors have written will help today's leaders navigate the maze of the digital world. They remove the mask of mystery to help understand where a business should focus its energy, people and capital. The retail landscape is littered with examples of businesses spending huge sums of money and thousands of hours only for sales to go backwards. *Optimizing Digital Strategy* perfectly illustrates that technology alone is not the answer – the answer of course is the customer.' **Darren Topp, Chairman, Retail Executives Limited, and experienced retail CEO**

'*Optimizing Digital Strategy* gives business leaders a practical toolkit for thinking about and executing their digital strategy. The Good Growth team have condensed years of research and experience into a genuinely useful handbook.' **Alex Murray, Digital Director, Lidl UK**

'A practical handbook on running an online business, this is a must-read for the online practitioner through to the executive. Clear models, simple language, with plenty of examples across sectors make this an invaluable asset – it sits permanently on my desk! Importantly, *Optimizing Digital Strategy* offers good insights, perspective and practical advice on leadership and organizational challenges as a business develops.' **Ann Steer, Chief Customer Officer, N Brown Group plc**

'An informative and insightful book that should be read by all directors and business leaders. The distinction between good and best practice in this fast-moving area is a point well made. The case studies add richness and amplify the content.' **Helen Pitcher OBE, Chairman, Advanced Boardroom Excellence; President, INSEAD Directors Network; Chairman, pladis; Chairman, KidsOut**

'An essential read for any executive seeking to leverage the opportunities and mitigate the risks posed by digital transformation. This is a book that lays out a clear road map for how organizations can deliver on their digital strategies, recognizing that customer experience has become the primary basis for sustainable growth in today's hyper-competitive marketplace.' **Professor Michael Hartmann, Executive Director, EMBA in Digital Transformation, McMaster University**

'It would be hard to imagine a more authoritative guide to the pitfalls and opportunities of multichannel transformation.' **Ian Shepherd, former COO, Odeon Cinemas Group**

'This is a compelling guide to the creation and execution of business growth strategy in a high-rate-of-change digital age, rather than being about digital strategy in a purist/technical sense. It takes a systems-thinking approach and draws out the criticality of active and accountable business leadership, culture, ethics and, above all, the need for ruthless customer-, consumer- and marketplace-centricity.' **Stuart Fletcher, Portfolio Director and angel investor, former Global CEO, Bupa, and President International, Diageo plc**

'An excellent guide, full of insight, for those of us working in digital leadership. The authors have highlighted not the "best practices" but the "good practices" to be aware of – as they quite rightly mention, anyone who claims to follow best practice is fooling themselves in this fast-moving sector. The digital world is comparatively young and there is always something new to learn. Thus, whether you're starting your journey in digital leadership or have a few years under your belt, this book is a must-read.' **Tom Weeks, Sales Director UK, AB Tasty**

'The globalized, networked nature of the "Fourth Revolution" means that no organization can opt out of its impact. *Optimizing Digital Strategy* is therefore a must-read for all leaders trying to make sense of the decisions they need to make to transform their organizations. The book is a practical, step-by-step guide to how to oversee the successful execution of these decisions, and given that so much technology transformation ends in failure, a text that helps lift the fog is a rare jewel.' **Baroness Margaret McDonagh, Chair and Co-founder, The Pipeline – Executive Leadership Designed for Women**

'This is *the* book to read for leaders who are considering their future digital strategy and subscribe to the idea that those who cannot remember the mistakes of the past are condemned to repeat them. Including a wealth of historical and statistical data, as well as detailed management advice, *Optimizing Digital Strategy* will be the go-to resource for any executive on the road to a new digital future. Written in a clear no-nonsense style, and drawing on detailed research, it includes case studies and examples of digital projects from companies including the BBC, Poundland and Marks & Spencer, and analyses past failures to inform future successes. Structured as a cover-to-cover read, and a handy reference guide, this book will assist leaders in defining digital strategies that address their market, their customer and their company. An indispensable management resource.' **Anthony Harris, Mentor and Team Coach, Accelerate Cambridge, University of Cambridge, Judge Business School**

'*Optimizing Digital Strategy* is a great resource for any marketer, whether a relative novice or highly experienced, who wants an effective digital strategy at the heart of their business's growth engine. The book is nicely chunked into relevant chapters so you can dip in and out, focusing just on the topics pertinent to the latest knotty conundrum you're grappling with. It gives direction on how to frame an issue, practical examples of success and failure, and lists of what to ensure you think about on your path to success. A chapter on the "Dark Side" is particularly valuable in this day and age, where your consumers care as much about the ethics of your engagement with them as the efficacy of that engagement.

The rate of change in this area continues exponentially, but there are some universal truths the book points out that you need to hang on to. Everyone should have a copy in their favourites.' **Andraea Dawson-Shepherd, Senior leader, global consumer goods, Coty, Carlsberg, Reckitt Benckiser, Cadbury Schweppes**

'This book makes the case for leaders to get their organization strategy correct in digital. Culture as well as capability makes a significant difference in the ability of a business to grow online. The authors' approach to developing outstanding customer experiences cuts through the noise and provides leaders and their organizations the framework, tools and techniques to deliver sustainable results.' **Carina Conaghan, Director, UK Partnerships, Optimizely**

'Delivering growth in a dynamic digital world requires innovators and learners, not just experts. This book offers an inspiring leadership blueprint for essential good practice, including focus on returns, an obsession with the customer and, more than anything else, making the right informed choices at every key moment.' **Feilim Mackle, Independent Non-executive Director, Ardonagh Group**

Optimizing Digital Strategy

How to make informed, tactical decisions that deliver growth

Christopher Bones,
James Hammersley and
Nick Shaw

KoganPage

First published in Great Britain and the United States in 2019 by Kogan Page Limited

2nd Floor, 45 Gee Street	c/o Martin P Hill Consulting	4737/23 Ansari Road
London EC1V 3RS	122 W 27th St, 10th Floor	Daryaganj
United Kingdom	New York NY 10001	New Delhi 110002
www.koganpage.com	USA	India

© Good Growth Limited, 2019

The right of Good Growth Limited to be identified as the author of this work has been asserted by them in accordance with the Copyright, Designs and Patents Act 1988.

HARDBACK	978 0 7494 8781 2
PAPERBACK	978 0 7494 8372 2
E-ISBN	978 0 7494 8373 9

British Library Cataloguing-in-Publication Data

A CIP record for this book is available from the British Library.

Library of Congress Cataloging-in-Publication Data

Names: Bones, Chris, 1958- author. | Hammersley, James, author.
Title: Optimizing digital strategy : how to make informed, tactical decisions that deliver growth / Christopher Bones, James Hammersley and Nick Shaw.
Description: 1 Edition. | New York, NY : Kogan Page Ltd, [2018] | Includes bibliographical references and index.
Identifiers: LCCN 2018033619 (print) | LCCN 2018035132 (ebook) | ISBN 9780749483739 (ebook) | ISBN 9780749483722 (pbk.) | ISBN 9780749483739 (eISBN)
Subjects: LCSH: Business networks–Computer network resources. | Strategic planning. | Electronic commerce. | Organizational change.
Classification: LCC HD69.S8 (ebook) | LCC HD69.S8 .B646 2018 (print) | DDC 004.068/4–dc23

Typeset by Integra Software Services Pvt. Ltd, Pondicherry
Print production managed by Jellyfish
Printed and bound by CPI Group (UK) Ltd, Croydon, CR0 4YY

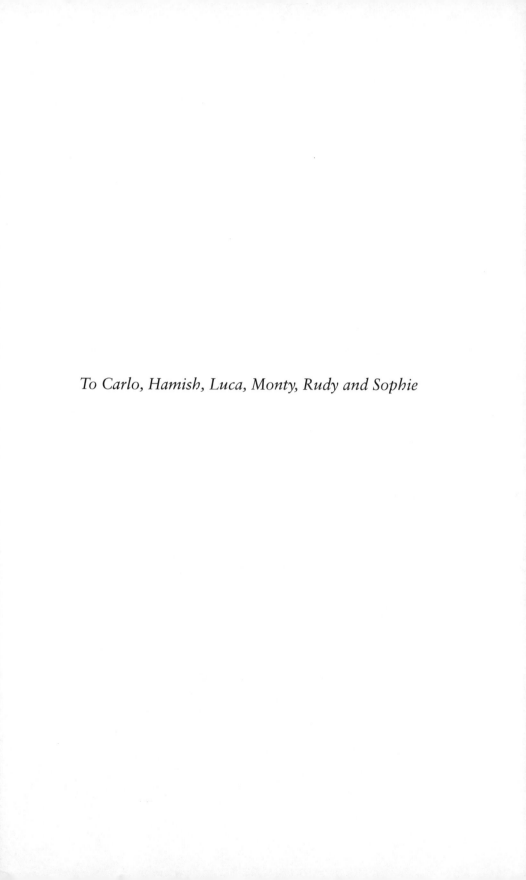

To Carlo, Hamish, Luca, Monty, Rudy and Sophie

CONTENTS

ABOUT THE AUTHORS

Christopher Bones

Chris Bones is Dean Emeritus, Henley Business School, Emeritus Professor of Creativity and Leadership at Alliance Manchester Business School and Chairman of Good Growth, which he co-founded with James Hammersley in 2011. Educated at Aberdeen University, his industry career spans time at Shell, Diageo and Cadbury Schweppes and he has developed the strategic thinking that has supported client engagements since the foundation of the business including those described in this book. Co-author of *Leading Digital Strategy* with James Hammersley, his book *The Cult of the Leader* won the UK Management Book of the Year Prize in 2012.

James Hammersley

James Hammersley is CEO of Good Growth. He is a serial entrepreneur with experience across a range of industry sectors before moving into digital in the late 2000s. Educated at London Metropolitan University and Cambridge he has also worked in Africa and for a World Health Organization programme aimed at eradicating malaria. He is a regular keynote speaker at major conferences in Europe and the United States on digital performance and growth and co-author of *Leading Digital Strategy*.

Nick Shaw

Nick Shaw is Chief Operating Officer of Good Growth. He is an engineer by discipline and holds a doctorate in innovation management from Loughborough University. His career started in design management and then moved into engineering process design, innovation management and finally into the leadership of commercial bids for major engineering and facilities management projects for one of the world's largest construction engineering firms. He has led the vast majority of client engagements over the last four years and has developed the processes and systems that sit behind the case studies explored in the book.

PREFACE

The biggest challenge with strategy in any sphere is making it happen. When making it happen relies on unfamiliar expertise, leaders are at an immediate disadvantage. This book gives leaders the structure to understand the issues, frame the choices and steer a thoughtful path to make their digital strategies happen.

In our work with over a hundred organizations on three continents we have met challenges and mistakes in the implementation of digital strategies that seem to be common, regardless of sector or geography. This book pulls these together into a set of recurring themes and offers a way forward that combines process, standards and commercial rigour into a blueprint for success.

There is no silver bullet: digital is a fast-moving world and is fraught with the now evergreen risk of investment in technology where projects regularly spend more, take longer and deliver less. It is also one where until recently many leaders have acted to empower digital experts and trust in their expertise, often with negative consequences. More recently, we have seen a trend for a more demanding, commercially oriented approach to all activities along the value chain and a reassertion of leadership. Certainly in our own client work we look to empower leaders to make better-informed decisions that focus on returns and growth rather than technology.

All our experience points towards one core truth about making digital happen: you have to put the customer at the heart of everything that you do. Unless you do this you will increase the risk that your investments in technology and marketing activities do not provide the returns or the growth that you were promised when you agreed them.

The starting point for this book is that leaders should look for ways to drive more return from investment in technology and digital marketing before they agree to invest further. It explores how best to do this, where to focus leadership opinion and shares some cases where applying the principles has changed performance.

It also looks at some of the wider issues associated with digital in business and explores the darker side of digital: the monopolistic behaviour of 'big tech', the challenges around the application of AI algorithms and the ethics in how business leaders address the implications of personal security, privacy and data ownership. Making digital happen comes with a responsibility as well as opportunity and leaders cannot abdicate their accountability for ensuring they do good for all stakeholders, not just the bottom line.

Finally, it shares examples, good and less so, and looks into at least the near future to think about where decisions today could impact future performance.

As with *Leading Digital Strategy* this book would not have been written without a great deal of hard work and support from our amazing team at Good Growth in both Exeter and New York, and the willing collaboration of some of our clients and contacts who have shared their insights and experiences to illustrate the major themes. A special thank you goes to industry leaders, John Boyle of Ann Summers, Simon Whittaker of Time Inc., Nicholas Spitzman of Regus Inc., Kevin Barrett of Howdens PLC, Rob Hattrell of eBay and Brett Moore of TripAdvisor.

All our Good Growth colleagues have played a role in creating the thinking in this book and some in particular deserve recognition for their role in building our thinking: Dave Cannell, Sarah Znideric and Johnny Gedye should take the credit for the work on Trust and Performance Marketing; Nicky Cunningham's work on organizational maturity and culture and capability mapping pushed on the thinking considerably; Hamish Bones worked on many of the cases shared and his experience has shaped much of our optimization approach and finally, Mike Duke is responsible for all our data points and a great deal of the thinking on testing approaches and modelling e-commerce performance. Simon Rix conducted the leader interviews and wrote them up with his usual aplomb. Credit should also go to senior associate Oliver Mack, for his contribution to the leadership and change thinking and to Tom Deakin who has worked tirelessly on ensuring we kept to time and has helped in the production of all the figures. The stories of success would not have been possible without the commitment over the last couple of years from the rest of the delivery and business development team: Leah Holland, Simon Banks, David Watkins, Matt Evans, Becky Brennan, Annaliese Mason, Dan Kendall, Matt Abbott, James Bennett and Drikesh Etoar.

Producing books requires two other elements of support: we are incredibly grateful to our editor, Charlotte Owen who supported us through the process with constructive criticism and encouragement and, as with the previous book, we want to acknowledge the support we have received from our families as well as our colleagues. Without their understanding and acceptance, we would have found it far more difficult to write this book.

This book explores good practice not best practice. In such an immature and fast-moving sector anyone who claims that what they do is best practice is fooling themselves as well as others. This is a sector where continuous learning is a core capability. As new technologies appear, regulatory frameworks are developed and insights deepened, how to make digital happen will change. Experts pass their 'use by' date very quickly in our world: learners and innovators don't.

ACKNOWLEDGEMENTS

We would like to thank our interviewed leaders for the use of their quotations.

Building digital strategy that works

Executive summary

The most challenging aspect of leadership is not necessarily that of making the choices as to where to allocate scarce resources, but more likely to be the art of ensuring that, once the choice is made, the organization can deliver an effective execution. The pace and the potential scale of change presented by digital in most organizations means that the execution challenge is even greater than before, putting a significant burden on leaders who are often less expert than those on whom they rely for expertise. Making digital happen requires confident leadership willing and able to get to grips with the issues and to spot the drivers of failure before they take hold and ensure any transformation is an exercise in failure management. So, what drives failure, what is the 'golden thread' of success and what are the building blocks of a digital strategy that works?

Digital strategy

Strategy is the art of making choices. Well-informed choices come from analysis, clarity on the proposition and how it fits into its market, and from a deep understanding of the customer in the market. The best choices are distinctive and achieve this through the leverage of differentiation, core capabilities and any structural advantages.

Getting this right is tricky and many a good strategy has been thrown by significant changes in the environment, technology or competitor product/service. Despite this, strategy fails less often because it is wrong, than because it was badly executed or the execution failed to take account of changing circumstances. A study published by Forbes (2009) based on work carried out with the Association of Strategic Planning in the United States[1] identified the main reasons for failure as:

- unforeseen external circumstances (24 per cent);
- lack of understanding among those involved in developing the strategy and what they need to do to make it successful (19 per cent);
- the strategy itself is flawed (18 per cent);
- poor match between the strategy and the core competencies of the organization (16 per cent);
- lack of accountability or of holding the team responsible (13 per cent).

Digital failure is more likely

In digital, these drivers of failure are even more likely to trip you up, whether you are an incumbent business with a heritage in non-digital business models or a pure online player. There are some spectacular failure stories and all of them point to a common thread of things that tend to go wrong in the execution.

Computerworld (2013) reported that £100 million was written off by the BBC after a failed digital transformation project.[2] The goal was to 'improve production efficiency by enabling staff to develop, create, share and manage video and audio content and programming on their desktop'. A subsequent external audit by PwC completed in 2013 heavily criticized the BBC for 'serious weakness in project management and reporting', as well as 'a crippling lack of focus on business change'.[3] The key criticism was an assumption that digital transformation was all about technology whilst failing to realize that a cultural, behavioural and capability transformation was also required.

In 2014 general media and trade paper headlines reported the then Marks & Spencer CEO as pointing the finger at the introduction of a new website for a significant drop in sales in 2014.[4] 'M&S CEO blames new website's "settling in" period for 8.1 per cent online sales drop' was the headline in digital marketing paper The Drum (2014).[5]

An Econsultancy analysis (2014) identified that the site was certainly peppered with a whole series of customer experience failures;[6] the biggest question for many commentators like John McGarvey at Tech Donut (2014) was the size of the cost – quoted at £150 million.[7] Whilst no doubt a chunk of that investment came in redesigned processes and systems that supported the back end, it was also clear that a significant amount had gone into upgrading the customer interface with gadgets and gizmos that many customers just didn't value over the ability to make a simple purchase.

It's not just heritage businesses that can get this wrong. In North America, online pure-play retailer Shoes.com invested around US $30 million, according to a report in Forbes (2017), before going bankrupt in 2017.[8] Retail analysts interviewed for the report suggested that there were several reasons for this failure and not just the obvious challenge of going toe-to-toe with Amazon-owned Zappos. These included: failure to meet customer satisfaction; poor customer experience during the shopping journey; and a failure to communicate its USPs over those of other bigger, broader shoe propositions.

Nor is failure confined to those with bigger margins. Discount retailer Poundland, a mainstay until mid 2018 of many UK high streets, launched an e-commerce channel in 2015, only to close it less than two years later in 2017 as it failed to catch on with core customers or attract new ones online. At the heart of the failure, according to a blog analysis by Econsultancy analyst Nikki Gilliland,[9] seems to have been a combination of not understanding how customers shopped, getting the delivery structure wrong such that the price for delivery became a disincentive and an online execution that, whilst trying to replicate the 'surprise' nature of bargain finding in its high street stores, ended up confusing more shoppers than it helped.

The thread that pulls these stories together is that of the failure of the organization to work out how to operate successfully in order to give the chosen strategy the best chance of success. These are, of course, extreme examples, but at a lesser level the same drivers sit behind the failure of many digital projects, changes and investments to deliver their promised return.

As with *Leading Digital Strategy* our focus on digital transformation is at the customer interface. We chose to operate here as, in our experience, this is the point of greatest failure and easiest remedy. There are pitfalls to technology, however, and although we don't deal with the detail here, it is worth noting down the most obvious that drive cost up, scope down and timescales out.

Technology frequently gets out of control; this is a combination of the decision by those who lead the channel to create a complex specification to meet a myriad of customer requirements, many of which do not materially affect revenue, and the delight of the vast majority of development specialists in the complex and the challenging that make a routine job more interesting for them. A good example of the former is the over-personalization of content for what is often an inaccurate, and at worst random, array of customer personas that have little or no relevance to the real customer in the market. Another is the insistence on building an omni-channel experience where customers are choosing to engage only through specific devices for specific needs. Examples of the latter include decisions such as the development of a customized split testing software tool instead of buying a proven off-the-shelf solution and the addition of complex predictive recommendation algorithms as opposed to the far simpler reporting of what others who bought product 'A' also purchased.

Technology is costly and rarely delivers the promised scope, to cost and to time. In an interview in *Forbes Magazine* (2016) one commentator suggested that in research right across the Forbes Global 2000 index, seven out of eight companies reported that they were not succeeding in their digital transformation plans.[10] However, to lay the blame for failure at the feet of technology would be a mistake. The responsibility rests firmly with people. It's people who agree the specification, allocate the resources, plan and manage the projects. It's people who run the channel and other people who measure their performance and hold them to account. To misquote a former US president: it's the organization, stupid. And organizations can indeed be stupid. In the absence of leadership, they fragment, creating smaller units that lose focus on the customer and drive forward with their own agendas. This is what happens when digital doesn't work.

So, what should leaders watch out for? We think the drivers of failure can be grouped into three categories:

Cultural drivers

These are organization-wide and sit with the leadership of the business as a whole. Often, they are deep-seated and require significant effort and time to address and resolve. They include:

- **A failure to establish the customer as the primary stakeholder** – to be customer-centric and to ensure that the whole organization thinks customer-first transforms performance.

- **Assuming that digital transformation programmes have an end** – to be competitive, organizations must improve and innovate continuously.

- **Abdication of ownership and responsibility for 'digital' to an 'expert' or team of 'experts'** – no one is an expert in digital, some people have more experience in it, some may have more success, but unless leaders engage and learn and are willing to become vulnerable such that they question everything and build their own knowledge and insight, they are likely to preside over more digital failures than successes.

- **A failure to encourage learning by doing** – this is what we call test and learn and involves having the courage to accept short-term failures as a means to achieving longer-term success.

Capability drivers

These tend to sit closer to the functions on which the organization relies to execute the agreed strategy. They include:

- **Getting the business model wrong** – understanding where you will make money and understanding where margins are at risk and how to mitigate that risk separates out the successful from the less so.

- **Working a new channel using ways of operating that support an established one** – using digital to deliver products or services requires new ways of working, new standards and new behaviours.

- **Failing to operate to a single process and common standards across all key functions involved** – the most obvious example here is the failure to set a drumbeat for IT support such that business critical changes take weeks if not months to make, impacting revenue and/or profitability.

- **Assuming that digital transformation equates to a new website** – a new website does little in itself for a business and can often be followed by a drop in performance as it beds in. Transformation comes from the application of digital technology to the business such that it either makes more money or saves costs, or ideally both. This requires a change strategy, engagement and significant management effort to make it work during the early stages of adoption.

- **Failing to establish the primacy of customer insight as the key driver for change** – if the customer is going to drive your business then you need to ensure that insight about the customer and his or her needs, and problems in meeting them today, sits at the heart of any change you make to improve performance.

Capacity drivers

These are associated with the failure to think through resourcing, organization structures and how/where to use external expertise. They could also be seen as planning failures. They include:

- **Not thinking through the transition from project to business-as-usual** – it is rare for anyone with the capabilities to deliver a technology platform to be able to run it commercially, for example.

- **Not agreeing a long-term understanding of functional alignment to the new ways of working and where the ownership of key processes will sit** – functions work in tribal silos, especially IT, marketing and sales and yet all three will need to work seamlessly in any e-commerce operation, for example.

- **The absence of principles against which key commercial and operating decisions will be made and where they will be made** – too far up the line and you create bottlenecks in a world that moves far faster than any heritage business model, too decentralized and the tail will end up wagging the dog with the inevitable consequences associated with inefficient operations.

- **The lack of a test and learn process that creates the evidence that justifies investment in change** – expert-led change is the antithesis of a business driven by data. Making sure there is a robust framework, process and adequate resources to support test and learn is a differentiator of superior performance.

The opening examples at the head of this chapter are such that one can only imagine a pretty significant combination of many of the above being allowed to continue unchecked. But it would be unfair not to recognize the context within which leaders are trying to operate. The pace of development in digital technology is faster than at any time in the past. Reacting to this pace and letting this drive internal decisions can become an overwhelming pressure. As sales falter or margins decline it is easy to think that technology can provide some kind of silver bullet.

Doing so presents leaders with a risk that they could drive decisions that will destroy shareholder value; in so doing, they eventually threaten company success, jobs and general prosperity. In the face of this risk, leaders need to check that they are not drinking the digital Kool-Aid and investing mindlessly in response to fad and fashion.

Just as we can cite significant failure there are also many stories out there of how to drive digital transformation effectively. In e-commerce standout examples from around the world are not just the obvious Amazon, Flipkart, eBay and Alibaba but would include: US companies such as Home Depot, Best-Buy and QVC; UK companies such as ASOS, John Lewis, Argos and Shop Direct; and others like Germany's Zalando. Our analysis of their benchmark performance indicators suggests that what holds them together is the following:

- an obsession with the customer and investing in ensuring the customer experience meets or even beats expectations;

- a belief in design thinking and applying this to creating solutions to real problems faced by real customers;

- an understanding about how to use data to create insight and how to use that insight to drive experimentation and innovation to improve performance;

- the adoption of agile customer-led processes that move fast and put the customer at the centre of the conversation;
- a focused use of creative to support the design of solutions that work for the customer;
- measuring the commercial outcome and demanding quality returns from the investment they make in technology, infrastructure and people.

The work we have done with our clients over the last six years reinforces these lessons and those who have focused their efforts in the same way have seen growth at rates significantly ahead of their competitors.

The value chain in strategy

The way we think through strategy in looking at digital business is through four sets of choices – these are laid out in Figure 1.1.

Each of these elements defines how value is created and, in terms of a digital channel, need as much clarity as for any other part of the business. Specifically, in each element the key questions have to be well understood throughout the organization and used to define the detail of how things will be done to ensure that the expected value materializes.

Figure 1.1   The key choices in digital business

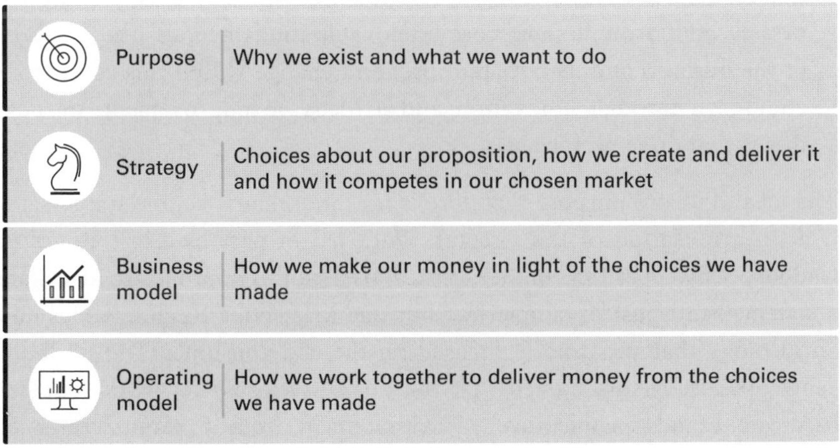

(icon)	Purpose	Why we exist and what we want to do
(icon)	Strategy	Choices about our proposition, how we create and deliver it and how it competes in our chosen market
(icon)	Business model	How we make our money in light of the choices we have made
(icon)	Operating model	How we work together to deliver money from the choices we have made

SOURCE © Good Growth Ltd

Purpose

Purpose is what the business exists to do. A great deal of work has been done on the idea of a core or common purpose, most notably by Jim Collins and Jerry Porras (1994)[11] in the United States who identified this amongst six timeless fundamentals that differentiate longer-term successful businesses. These were:

- Make the company itself the ultimate product – building the right organization that is able to grow with the market and innovate and change in response to customer changes.

- Instil a core ideology – make your values and a clear sense of shared purpose the guiding thread for your company beyond making money.

- Build a cult-like culture – reinforce what you value and believe generates value, and do not tolerate deviation from these core beliefs.

- Grow your own future top management – the best insiders preserve what is core to the belief system, culture and purpose of an organization; succession of the best is less expensive (no recruitment fees, less of a learning curve and so on).

- Stimulate progress through 'big hairy audacious goals', experimentation and continuous improvement – 'bhags' as an idea may be old hat but there is nothing wrong with putting a stretch goal into an organization to drive innovation and change, and experimentation and continuous improvement are core tools in driving digital performance today.

- Embrace 'the genius of and' – think about growth and progress in business as built around some core immovable fundamentals (the ideology of the business and its core purpose) and change within this context by adding on through innovation and a focus on improvement are new things that drive performance.

The idea of a core purpose therefore is far more than a simple statement – it is an articulation of the visceral. Work led in part by Chris Bones in Cadbury Schweppes PLC in the early 2000s used this approach to articulate a statement not just of simple fact but one that spoke to core values and an ideology that was totally focused on the end consumer. The Cadbury Schweppes leadership agreed that the business existed to 'work together to create brands people love'. This statement from a manufacturer of confectionery and beverage reflected not just that they made products for consumers but also three key ideological fundamentals for the business: a desire to improve living conditions and health and the working environment for those employed by the organization and a commitment to working with employees and customers alike to make things better (working together); a track record of innovation in product and marketing communications (to create brands); and a total commitment to consumer satisfaction (that people love).

Cadbury Schweppes chose to do this as it faced an organization-changing decision to acquire a huge global confectionery business, Adams Inc. It knew that this was a major addition to its business with significant implications for organizational change. It also knew that it would fail unless it ensured that in any way possible the resulting entity was able to hang on to what had made Cadbury Schweppes one of the most successful global businesses in its sector. Building the new integrated organization around this statement of the 'essence' of the core business helped deliver a very successful acquisition.

For any business, understanding purpose is a critical part of ensuring that any digital organization or e-commerce structure put in place understands not just its commercial aim but the ideological fundamentals required for every part of the business to hold to. That's how to ensure that every part of a business in a fast-changing and uncertain world can operate effectively and deliver strategy.

Strategy

As we have already said, strategy is the art of making clear and distinctive choices that define where you will allocate scarce resources. It is not our purpose to map out in detail how to define and make the choices; this is a book that focuses on making a strategy work: our first book, *Leading Digital Strategy* (2015)[12] helps leaders think through strategy choices for e-commerce channels. However, it is worth reflecting here on what makes an effective strategy and how you can identify when the strategy you have may not be making enough of a choice to ensure that you win in the market. Ultimately, strategy defines how you think you can optimize value for capital employed in the business; the tell-tale clues that suggest you may want to review current strategy are:

- it also describes the strategy of most/all of your main competitors;
- it fails to employ capabilities that are in the organization and recognized as superior to other players;
- the choices are so broad that there is no real choice made in any of the four major areas: proposition (including market choices), product, price and operations;

- it doesn't pass the 'not' test – in other words when you put the word 'not' in front of it (or key elements within it, for example product or operations) it offers a credible alternative decision that could be made by a competitor.

As far as a digital channel is concerned, there are some key leadership questions that need to be addressed when thinking through strategy:

- Proposition
  - What is it that makes your online proposition distinctive from others competing for the same customers in the market?
  - On what markets (or market segments) have you chosen to focus? What markets (or market segments) are not priorities?
- Product
  - What products for which segments? What won't you sell?
  - What differentiates your product range from competitors?
- Price
  - What price points are you choosing?
  - Is price a differentiator? If so, how?
  - What are the principles of promotions/discounts and how do they operate?
  - What makes promotions/discounts different from competitors?
- Operations
  - How are you fulfilling orders?
  - How are payments processed and cash collected?
  - Are there core capabilities that differentiate operations and are these being fully utilized?

The more you believe that your current strategy looks like every other competitor in the market, the more you might like to review it critically. Little or no differentiation at this level makes it very difficult to create distinctive and compelling sales and marketing executions that attract attention and run through into sales revenue.

Business model

A business model is simply a description of the value chain and how you make money, assuming customers buy your product or service. For many if not most incumbent businesses the places where value can be created online will be different from those in the 'bricks and mortar' or catalogue/voice channels. Less so compared to catalogue but even here the way the digital channel can interact with a customer (for example, through remarketing activity after a failed purchase journey, or by sharing what other people also bought) will offer different places to create value.

In digital the significant difference is the measurability of impact right through the value chain. Every action and reaction has both a trackable cost and a trackable, attributed impact. Our value chain model (Figure 1.2) helps leaders understand where they are allocating resources and where there are opportunities to improve performance and drive greater value from the channel:

- Location – the cost of appearing in front of your target customer. This includes the cost of media strategy and media buying as well as the cost of email marketing, remarketing and other direct to known email/social media account communication.

- Acquisition – the cost of the creative execution and the activity undertaken to attract engagement such that your proposition generates target engagement (most often a click through).

Figure 1.2   E-commerce value chain

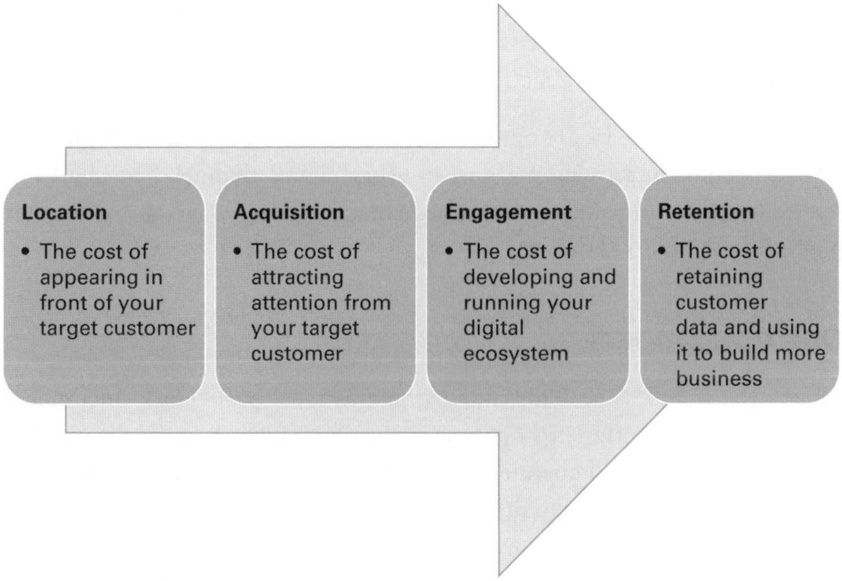

Location	Acquisition	Engagement	Retention
• The cost of appearing in front of your target customer	• The cost of attracting attention from your target customer	• The cost of developing and running your digital ecosystem	• The cost of retaining customer data and using it to build more business

SOURCE © Good Growth Ltd

- Engagement – the cost of the development, build and running of your digital ecosystem, its optimization and associated back-office and fulfilment processes.

- Retention – the cost of CRM technology and management, loyalty and referral programmes.

These costs can be put against the direct revenue stream through the channel and against indirect revenue where the journey started out online, even if it was finished though a direct interaction (click and collect or completion via the phone due to a failure or complexity that cannot be resolved online).

Value erosion through the chain will come from:

- Location – poor media buying – often associated with automation or what is called programmatic marketing – ineffective direct and remarketing marketing activity and mishandling of investment in social media channels.

- Acquisition – poorly performing organic and paid search performance, conflation of activity between customer consideration and conversion, leading to poor creative execution.

- Engagement – over-spending on technology and development support; badly modelled delivery and fulfilment thresholds; ineffective fulfilment execution; poor merchandising; under-optimized web estate; over-manning; resource duplication between agencies and internal teams.

- Retention – underperforming loyalty programmes, no incentive for referral and endorsement, over-spending on CRM technology and failure to utilize customer data effectively.

In our experience, there are opportunities to enhance value through growing revenue and/or improving margins in every digital channel. The challenge for leaders is to understand the value leakage at every stage and what they might be able to do about it.

Operating model

This is the Achilles' heel for many organizations, particularly incumbent ones who often continue to operate as they have done historically, pasting on top of this a digital channel. Our definition of an operating model (see Figure 1.3) is 'the way we work together to deliver value from the business model'. It is the combination of formal and informal processes, support technology (for example, analytics or testing software in e-commerce) and

Figure 1.3 Elements of an operating model

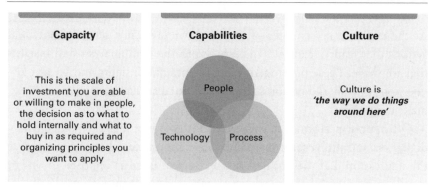

Capacity	Capabilities	Culture
This is the scale of investment you are able or willing to make in people, the decision as to what to hold internally and what to buy in as required and organizing principles you want to apply	People, Technology, Process	Culture is *'the way we do things around here'*

SOURCE © Good Growth Ltd

skills that are required to execute successfully. On top of these it is also the structures within which we decide to group resources to deliver the value and, probably most importantly of all, the culture within which we expect people to operate.

We deal in detail with how to create, develop and sustain an operating model in Chapter 8. It is the single biggest determinant of strategic success and to do it well requires leaders to make positive choices about the three 'Cs': culture, capacity and capability. In our previous book, we shared our definition of culture as 'the way we do things around here'. It sets the tone, defines the prevailing attitudes and shapes the ability of an organization to respond to changes in the world in which it operates. Capacity decisions are resource allocation choices. What is bought in and what is retained inside are important choices in digital given the pace at which practice and technology moves. Capability comes from thinking through not just the skills and experience required to create value within the business model but also how people will work together within and across functions to deliver value and what technology is employed to enhance their performance.

The strategic choices about how the organization will work can cripple the chances of success before execution gets underway or accelerate the pace at which value is created. They should not be left to those with a partial view or specific agenda. Those accountable for the performance of the organization as a whole need to make sure that there is complete alignment, not just at an enterprise level but also within their digital channel, from purpose through strategy and business model to how their organization is going to work to ensure that value creation is optimized.

Leadership actions

At the end of every chapter of the book we lay out a series of potential actions that leaders can take in response to the data analysis and insights that we share. These pull together the themes and insights and set out key questions that should be considered as part of a structured process that can make digital work.

Often, poor performance isn't easy to isolate in a digital channel. Many digital organizations seem incredibly busy and stretched and this can give the impression that the business has a resource issue as opposed to one of capability. In fact, what you may be looking at is a 'hamster wheel' effect – everyone is spinning but nothing is being achieved. More resources in these circumstances will only make the wheel go faster.

It is in these circumstances in particular that major investment decisions become even more risky so it's critical that you get the most out of what you already have before you look to invest significantly more. Our rule of thumb is that when a leader is told that he or she needs a new website or to invest more in digital marketing or CRM software, warning bells should sound. If you hear this, the first thing you should do is ask why, and the second thing is to have a thorough review of the digital value chain to see where you can extract more value from what you already have.

There is no silver bullet, technological or organizational, that can make digital work. Success comes from making a deliberate set of strategic choices that ensure alignment across purpose, strategy, business model and organization. Without it comes an increased risk of failure, both operational and strategic. With the scale of cost that can be incurred through technology change the impact of failure can be significant and could even result in long-term value destruction. Making digital work is as much about mitigating this risk as it is about innovating to open up new sources of value. These mitigating actions may well be worth considering:

- Make sure the customer is driving the choices being made in the business not the reverse. Don't let technology (and those promoting it) drive the business agenda. Ask for insight every time someone suggests a change (particularly one that is going to consume scarce resources) and demand an experimentation or 'test and learn' process to demonstrate value creation before changes are made.

- Put your current digital strategy under the microscope. The less differentiated it looks and particularly if it doesn't pass the 'not' test, the more you might want to review it carefully and analyse the quality of the choices being made.

- Do a value chain analysis right across the digital channel. Look for areas of poorer performance and identify where revenue is being lost or costs seem excessive.

- Take a long hard look at the three 'Cs'. If you are unsure then carry out an organization effectiveness audit to help identify what is getting in the way of optimizing value.

References

1 https://i.forbesimg.com/forbesinsights/StudyPDFs/PowerfulConvergenceof Strategy.pdf [accessed 28 December 2017]

2 https://www.computerworlduk.com/it-management/pwc-slams-bbc-for-failed-100m-digital-transformation-project-3494357/ [accessed 28 December 2017]

3 https://www.computerworlduk.com/it-management/pwc-slams-bbc-for-failed-100m-digital-transformation-project-3494357/ [accessed 28 December 2017]

4 https://www.retail-week.com/topics/technology/multichannel/analysis-why-did-mss-new-website-fail-to-click-into-place/5062287.article?authent=1 [accessed 28 December 2017]

5 http://www.thedrum.com/news/2014/07/08/ms-ceo-blames-new-website-s-settling-period-81-online-sales-drop [accessed on 3 February 2018]

6 https://econsultancy.com/blog/65244-where-did-the-marks-spencer-website-relaunch-go-wrong – one of a number of analyses done at the time of the issues on the site [accessed 27 December 2017]

7 https://www.techdonut.co.uk/blog/14/07/ms-shows-dangers-of-redesigning-your-website [accessed 30 December 2017]

8 https://www.forbes.com/sites/susanadams/2017/03/17/seven-lessons-from-the-failure-of-shoes-com/#4a4cc74e4009 [accessed 29 December 2017]

9 https://econsultancy.com/blog/68787-why-did-poundland-s-ecommerce-trial-fail/ [accessed 29 December 2017]

10 https://www.forbes.com/sites/brucerogers/2016/01/07/why-84-of-companies-fail-at-digital-transformation/ [accessed 31 December 2017]

11 Collins, J and Porras, J (1994) *Built to Last: Successful habits of visionary companies*, HarperCollins, New York

12 Bones, C and Hammersley, J (2015) *Leading Digital Strategy*, Kogan Page, London

Why digital strategies fail and how to recognize failure

Executive summary

In Chapter 1 we shared some significant digital failure stories. From research reported by Forbes in 2016 it would seem that failure in digital transformation is a more common experience than success. The headline for the piece in Forbes.com suggested that 84 per cent of companies then engaged in some form of digital transformation did not believe that they were succeeding.[1] From our experience of working globally with some of the world's leading brands, we believe that digital strategies fail most frequently because organizations fail to listen and respond to customers. This might sound like a 'basic' requirement but it is clear that many businesses do not even invest in the software that allows them to engage customers online, let alone do so effectively and on a routine and regular basis. In our annual reporting on comparative e-commerce effectiveness in the United Kingdom for 2017, we highlighted that 65 per cent of the companies reviewed did not have a tool that could survey people visiting their websites and gather feedback on their experience as customers.[2] This chapter looks in detail at the drivers of failure and how leaders can evaluate whether what they do today is more or less likely to fail.

Poor projects drive failure

With a wide range of available commercial and comparative metrics for digital and e-commerce performance, the assumption is that organizations can judge the effectiveness of their digital investments earlier and more effectively, to drive a better commercial outcome than they can for similar offline investments. However, in reality, the risks of failure seem to be the same if not greater in digital and there is a common refrain in many businesses that they are failing to generate promised investment returns. This brings into question not the credibility of the strategy necessarily, but the effectiveness of the execution. In our experience, there are three execution issues at the heart of the problem: first, a technology failure in many organizations to be able to scope, de-risk and deliver to time and quality, complex projects; second, a commercial failure to understand why customers in the market do and do not respond to the proposition and a subsequent failure to agree how to respond; and third, a tendency to fad and fashion in digital that inevitably drives cost with very variable returns.

In 2015, a report suggested that large organizations wasted around US $400 billion on digital transformation projects and linked this to a finding that two-thirds of projects in the study failed to meet expectations.[3] However, despite this scale of failure organizations feel compelled to invest in digital transformation or fail. In 2017, Couchbase[4] surveyed 450 heads of digital transformation in the United States, United Kingdom, France and Germany and found that:

- 89 per cent said their industry is, or is about to be, disrupted by digital technology;
- 95 per cent said the goal of digital innovation should be unique customer/ end-user experiences;
- 84 per cent reported projects being cancelled or hindered because of legacy database limitations;
- 80 per cent felt their organization was at risk of being left behind by the competition;
- 54 per cent said organizations that don't keep up will be gone in under 5 years.

There is no doubt that many organizations believe that digital presents an existential threat and that the strategic response is to allocate significant capital spend to create infrastructure that can transform performance – often measured in terms of reduced operating costs. The pace of change in technology is also a significant issue with some projects, particularly those with a long time frame, having to be revised or even completely halted as they are overtaken by change. There are endless sources of analysis as to why large IT projects fail but if you boil them down five reasons stand out:

- **Scope creep** – this is a serious issue in digital transformation projects and organization leaders are often more guilty than any other group for either initiating this ('would it be a good idea if...') or letting themselves be persuaded by others that extending a project is a good idea.

- **Poor methodology** – process indiscipline above all other things can derail projects, add cost and extend time. Leaders must insist on a strong and coherent approach to the chosen methodology and take careful stock of the capability in the organization to deliver it.

- **Organizational blinkers** – not looking carefully outside and learning from others in a range of sectors who have gone before will mean you are more likely to fall down the same elephant traps – including those brought in by your chosen partners.

- **Risk register reliance** – a risk register is the least likely tool to prevent project failure. We are inclined to believe the existence of a register can provide far too much comfort and is only brought out after disaster to allow a project team to claim that they flagged the risk months ago.

- **Cultural calamity** – a failure to engage the organization in the process of changing how it works such that both the transition to and the adoption of new technology fails to deliver both the project in full and the promised benefits.

These combine to create an outcome where the project will deliver less in terms of functionality, take longer to complete and cost more/deliver less value than the business plan. Research done globally by McKinsey (2017)[5] across all key sectors suggests that nearly half of all digital investments fail to deliver a return on investment above the cost of capital and a further 25 per cent only manage a modest return. They argue that this suggests that organizations are investing in the wrong places or too much or too little in the right ones. In looking at the winners from this analysis the importance of organization and culture comes through particularly in three areas: rejecting silo thinking and behaviour; building a common culture across business units and investing in a single view of the customer.

Their research also identified that in every industry sector there were high performers – this suggests that some are getting it right. Intriguingly, this analysis identifies the areas of highest and lowest return at an earnings level based on the observation that for those in the survey there was little momentum in top-line growth overall but a significant impact on earnings before interest and taxes (EBIT) with the biggest opportunity coming from investing in digitizing supply chains. Where there was revenue impact in the digitization of products and services, EBIT growth was significantly lower, and in marketing and distribution it was only slightly higher than the revenue growth, suggesting an earnings drag. We think there is a link between this high-level analysis of corporate performance in the digitization of products, services, marketing and distribution and the issue that sits at the heart of this book – the challenge of optimizing digital strategy such that it delivers the best possible growth in revenue and margin. It begs the question: what happens to undermine value creation in the execution of product and service innovation and the execution of sales and marketing activity online?

We are not arguing here that organizations should be wary of investing in technology projects. It is important to stay current and invest in change and indeed, where possible, to future-proof investment by looking for solutions that can absorb known change ahead; but the greater the scope and the greater the complexity, the greater the chance of failure. Leaders need to think hard, not just about the outcome, but also about how capable their organizations are to work effectively in this type of change and how best they can help transformation projects deliver. Whilst no IT project ever goes perfectly and there will be bumps along the way, focusing on the five areas above in the leadership of digital change will go a long way towards reducing the risk of a strategic failure.

It's the customer, stupid

Our research and analysis and our experience in what some call the 'front-end' of e-commerce – the web sales and marketing platforms, self-service portals, loyalty platforms and digital marketing – suggests that many businesses are not getting the returns they had hoped for from their investment into these activities. The McKinsey data shared above also suggest that even when revenue grows, earnings are not responding as positively to investments in these areas as they do in areas in the 'back-end' – possibly because in these areas much of the gain comes from cost reductions that are much easier to deliver. The difference with investments into products and services and sales and marketing is that they have traditionally been evaluated against a set of assumptions about the behaviour of consumers or businesses as customers and their propensity to buy.

In digital, done well, this propensity can be tested and plans changed before there is a commitment to significant investment. Not getting expected returns in growth investments suggests that one of the main reasons for failure in digital strategies is a lack of understanding of the customer and of testing to learn how best to meet their needs. What is fascinating is that given traditional industries are still dominated by legacy brands, many of whose successes have been built on their ability to understand a market and to then sell into it effectively, why do so many of them fail to do this online? In retail, for example, for the top 500 retailers in the United Kingdom in 2017, IRUK[6] reported that fewer than 5 in the 'elite, leading and top 50' are new online-only entrants – two of whom are the behemoths, Amazon and eBay.

Therefore, whilst the multi-channel retailers are being challenged by digital, customers in their millions are engaging with their brands online. This is one of their biggest advantages – and indeed the growing advantage of Amazon, which has invested huge amounts in marketing, recently moved into grocery and pharmaceuticals, introduced value added services (such as Amazon Prime), and developed its Marketplace platform to establish itself as a 'go-to' site for all categories of goods. What Amazon has learned from established retailers is that brand recognition and awareness is still a powerful driver of customer interest when shopping.

Focus on the customer

The strategic challenge for any e-commerce proposition is to capitalize on the customer interest and address the key reasons why customers don't buy. Every year we pull together an e-commerce effectiveness ranking based on the companies we run through our online benchmarking tool[7] whose results are subsequently published by digital marketing magazine *The Drum*. In 2018 this Good Growth ranking covered around 80 e-commerce organizations. We spilt the outcome into four quartiles against a maximum rank score of 10/10. Whilst none found themselves in the bottom quartile (2.5/10 or lower) in the next-to-bottom quartile came a slew of major brands, particularly from financial services and retail. These included the Royal Bank of Scotland, Liverpool Victoria Insurance and insurance aggregator Compare the Market through to international retail brands H&M, Abercrombie & Fitch and Hollister.

Let us share one example of the potential impact of being at the bottom of the pile for e-commerce effectiveness. According to *Retail Week*, the United Kingdom is the third-largest market for H&M. In November 2016, sales grew by 2.7 per cent to £1,040 million (including wholesaling). UK profits fell in the period to £50 million.[8] Now, there is nothing to suggest this is anything but a correlation, but nonetheless, one that should encourage leaders in this position to look carefully at their e-commerce operation to understand how it is operating.

Overall, in the effectiveness ranking the best performers – they included global electronics business Samsung and insurance giant Aviva – are not only well equipped from the point of view of analytics and testing but they also actively listen to customers in the market as they attempt to engage and/or transact on their websites. Whilst all had analytics software that tracks customer activity on their websites, and many had invested in tools that would support the testing of alternative executions, only 35 per cent had tools that captured online customer feedback about their website in real time. Only with this customer data can an organization be confident that it can build quality customer insight and answer the question: 'Why are customers in the market not buying/engaging with the proposition?'

If failure comes first and foremost from a lack of customer insight what it also comes from is a failure to locate and acquire the right customers, a failure to engage customer interest and a failure to build quality insight that can drive investing in testing to solve customer problems.

Spotting failure from comparative data

To help the leaders we work with to identify the drivers of failure we built a benchmarking tool that is now available for general use through our website. This identifies five key data points where comparative external data are available via various tools that extract data from the back-end of Google. Using Google as a proxy for all traffic is a credible assumption, according to Net Market Share[9] who report that in 2017 the global marketing share percentage, in terms of the use of Search Engines by desktop/laptop users, showed Google averaging a net share of approximately 75 per cent. When it comes to mobile users Google still dominates holding more than 90 per cent market share. This is not surprising considering the ubiquity of Chrome on mobile devices and that it has made changes to mobile indexing to provide higher quality search results, and in our view a better user experience. No other search engine is remotely close; with Baidu having a net share of around 11 per cent, Bing 8 per cent and Yahoo 5 per cent, and the rest less than 1 per cent each.

Our benchmarking tool exploits one of the advantages of digital: the availability of data that can reveal relative performance in a market to identify the tactical choices organizations are making to gain market share. The comparative data that can be sourced includes sales effectiveness, marketing effectiveness and investment in technology to drive performance. We have tested the data reported through the tool with the actuals for our clients and broadly the data source used is around 80 per cent accurate – in other words it generally under-reports visits by about 20 per cent. This is consistent and therefore provides a credible base for comparative assessment – the question for leaders when looking at this data is: Am I leading the competitor set or am I behind? To demonstrate how leaders can understand performance and identify areas of potential failure relative to their competitors here are the data for four of the UK's top high street multiples.

An example benchmark from September 2017

The first metric to review is a simple one: how many shoppers who search for goods or services choose to respond to a proposition when presented with the results of their search enquiry? This is a very effective comparative measure as it ignores customers who choose to come direct to a company website (that is, typing the website address into the browser bar or using a bookmark) so focuses on what happens when propositions compete for attention. We call this total search traffic and as at May 2018 (Good Growth) it normally counts for about 60 per cent of traffic to websites, according to our all client database. This number includes visits from people who clicked the 'organic' (unpaid) search result or those who click an advert at the top of the search results (paid).

Keeping this example straightforward we are looking at the relative performance of visits from desktops/laptops (that is, non-smartphone or tablet visits) to John Lewis, Debenhams, House of Fraser and M&S. For this example, we are excluding smartphone visits as the available data, including our own, suggest that visits to websites from smartphones (as opposed to visits to apps) are dominated by people browsing rather than those with intent to transact. To give you a sense of scale, in 2017, there were around 650 million visits per month from desktop and laptop to the top 150 retailers in the United Kingdom.[10]

For these high street multiples the 'search visit' data for the month of September 2017 were reported by our tool as shown in Figure 2.1.

In September 2017, therefore, the total visits through search results in Google for this competitor set were at least 43 million. Their comparative performance is telling – on this measure House of Fraser look like they are losing out against their high street competitors. Reasons for failure here could range from poor proposition advertising (un-compelling search result presentation through to poor headlines or copy) through poor paid marketing campaigns (under- or over-paying for significant keywords) to a failure to compete for interest (not having quality responses to searches in either organic or paid).

Figure 2.1   Total search traffic (paid and organic) to leading UK multiples

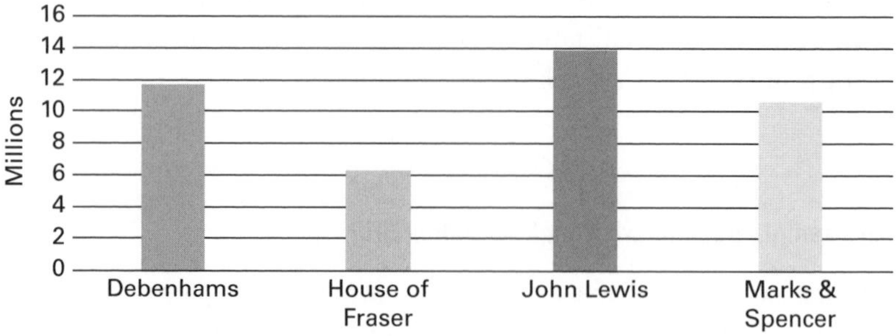

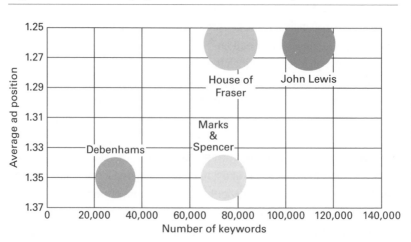

SOURCE © Good Growth Ltd

So, having established which of these competitors capture customer interest effectively, we go on to look specifically at the performance of paid marketing. This is the next area of potential failure – for example, it may be that House of Fraser is failing to buy interest and is falling behind as a result. The data for paid advertising (Figure 2.2) look at two drivers: the scale of investment into keywords and the outcome in terms of average advert position in search results for the top 100 keywords (defined by the level of customer interest).

For the first point, the data are telling us something quite significant about the performance of House of Fraser. It is attracting the second

Figure 2.2   Paid campaign effectiveness for UK multiples

SOURCE © Good Growth Ltd

highest level of paid for visits of this competitor set. What can be inferred from this data is that House of Fraser is attracting a great deal of interest in its proposition through additional investment in marketing. If as a leader you saw this combined with a significantly lower level of traffic you would have to ask yourself why are we generating so much less interest than our competitors without paying for it? Are we offsetting a poor performance by spending additional resources only to be significantly behind our competitors?

For the second data point, advert positioning – this is far more nuanced. What effective paid campaigns achieve is the best sales return for the available budget. Whilst there are advantages for getting into the number one slot (in terms of click through to a landing page), the cost of doing this may mean you end up paying far more per sale than your competitors or burning through your budget so quickly such that you don't appear for significant parts of a day, week or month. As at May 2018 (these things do change), there are a maximum of four adverts that appear on any Google search above the organic (unpaid) results. For this data set both Debenhams and M&S are getting pretty high placements on average but the others are doing better. The question for all four leaders is the same: What is our cost per acquisition? If you are a leader in an organization at the top of the pile you may want to test spending less and see if sales remain and the cost of acquiring them falls. If you are towards the bottom then you might want to see if you can improve ad quality, landing page relevance or indeed spend more to grow sales and retain or reduce your cost per sale.

The next key metric is the use of segmented landing pages. It is difficult to judge effectiveness of competitor landing pages but you can use a proxy of the previous measure – if you are being beaten to a high advert position for a keyword by a competitor and this is sustained over time, you would probably be right to assume that their landing page is working better than yours. After all, advert position is driven by the performance of the landing page (that is, does it generate engagement) as well as the amount you are willing to pay. As a leader you want to ensure you understand why this is happening. Having done this you will want to know what is being done to test alternatives to improve advert and landing page performance and what the financial implications might be of changing budgets.

The thing that is easier to assess is the effectiveness of your organization in using landing pages to ensure that, as customers land on your website, they feel that you are responding to their needs. Again, there

Figure 2.3   Landing page comparisons (number of unique landing pages for top 100 keywords): UK multiples and Amazon

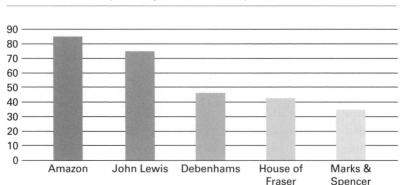

SOURCE © Good Growth Ltd

are data sources that can count, for the top 100 keywords, the number of individual pages employed by an organization. Why is this important? Personalization is difficult, if not impossible, for customers that you do not know (see below), but thoughtful segmentation is both possible and profitable. As an example: if a customer is looking for a white short-sleeved T-shirt, retailers should not send the customer to their general landing page. It sounds obvious – but is often overlooked. Figure 2.3 shows the data on the number of landing pages for their top 100 keywords for our multiples with the addition of data from Amazon.

Amazon has a landing page ratio of 84 per cent. Against this only John Lewis can get close at 74 per cent whilst House of Fraser at 41 per cent and M&S at 34 per cent look comparatively less effective.

Finally, we come to the capability to build deep insight into the customer experience. To do this effectively organizations need four pieces of technology attached to their websites and their apps. These are:

- analytics software – this enables the tracking of visits, the number of users, interactions with key actions such as add to basket, filling in forms and transactions;

- page analytics software – this enables the tracking of customer interactions with individual pages;

- voice of the customer software – this enables customers to leave live feedback in real time about their experience whether or not they have bought anything or become a lead;

Figure 2.4   Performance technology on websites

	Debenhams	House of Fraser	John Lewis	Marks & Spencer
Analytics	Adobe Analytics Google Analytics	Adobe Analytics Google Analytics	Adobe Analytics	Adobe Analytics WebTrends
On-page analytics		SessionCam	SessionCam	Adobe Marketing Cloud
Voice of customer	ForeSee		Bazaarvoice	Bazaarvoice
Split testing	Maxymiser	Maxymiser	Monetate Qubit	Adobe Target WebTrends Optimize

SOURCE © Good Growth Ltd

- testing software – this enables the organization to develop alternative sales and marketing executions on the website to test against the current execution to see if they can improve performance.

The data for the UK multiples (Figure 2.4) suggest that two of them may be missing out on valuable data to help them understand why parts of the customer experience are not performing as well as they might want them to.

Organizations can kill strategy

The more gaps that are apparent in the capability to build insight, the more leaders need to question how important the customer really is to their organization. If the answer comes back to the challenge that you need a new website then you need to look hard at the outcome from this type of comparative performance and at the internal commercials, and think long and hard about whether this is the answer, or whether you shouldn't focus first on getting a greater return out of what you have already invested in. There are very few digital platforms that can't be made to perform better before having more money spent on them.

Indeed if you've responded to requests for more investment in the past and these haven't delivered the promised returns then why would you think that the next time things will be any different? If you're on your second or third iteration of these conversations you are probably less and less confident that anything significant is really going to happen. Yet for some reason

– and despite this being a pretty common experience – organizations seem to feel compelled to keep handing over significant amounts of cash in the hope that 'this time things will be different'.

In Douglas Adams' book *The Hitchhiker's Guide to the Galaxy*,[11] the computer Deep Thought memorably presented the answer to the great question of life, the universe and everything as '42'. It explained that this conclusion had been reached as a consequence of its programmers not knowing precisely what the question was. Unless the website is constantly taking feedback and testing to find the best execution, it will have as much chance of coming up with the optimal commercial outcome as Deep Thought had in reaching a profound conclusion. This is because, like the great computer, they have been constructed on unproven assumptions, unclear goals and untested expertise.

The real answer to your questions about the commercial performance of your website lies less with the technology and far more with the organization. Unless the organization can articulate the precise question and then develop and test a range of hypothetical answers until it finds the one that best answers that question, then your website will continue to underperform, regardless of how much you spend on it. Often, an underperforming website is a symptom of an underperforming organization where, despite a clear and well-thought-out strategy, its people coalesce around processes, policies and practices that conspire to undermine its ability to achieve its goals. In our previous book, we introduced the idea that organizations where this occurs are suffering from mis-organization.

The inclination to blame the technology, rather than the processes, policies and practices that created it, is the age-old trap of the poor workman blaming his tools. In the traditional channels through which organizations transacted, leaders were able to spot this trap pretty effectively, partly through having had direct experience of working with the tools themselves and partly through their position in the organization. In digital channels many leaders find themselves at a disadvantage: few have direct experience of working with the tools themselves, and the way in which the channel presents itself and reports its activities is often opaque to the uninitiated. To address the shortfall in their own appreciation leaders appoint 'experts' on whom they rely; not just to develop and deliver an effective website but also to be the source of benchmarking and external validation. These experts may well understand how to manage the technology, but do they understand the market and the customer sufficiently to ensure that it is focused on the right questions? If we take our experience across 7 sectors over the last 18 months, we would suggest that this is a significant area of risk.

There is one other area where organizations can be the driver of failure and that is in choosing to measure the wrong things. There is no shortage of data in digital. The one thing leaders complain to us about, however, is the shortage of information. Leaders need information against which they can evaluate the relative performance of one channel over another and the return that can be achieved by resources when allocated to a particular activity or set of activities. In *Leading Digital Strategy* (2015) we identified a set of key measures that leaders should adopt in e-commerce to understand the performance of their channel.[12] We won't repeat these here but they were driven by a focus on commercial performance and return on investment, from initial attraction of customer interest (digital marketing) right through to the effectiveness of self-service and known customer engagement (loyalty marketing). It's not just right measures, however, that help drive performance: it is also how they are measured. Don't let agencies or internal teams mark their own homework. Establish firm standards and impose them transparently, internally and externally, such that you know what and how data are being presented.

What we see increasingly is mis-organization: significant investment in capital and resources in order to achieve commercial goals being fed into platforms, web design, sales execution and analytics software that fail to deliver. In traditional channels, organizations would have acted swiftly to change activity, processes or people at the first sign of under-delivery; in digital channels, we seem to be more willing to make the same mistakes again and again and repeat the cycle with the same inevitable outcome. Expertise, it seems, only takes us so far. What differentiates the superior performers is that they have realized that their digital channel is the same as any other – to make it work well requires customer insight and understanding such that specific channel expertise is applied to the real problems and opportunities.

Dedicated followers of fashion

The final area that drives failure in digital is associated with the immaturity of the discipline inside organizations, the high level of turnover in many digital teams and the consequent over-dependence on agencies. This dependence in our view makes organizations more vulnerable to ideas and approaches that extend agency engagement and fee income but have very variable impact – sometimes requiring considerable investment without ever delivering a credible return. Here are three examples that, at the time of writing, are currently fashionable initiatives.

Propensity modelling

There are many areas where propensity modelling can play a very important role, for example in epidemiology, but its application into areas of human behaviour is more complex. Propensity modelling in digital seeks to measure and understand a customer's likelihood to convert into revenue. To do this, proponents apply machine learning principles to standard customer journeys and, using historical data, try to predict the ideal customer or the ideal journey or both to grow revenue. There are two key issues facing organizations being asked to adopt such an approach. The first is the lack of differentiation between marketing (communicating to customers who may not be interested in your proposition) and selling to those who have actively chosen to engage and have entered your e-commerce world. No machine can predict intention behind a customer visit. A question we always ask is: How often do you buy products that are recommended to you when you visit a website? Even when we narrow the question and say Amazon's website, the number of affirmative answers we get is far fewer than those who report that they do not buy.

The second, is that for this to have any potential value requires a significant scale so that the organization can benefit from the statistically small likelihood that any algorithm can predict accurately customer behaviour. This point was well made by renowned statistician Tim Harford in a major piece on big data in the *Financial Times* (2014),[13] where he pointed out that the value to a very large organization of a very small increase in targeted offer accuracy could still be significant. Given the scale of data held on customers by organizations the size of Amazon, Walmart, Tesco or Target, they have to get this type of guessing right some of the time and even a very small increase will generate an increase in profitability that is well worth having.

A final point: the investment to generate this very small increase is significant and it is not relative to your size. If the small increase in accuracy of offer targeting delivers only a small increase in earnings then your payback period will probably end up being way beyond what any rational finance department would consider reasonable. Even worse: applying this to unknown customers, where the data you have are minimal, is very unlikely to generate any sort of acceptable return regardless of the scale of data in your sales funnel.

Social media marketing

We run twice-yearly reports on the commercial effectiveness of investing in social media marketing. These pull together our own experience with research reports from across Europe and North America and look to present the reality of the commercial returns for social media marketing investment. Our report for the second half of 2017[14] identified a continuing issue that has been evident ever since we have been advising clients on digital marketing: social media marketing continues to be the worst performing channel in terms of sales compared to any other available digital marketing choice.

One of our most intriguing findings is the continual shift from moving marketing budgets from other channels into social media marketing (Facebook generated US $26 billion in ad revenue last year, up 57 per cent from 2015[15]), even though there is still little evidence of an effective direct commercial return. This is especially true when you compare social to other channels including other digital platforms, but also non-digital channels such as television. So, whilst it is understandable that brands want to shift to social channels to test social media's effectiveness in encouraging 'consideration' (given a lack of evidence for sales 'conversion' compared to display or search, for example) it is surprising that some marketers are so insistent that there is a credible ROI, even enough to favour it over more proven channels.

One of the primary issues is the challenges brands face in measuring the impact of social media. Identifying the revenue resulting directly from investment into social channels continues to be extremely difficult. The most worrying piece of data from our research over the last six months is that 67 per cent of marketers are optimistic that they will be able to measure social in the next two years and that 50 per cent will increase their resource and budget for this in the next 12 months.[16]

Why do we think it's time to stop and reflect? Just look at these outcomes from third party reports published in 2017:

- 76 per cent of retailers are spending more on social media marketing this year, yet the same survey suggests that whilst they do this, the most cost-effective channel is email marketing.[17]

- 89 per cent of marketers believe social media marketing increases exposure and drives traffic but only 51 per cent believe investing in social media improves sales.[18]

- 48 per cent of marketers say social media marketing is the most difficult channel to get right.[19]

- 90 per cent of marketers believe social media is important[20] but 92 per cent do not know which social media management tactics are effective.[21]

- 60 per cent of consumers have concerns over the social media channels being at risk of phishing attempts or fraudulent profiles.[22]

- 43 per cent of marketers questioned on their experience of investment in social media marketing said they 'haven't been able to show impact yet'; 38 per cent claim to have a 'good qualitative sense of the impact, but not a quantitative impact'; whilst just 18.4 per cent have proved the impact quantitatively.[23]

That's not to say that there haven't been reports of a commercial impact:

- 68 per cent of respondents to one survey said Facebook ads increased sales.[24]
- Sony announced in February that through Twitter it had earned an extra £1 million in sales and Dell announced in June 2017 that its presence on Twitter accounted for US $3 million increase in sales.[25]

But these are statistics that are in a vacuum: there is no comparison against other choices – would this investment have generated more if spent differently? After all, there are sales to be got through this channel but if the return on advertising spend is significantly poorer than in other channels and you are looking for sales, then why do it?

We think investment in social media generally should be seen in the same way as investment in TV, newspapers and magazines, cinema and outdoor activities – brands are choosing to insert themselves into consumers' lives and they may, or may not, get them to consider their proposition. Just a word of warning: the last time anyone asked the consumer, the majority of them said they didn't want brands in what they consider to be their personal social space.[26]

Programmatic marketing

Despite concerns in the trade and mainstream media about the use of machine learning to place advertising, marketing agencies in particular are still pushing this heavily and digital marketing teams are still putting resources into this process. In the first half of 2018, an increasing number of major brand companies pulled out of this type of marketing for a whole range of reasons that range from concerns over where their brands are placed (this has hit YouTube particularly), to a growing belief that this approach to digital marketing is poor value for money. A 2018 report in the *Wall Street Journal* quoted P&G's Chief Marketing Officer as identifying a number of significant issues with programmatic digital advertising generally such as advert fraud, banner visibility and brand links to inappropriate material.[27] Quoted in the article his conclusions are worth recording here:

The push for more transparency into its digital ad outlays has taught P&G that marketers need to be more in control of how their dollars are spent online, he said.

As we all chased the Holy Grail of digital, self-included, we were relinquishing too much control – blinded by shiny objects, overwhelmed by big data and ceding power to algorithms.

Quoted in a separate report (2017)[28] was the JP Morgan Chase CMO who had cut the number of sites on which the brand's programmatic display ads appeared from 400,000 to 12,000 that actually generated clicks, then to 5,000 that they thought were trustworthy, so the brand would not risk advertising next to fake news and objectionable content on platforms like YouTube. In the same report, she was quoted as saying that they had not seen any deterioration in campaign performance. Interestingly, they also were reported as having moved the execution of their programmatic activity in-house to protect the integrity of their brand.

The continued lack of trust in programmatic solutions should act as a warning to leaders when asked to approve investments in this activity. A late 2017[29] survey of marketers across North America, Asia Pacific, and Europe and the Middle East found that marketer mistrust of the programmatic supply chain is significant. More than half described agencies as 'untrustworthy' and over two-thirds believed that their media agencies have 'struggled' to adapt to the demands of programmatic media buying, with concerns over financial disclosures and measurement in particular. The same amount said agencies don't fully report financial data and do not accurately measure the performance of their programmatic media buys. From our perspective, the most concerning finding was that two-thirds believed that the status quo means they lack the control over their relationships with premium publishers.

Whilst machine learning solutions provide agencies with revenue cost savings, they turn significant relationships into transactions and remove the quality of judgement from the decision as to where an advert is shown, to whom and for how long. There are some significant questions as to the accuracy of programmatic data sources that identify 'target customers' – if you are interested in this, find out who your marketing team are using to inform such activity and run yourself through it. We did this in one of the leading providers and discovered two out of three of us were listed as young women under the age of 35.

There is value to an advertiser in a smart and actively managed programmatic activity. But in our view the moves to remove the intermediary taken by firms such as JP Morgan Chase will start to be replicated across industries as brand owners look to protect their brands and maximize their performance.

Personalization

Since 2015, personalization has become a key driver of investment in e-commerce. In 2017, *Adweek*[30] reported 90 per cent of Forbes global 500 executives believe that improving customer experience was key, and 73 per cent of global marketers believe they had to deliver a personalized experience to be successful. There are some UK retail reports that would appear to support the view that personalization can drive a more effective commercial outcome:

- Marks & Spencer reported a 6 per cent increase in conversion after introduction of personalization to account holders.[31]
- Both Misguided and N Brown PLC, owners of fashion and lifestyle brands JD Williams and SimplyBe, reported a similar level of performance improvement through the introduction of personalization.[32]

However, further research brings to life the challenge of building effective personalization campaigns. The *Harvard Business Review* (2015) outlined an approach to personalization, which placed 'test and learn' at the heart of campaign success.[33] The *HBR* authors found the best way to achieve meaningful personalization is by systematically testing ideas with real customers, then rapidly iterating. The focus on testing ideas and building the organization structures that enable successful personalization is supported by Gartner research.[34] All these examples are focused on the 'known' customer: a person with whom the organization has history, holds probably quite significant data, and can recognize the customer when they 'log-in'. Even then, do not expect significant returns, and if you do not have the scale of some of these very large retail sites then accept that the investment required could make it a very inefficient use of scarce resources.

Investment in personalization for unknown customers based on propensity modelling or some other approach is just very unwise. No organization knows enough to risk significant expenditure on something that has the probability of generating little if any real return.

Leadership actions

Digital strategy carries a higher risk of failure than many other parts of business transformation. Partly, this is due to the fact that it is inextricably linked to technology and the more organizations invest in technology to help them transform performance the more complex the change becomes.

From a leadership perspective, the two key issues in technology projects are scope and scope creep, and the failure to get the culture of the organization aligned to the change you want to achieve. The second reason for the higher level of risk is a failure to put the customer at the heart of the conversation and decision-making about the e-commerce execution, particularly the failure to ensure there is genuine insight as opposed to 'expert' opinion. The final reason is the organization itself. Organizations, regardless of leadership direction, have a habit of doing the wrong things unless they are managed tightly, measured appropriately and challenged quickly. If you don't do this in digital you get mis-organization – often spotted when your e-commerce team starts proposing investment in fashion and fad as opposed to understanding and responding to the customer agenda.

This chapter has focused on what drives failure behind even the best of strategies. The drivers can be classified as: capability, particularly in the scoping, management and delivery of complex technology projects; process, particularly in the generation of deep customer insight that can create powerful hypotheses against which tests to improve performance can be devised and executed; and culture, particularly the development of expert cultures that push the customer out of the conversation and instead focus on technology change or the latest fashion to find a route to growth. Some of these drivers are far bigger than e-commerce – there is a real understanding now in the most effective organizations, for example, that large technology projects can be an existential risk. Some of them arise through a lack of detailed understanding about what good looks like in e-commerce. The challenge for leaders is to be able to spot the potential for failure and know how to act to get the business back on track. In thinking about optimizing digital strategy, leaders might like to reflect on these key questions:

- What has been your organization's track record in technology project delivery? How many of your projects meet or beat their promised returns within the timescale agreed in the business plan?

- What happened as a result of the last major change to the website? Where has performance as measured by sales gone since the change? What about other key measures such as revenue per user, conversion, traffic and so on? Did it meet its business plan?

- Have you put your business through the benchmarking app? If you have, what does it tell you?

- How much insight is being shared with you about the customer experience online? Where does this come from? Is it really from the customer gathered in real time on the site or is it from research or from an 'expert review'?

- What is the testing strategy to drive performance improvement in digital marketing investment and online sales/lead generation? Does it work – that is, is it delivering a performance improvement and if so how is this being measured?

- What investment proposals or decisions have been made in e-commerce over the last 12 months? What have they been for? How many are aimed at improving performance of the technology you already own and how many at new technology or additional functionality or products aimed at changing performance?

- Where are you spending your digital marketing and what return on investment does each channel give you?

- Are you using programmatic solutions? Who runs them? How are they reported? What brand protection is being undertaken to ensure that your marketing appears where you want it and is presented to those you want to see it?

- How often do you have e-commerce conversations about the customer agenda and the customer experience?

References

1   https://www.forbes.com/sites/brucerogers/2016/01/07/why-84-of-companies-fail-at-digital-transformation/#1e6d35a4397b [accessed 27 February 2018]

2   https://goodgrowth.co.uk/wp-content/uploads/2018/05/Infographic-Review-2017.pdf [accessed 17 May 2018]

3   https://www.consultancy.uk/news/2656/two-thirds-of-digital-transformation-projects-fail [accessed 27 February 2018]

4   https://info.couchbase.com/2017_CIO_Survey_Report_LP.html [accessed 27 February 2018]

5   https://www.mckinsey.com/business-functions/digital-mckinsey/our-insights/the-case-for-digital-reinvention [accessed 27 February 2018]

6   https://ecommercenews.eu/top-500-ecommerce-retailers-uk/ [accessed 24 February 2018]

7   https://goodgrowth.co.uk/wp-content/uploads/2018/05/Infographic-Review-2017.pdf [accessed 17 May 2018]

8   https://www.retailweekprospect.com/retailers/hm [accessed 24 February 2018]

9 https://www.netmarketshare.com/search-engine-market-share.aspx? [accessed 24 February 2018]

10 Sourced from SEMrush, May 2018

11 Adams, D (1979) *The Hitchhiker's Guide to the Galaxy*, Pan Books, London

12 Bones, C and Hammersley, J (2015) *Leading Digital Strategy,* Kogan Page, London, pp 151–58

13 Harford, T (2014) Big data: are we making a big mistake?, *FT Magazine,* 28 March

14 https://goodgrowth.co.uk/wp-content/uploads/2017/08/Good-Growth-Social-Media-Report-August2017.pdf

15 http://www.campaignlive.co.uk/article/facebook-ad-revenue-rockets-57-26bn/1422945 [accessed 1 August 2017]

16 http://www.thedrum.com/news/2017/04/07/more-half-b2b-marketers-struggle-measure-value-social-media-0 [accessed 4 April 2017]

17 https://www.internetretailer.com/2016/09/29/why-76-retailers-are-boosting-their-social-media-budgets [accessed 1 August 2017]

18 https://www.socialmediaexaminer.com/wp-content/uploads/2016/05/SocialMediaMarketingIndustryReport2016.pdf [accessed 1 August 2017]

19 https://komarketing.com/industry-news/seo-social-media-effective-difficult-execute-3238/ [accessed 1 August 2017]

20 https://www.socialmediaexaminer.com/wp-content/uploads/2016/05/SocialMediaMarketingIndustryReport2016.pdf [accessed 1 August 2017]

21 https://www.searchenginejournal.com/top-dos-donts-effective-social-media-management/169626/ [accessed 1 August 2017]

22 http://internetretailing.net/2017/02/omni-channel-sales-throttled-shoppers-wont-buy-sms-social-chat-despite-loving-mobile-apps-email/ [accessed 1 August 2017]

23 https://www.marketingweek.com/2017/03/16/social-media-spend-failing-live-expectations/ [accessed 1 August 2017]

24 https://www.internetretailer.com/2016/09/29/why-76-retailers-are-boosting-their-social-media-budgets [accessed 1 August 2017]

25 http://www.josic.com/using-social-media-to-increase-sales-and-brand-awareness [accessed 1 August 2017]

26 https://www.theguardian.com/media/2011/nov/10/uk-facebook-twitter-brands-marketing [accessed 24 February 2018]

27 https://www.wsj.com/articles/p-g-slashed-digital-ad-spending-by-another-100-million-1519915621?mod=djemCMOToday [accessed 3 March 2018]

28 https://digiday.com/marketing/cmos-trust-issue-programmatic/ [accessed 3 March 2018]

29 http://www.thedrum.com/news/2017/11/16/study-finds-agency-model-broken-when-it-comes-programmatic-and-trust [accessed 3 March 2018]

30 http://www.adweek.com/digital/is-personalization-the-new-buzz-for-2017-infographic/n [accessed 1 August 2017]

31 http://internetretailing.net/2016/05/ms-sees-sales-lift-thanks-personalisation-returning-customers/ [accessed 1 August 2017]

32 http://internetretailing.net/2016/05/embracing-personalisation-bags-missguided-33-increase-revenue/[accessed 1 August 2017]

33 https://hbr.org/2015/11/how-marketers-can-personalize-at-scale [accessed 24 February 2018]

34 https://www.cmo.com.au/article/625674/7-things-high-performing-marketing-teams-do-differently-around-digital-marketing-personalisation/ [accessed 24 February 2018]

Levers for digital 03 growth and how to use them

Executive summary

For the vast majority of leaders, digital offers the greatest opportunity as a route to market. This may offer the opportunity to disrupt or shift through a discontinuity (for example, the move to online banking and the subsequent demise of the local branch and the creation of remote customer service hubs) but it is still a channel through which to engage the customer. Over time there may well be examples where it becomes the only channel through which business is conducted, but this looks to be some way off. The demise of print has been predicted for years now, yet there is still a market for news and analysis delivered in a physical form. This chapter looks at the structural challenges and the levers available to leaders who are looking to grow online. It analyses the available data to explore trends and then lays out the choices that leaders can make that enable their businesses to grow ahead of the competition. Finally, it explores the difference between thinking about consumers and thinking about shoppers and why the latter is the key to digital success.

The growth imperative

There is no doubt that digital has impacted every industry sector in one way or another. Whether through transforming supply chain and production management by creating transparency of raw materials and enabling more efficient scheduling and flow, creating data solutions that allow for radical change to back-office management or developing communication and connectivity solutions that are creating new opportunities for products and services, our lives are being changed beyond recognition.

This book is focused firmly on the customer and the engagement of customers to grow sales and margins. What concerns us is the risk of investment in technology for technology's sake and amidst the noise and the PR fluff that surrounds digital, it is sometimes difficult to establish clearly what drives greater sales and improved margins. We believe that the single biggest differentiator is how well an enterprise delivers the required customer experience. From first touch in the sales funnel to post purchase follow-up and engagement, getting it right for your target customer means that you will grow ahead of the market and be able to do so with better margins than competitors (driven by having to spend less to acquire customers as well as getting more of those you acquire to transact or become a lead that converts in another channel). The advantage of the online-only disrupter is obvious in this regard: they are set-up and led as digital organizations that can understand how the technology can help them understand the customer. It is undoubtedly more difficult to shift the organizational mindset of an incumbent or heritage business, but just as there are disruptors who get it wrong, there are heritage businesses that get it right.

As far as customer experience is concerned there are, in our experience, four industries that illustrate both scale of the impact of disruption but also the differentiation of what generates a successful performer from one that is less so: media, travel and tourism, banking and retail.

Media

This is probably the sector that we would argue is at the front line of disruption and it is true that many titles are facing existential challenges. We have focused in this section more on media than banking and travel as the emergent digital model – subscription – is one that has started to be adopted in a range of industries as a potential for growth, and it is worth understanding why it is so attractive.

But the media landscape has changed dramatically since the United Kingdom's vote to leave the European Union in June 2016 and the election of Donald Trump as US president in the November of the same year. Uncertainty has turned the tables on the seemingly inexorable rise of 'fake news' and subscriptions have soared in mainstream outlets as people look for ways of making sense of an emerging world, that is unfamiliar and potentially threatening of established 'norms'. Here are some of the statistics we came across in 2017 whilst researching this book:[1]

- *The New York Times* now has 130 million monthly readers and 3.5 million paid subscriptions, which is more than double the company's subscriber count since Q3 2015.

- January 2017 was the biggest subscription month ever for *The New Yorker* with a 300 per cent increase over January 2016. The magazine now has its largest circulation ever, at more than a million.
- *The Washington Post* reported it had 'doubled digital subscription revenue in the past 12 months, with a 75 per cent increase in new subscribers.'
- The *Financial Times* reported a 33 per cent increase in new subscriptions over the normal run rate in the two weeks following the US election, followed by a 20 per cent jump for the rest of the year. Brexit more than doubled that with a 75 per cent increase in the month around the vote.

Print continues to defy talk of an imminent demise

We can only hope that this is the beginning of a flight from fake news and conspiracy theories that seem to flourish in the undiscriminating melting pot of social media. In addition, it could also be a sign that FT CEO John Ridding may have put his finger on the value of the print product when he talked about the unique attributes of the print experience (*The Drum*, 2017). In his opinion, these are satisfaction of completion, the valuable service of selection and judgement for readers and an informed hierarchy of importance. His interview suggested that while personalization is an obviously powerful driver of engagement with audiences, 'serendipity should not be understated'.[2] Whilst it would seem that print is in a long-term decline, reports of its death might have been exaggerated. National readership data in the United States from Nielsen Scarborough showed 51 per cent of those who consume a newspaper read it exclusively in print (Nielsen Scarborough, 2016).[3]

But the money is missing out the publisher

The challenge for print, however, is that advertising revenue is declining much faster than sales and subscriptions. In the United States, newspaper advertising spend fell around US $5 billion in 5 years: from $20.7 billion in 2011 to $16.1 billion in 2017 (Statista, 2018),[4] and in the United Kingdom, the decline was from £6.4 billion in 2007 to £2.8 billion by 2014 (Statista, 2018).[5]

The growth, however, in digital subscriptions has also been significant. In our work with *The Economist* we demonstrated that there is still a significant underlying opportunity to grow revenues from subscription.[6] This is critically important as the challenge for digital is that it hasn't replaced print as the recipient of this marketing investment. Data from PwC and the Interactive Advertising Bureau comparing the first half of 2016 with

Figure 3.1   The percentage share of US online advertising revenue

Mobile takes bigger share of ad budgets

Percentage share of US online advertising revenues
■ Half-year 2016   ■ Half-year 2017

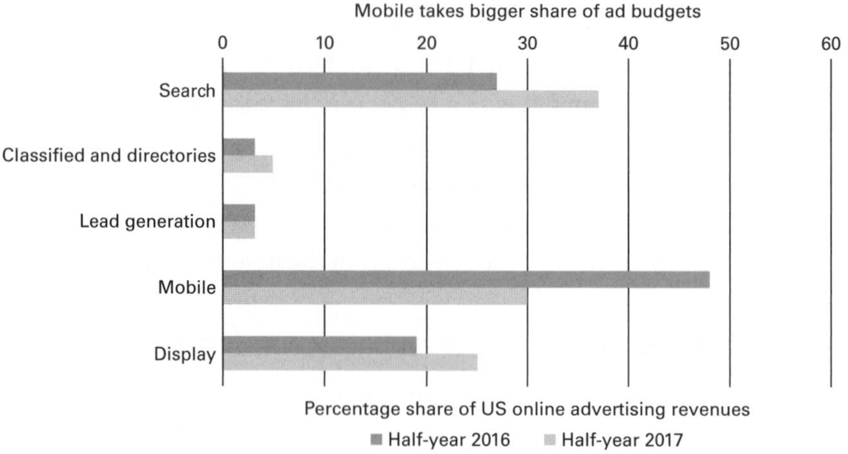

SOURCE Data from IAB/PWC Internet Advertising Report: Half Year 2017

the first half of 2017[7] (Figure 3.1) show that the percentage of advertising spend allocated to display adverts in the United States – the mainstream revenue generator for digital publishers – has fallen back significantly and is predicted to go further. This fall seems to have two primary drivers: a growing concern about the quality of advertising outcomes as agencies automate advertising delivery for their clients and the perceived shift of consumer attention to smartphones.

Whilst a superficial reading of this may suggest that display advertising has been the victim of the shift to engagement through smartphones, the move of media agencies into 'AdTech' and, in particular, the rise of programmatic marketing also plays a role. This technology automates the buying of advertising space and the delivery of digital display advertising and through no fault of the mainstream publishers has fallen into considerable disrepute with major advertisers.[8]

Not only has the application of technology shaken confidence in display advertising investment, through concerns about fraud and about the use of 'impressions' to determine whether or not the advertiser pays (and they pay when 30–50 per cent of pixels are presented to the browser) but also the insertion of these technology solutions into the transaction between advertiser and publisher has reduced income for the publisher and value for the advertiser. Some publishers are testing changes to their own models to provide advertiser reassurance – for example, the idea of 'attention metrics' being trialled by the *Financial Times*.[9] The challenge for them is to break away from the tyranny of the technology platforms to offer better value to advertisers.

Data published by AppNexus in 2015[10] suggest that technology owners are taking 60 per cent of the advertiser dollar from the publisher and, as a result, both the publisher and the advertiser get less: less 'consumer impact' for the advertiser and less revenue for the publisher.

Does mobile advertising make sense?

Well it depends, is the answer. A search for definitive studies, that show display ads aimed at mobile devices working better than say email or pay per click marketing, has yet to throw up any recent evidence that they drive sales better than these proven approaches. There is certainly considerable evidence from our own client base to suggest investing in social media advertising tends to generate low-quality traffic and, as a result, fewer transactions regardless of device. There is evidence out there, if rather dated (2014), to suggest in-app adverts do work better than desktop display ads,[11] however, in fairness that's only looking at commercial returns against a medium that has never performed that well as a sales generator.

Newer entrants such as Weve offer a highly customized direct to smartphone proposition, where data from consenting adults are utilized to target more 'personalized marketing messages'. This looks promising and, it has to be said, brand owners also invest to build awareness and engagement as well as sales, and this may explain the increase.

The challenge behind these figures is the inexorable rise of ad blockers. Estimates now suggest that in 2017 there were 86.6 million ad-blocking users in the United States.[12] As smartphone users close out their phones to advertisements it may well be that we see a return to more classic advertising solutions through publisher-distributed content. The irony is that the gainers out of all this are those who now stand accused of providing the platforms and communications channels for fake news. Google and Facebook currently dominate digital marketing – in 2017 the *Financial Times* reported a forecast from WPP/Group M that 84 per cent of digital marketing spend will go to these two technology giants.[13]

Even more worrying for publishers is that the 'distributed content model' offered by Facebook, Snapchat, YouTube and other content platforms utilized by publishers to drive value seems not to be delivering significantly either. A report cited by the *Financial Times* suggests that on average in the first half of 2016 publishers generated only about US \$1.2 million additional revenue.[14]

And do paywalls work?

There is no one defined route to market model for the old print industry. It is clear from this case study that high-quality curated content can be sold without a heightened context, which drives consumers to focus on ensuring they have the best news and analysis. Our work for *The Economist* and for the *Financial Times*, which has one of the most draconian access policies, shows that good quality content, sold well, can drive growth. The model that is most likely to fail unless trends reverse is the 'free content' model, as an online user just isn't as valuable as a print customer. *Management Today* (2017) reported that the *Daily Mail*, which had increased traffic to its website 550 per cent since 2009, now has over 14 million daily users, but that only brought in £73 million of revenue in 2016 (up 18 per cent), compared with £499 million (down 7 per cent) from its 1.7 million print customers.[15]

The Guardian Media Group revealed a full-year operating loss of £69 million in 2016. Their response has been to launch a membership scheme and again working alongside them in 2015, we demonstrated that a well-developed proposition with a clear target market could drive revenue growth. So much so, that you now cannot escape being encouraged to support their journalism at the bottom of every article.

Whilst a bleaker world has given quality publishers a respite, it doesn't signal a longer-term reversal, at least not yet. There is a market for both print and digital news and comment and one that is willing to subscribe. There is also no evidence that younger demographics are any less willing to become subscribers – they just need to know the benefits to them of making the commitment as our work with *The Economist* can attest.[16]

Travel and tourism

Not so long ago, most people booked holidays through a travel agent or bought a 'package' that included all the elements of travel and stay from an agent or holiday company. We bought train tickets from stations and bus or tram tickets from the driver (or even longer ago the conductor). If we wanted a taxi we hailed one on the street or pre-booked it. If we were touring by car and wanted a B&B or hotel we phoned ahead or drove around looking for the 'vacancy' sign. Today, we can do all of this and more from our smartphone on the move at any time.

Travel was one of the earliest sectors to be impacted by digital. It has been some time now since airlines offered to sell us tickets online and travel agents opened digital shops. Digitalization, aided in no small way by increasingly ubiquitous free high-speed Wi-Fi connections, ensures that we can book flights and hotels online, choose to stay in a stranger's house (with or without them being there) and, rather than booking any old restaurant, get online immediately and assess restaurants in our locality from the perspective of price, cuisine or other customers' reviews.

The general growth in population and in wealth in both developed and developing economies is certainly responsible for the fact that more people are travelling than ever before, but there is certainly an argument that digitalization has given us far greater choice by providing access to information and alternatives way beyond the capacity offered by any travel agent. It is also true that digitalization has enabled disrupter companies – for example, Airbnb, aggregators such as Booking.com and meta-aggregators such as Trivago – to enter the market and transform not just business models but also reduce the cost and, as a result, open the market to more travellers.

There are now far fewer travel agents on UK high streets than there were 20 years ago, mainly as a result of most of us not using them anymore. Fewer than 20 per cent of UK residents visited a travel agent in 2016 and nearly 75 per cent of them now regularly book their holidays online (Kayak, 2017).[17]

There has been much talk of the rise of the sharing economy – particularly in the context of the success of Airbnb; however, we have to remember that this is not a new phenomenon. Offering rooms for the night is a centuries-old tradition, but one that seemed to have died away somewhat as more and more people travelled through tour operators or wanted to stay in motels and hotels that offered a more private experience where the idiosyncrasies of your hosts wasn't a trip hazard. Digitalization has helped to rekindle our willingness to do this and has made it a far less random experience. In 2015 it would seem that 9 per cent of UK and US travellers had rented space in a private home or apartment and around 18 per cent of travellers had done the same in Brazil, Russia and China (Phocuswright, 2015).[18]

Banking

Banking would seem initially a sector where the take-up would have been slow but given the dreadful customer service experience in-branch of so many high street banks, customers have moved quite quickly into virtual transacting. What has been less obvious, due in part to the stringent rules on capital imposed by regulators after the 2008 financial crash, is evidence of disruptive entrants into banking.

In the United States, data (WWW Metrics, 2018) suggest that online and mobile banking is now embraced by nearly 80 per cent of internet-connected households (about 75 per cent of all US households). Moreover, the survey reporting this information also found that this practice is not restricted to any particular demographic group. It is growing across a deep and wide demographic that includes age, income and gender.[19] One of the things that makes disruption so challenging in this sector is, as the data suggest, the fact that those who are utilizing online or mobile banking are extremely loyal to their bank of choice.

Data for Great Britain – the United Kingdom excluding Northern Ireland – (Statista, 2017) suggest that nearly two-thirds of the population are now using online banking regularly.[20] Ever since the first secure internet systems for financial operations became available on the large scale, accessing of one's bank account online to carry out transactions, pay off credit cards, establish credit lines or invest savings has become one of the fastest-growing areas of internet activities. The same report suggested that by 2007 30 per cent were accessing their bank account online. The growth in this activity area has been steady over time and the degree of penetration can be seen in the rapidly increasing rate of branch closures in UK high streets.

Digitization is bringing further digital banking advancements including in mobile banking and mobile banking apps and in solutions for travellers, as well as an explosion in B2B finance solutions. The biggest potential disruption though is the creation of a digital wallet, which has the potential to change our millennia-old relationship with physical coinage and currency. The best illustration of this is the impact of innovation in China.

Driven primarily by WeChat and Alipay, the two major online payment platforms in China, cashless and cardless transactions are now an increasingly large part of daily life. A report in the *China Daily* in 2017[21] suggested that cashlessness was a new Chinese characteristic. It cites a report by Tencent, the Chongyang Institute for Financial Studies at Renmin University of China and French market research firm Ipsos, that suggested 84 per cent of Chinese were 'comfortable' going out with only mobile phones, no cash. It also reported more than 70 per cent saying that they could live more than a week with only 100 yuan (US $15) in cash, and 52 per cent only using cash for less than a quarter of their total monthly consumption.

The new payment pattern has won over Chinese consumers with its convenience and flexibility, squeezing the market share of card and cash payments. Data from the People's Bank of China showed a total of 157 trillion yuan of payments were made on mobile devices in China in 2016, more than 200 times that in the United States in the same period. The figure is expected to continue expanding by 50 per cent each year, it said.

The *China Daily* asserts that in a remote mountain village of central China's Hunan Province, one can easily buy a hen or groceries by scanning a QR code, and reports the Payment and Clearing Association of China stating that mobile payment users in small towns and the countryside account for half of the total in China. The percentage of mobile payment users in the countryside is even higher than in provincial capitals.

Retail

E-commerce sales in the United States tripled between 2007 and 2017 with the current rate running at about 15 per cent of all retail sales (Smart Insights, 2018 – e-commerce is defined as sales of goods or services directly to the end consumer and excluding transactions in cooked food, restaurants, cars and fuel).[22] In the United Kingdom, Europe's most advanced online market, the same report suggests that the share of all transactions in 2017 was just under 18 per cent.[23] Across the rest of the European Union, the picture is less advanced with only Germany and France having online sales above 10 per cent of the total retail market. The United States is still the leader in online retailing compared to Europe. The 11 largest EU members have a total population of 414 million (out of 520 million across the whole European Union) compared to the United States' 316 million; 66.0 per cent of the US public shopped online compared to 52.8 per cent across the leading EU economies in 2016. The Europeans also spend less: every online shopper in Europe spent an average of £921.83 (US $1,194.77 or €1,062.02) in 2016 compared to £1,477.71 (US $1,915.23 or €1,702.43) in the United States (Retail Research, 2017).[24]

At the higher end of these penetration statistics, for example in the United Kingdom, the impact on traditional retailers is now becoming significant. Many are asking themselves what they should do with what looks like an increasingly under-utilized amount of retail space: on the high street, in out-of-town shopping centres and in shopping malls. There is evidence of some reinvention in the use of this space – for example, the co-location of stores in the same space, the rise of in-store concessions and the development of more 'social' space. There are also signs of a more structural shift in the role of high streets themselves with Deloitte (2014) suggesting a focus on convenience and collection as shoppers look to stay local.[25]

Digitalization has also had a profound impact not just on preferred channels but also on where shoppers are spending their time and what attracts their attention. Data from Newzoo's Global Market Mobile Report published in April 2017[26] show that in 27 countries including China, India, Brazil and Russia, smartphone penetration was more than 50 per cent. Figure 3.2 shows the 10 countries with the greatest level of penetration of smartphones.

Figure 3.2   Smartphone penetration, April 2017

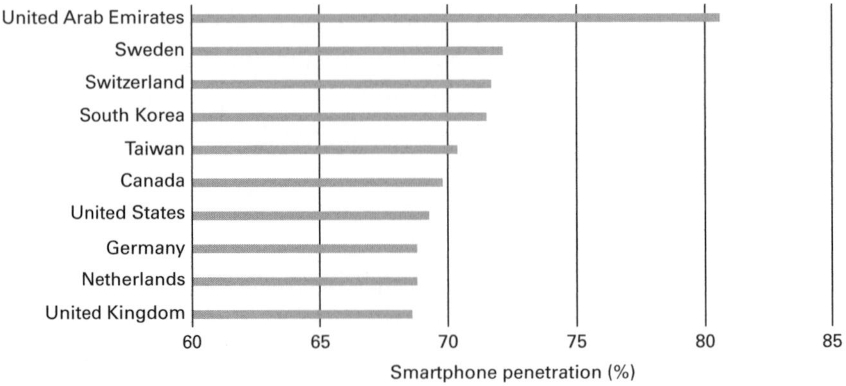

SOURCE Data from Newzoo: Global Market Mobile Report

The rapid adoption of the smartphone in these economies in particular is transforming how people live their lives and to some extent how they shop. Data from our all-client database (Figure 3.3) show how the smartphone has grown to become the primary channel for shoppers to reach e-commerce websites.

Two things to say about this data: first, these are proportional shares of a growing number of visits so the data are not suggesting that there is a massive drop-off in laptop/desktop visits; rather that, in a fast-growing market, the growth is coming from smartphones. Second, and more intriguingly, despite the growth in visits from smartphones people seem to be using them differently – they browse and then may well choose another device or channel to complete a transaction. Our all-client database suggests that for every completed transaction on a retail website from a smartphone there are two from a tablet and three from a desktop/laptop.

This shift presents another challenge for retailers as they have to think about segmenting visitors by shopping intent and being able somehow to spot this and satisfy it in the absence of human interaction. And before anyone says chatbot, there is a huge difference between a human interaction via LiveChat to deal with a problem and a random pre-programmed interaction that is trying to neutralize the inadequacies of a website. Whilst there is plenty of evidence to suggest the customers like to self-serve and simple automation to help them do this is welcomed, the vast majority want to know, if there is a self-service failure, that the human interaction that inevitably follows needs to be able to pick up from where they left off[27] – and today, that is still a big challenge.

Figure 3.3 The shift to smartphones, 2014–17

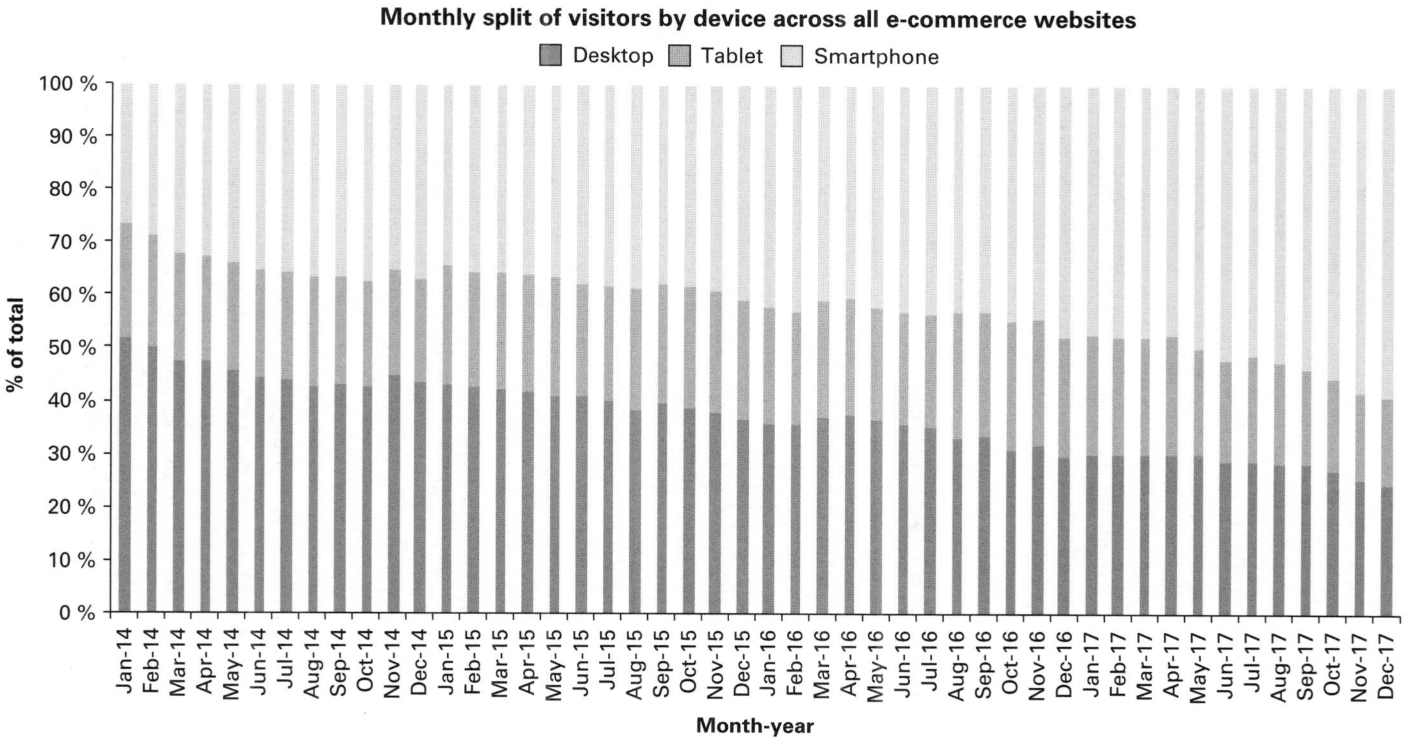

Monthly split of visitors by device across all e-commerce websites

Legend: Desktop ▮ Tablet ▯ Smartphone ▯

Y-axis: % of total (0 % to 100 %)

X-axis: Month-year (Jan-14 to Dec-17)

SOURCE © Good Growth Ltd

But it's not just structural changes that are putting pressure on retailers in the United States and the United Kingdom in particular: in these markets the impact of Amazon and the way in which it is dominating online retailing in an increasing number of sectors is creating a crisis of competition. We deal with the issues surrounding Amazon and the other big tech players in Chapter 5, but for now here are two data points[28] that show you the sheer scale of Amazon's reach in the two most developed e-commerce markets in the world:

- In the United States, Amazon attracted over 710 million monthly searches in 2018 from desktop and laptop devices.
- In the United Kingdom, the same data point was over 169 million – this was approximately 24 per cent of all monthly searches to the 150 top e-commerce retail sites in the United Kingdom in April 2018.

Customer experience

We believe that, regardless of sector, those who will thrive are the organizations that understand the customer in the market (not just those who buy but also those who are looking to buy but choose to do this with competitors, or don't buy at all) and work hard to put their priorities front and centre of everything that they do. At the heart of this is the need for organizational humility rather than expertise. When learning about a foreign culture, the wisest advice anyone can give you is that you need to become expert in explaining your own culture – that way, others will share similar insights and help you learn about theirs. The same strategy is the one that works best for customers: there is no such thing as a customer experience expert, rather you want to build expertise in getting customers to articulate their experiences and what they do and don't like about them.

This is the single most important driver of growth online and one where, despite all the investment, many enterprises fail to make the grade. Our work across the globe suggests that a significant proportion of customers feel let down by online shopping journeys, so much so that of those who look at a product page, 95 per cent do not buy.[29] There are many organizations that talk a good game but fall some way short of our expectations. Having worked with brands including *The Economist*, GAME, ODEON/UCI, Fitness First, Virgin Active, LK Bennett, JD Williams, the *Financial Times*, Channel 4, QVC, *The Telegraph*, Time Inc., Regus and BUPA over the past six years, we have been exposed to a considerable amount of customer feedback from all over the globe. From this experience, we can tell you a story of customer engagement against which you can judge how close your current online execution is to ghastly.

Maeve's moment of madness – a customer experience fairy tale

Maeve is looking for a gift for her partner Lesley. She's looking for a jumper and, because she wants to start with a range of potential choices, she starts by searching on Google. (Despite the hype about apps and social media, just under 0.6 billion searches that lead to a customer landing on a website for the largest 150 retailers are carried out in the United Kingdom every month[30] – that's 9.1 searches for every UK resident per month.[31])

She starts on her smartphone. (On our all-client index, traffic to websites from smartphones now sits at around 50 per cent of all traffic to websites.) She clicks the link for a smart-looking blue cashmere cardigan from a retailer from whom she's bought successful clothing items for Lesley before – this puts her, however, on a page that displays a range of women's fashion items. She then spends five minutes looking for cardigans in the specific style and colour she saw displayed in the search results and fails. The site is image heavy and takes ages to load so she's now frustrated and losing connectivity; she stops searching and makes a mental note to look when she gets home.

At home and on her tablet (on our all-client database, desktop/laptop/tablet users are twice as likely to be actively shopping compared to those on smartphones), it's back to Google and a classic search for the retailer's site takes her to the home page. Knowing what she wants, she explores the navigation options but can't find cashmere cardigans. She tries the search engine but it produces nothing apart from a helpful assertion that she made a mistake and could try spelling cardigans correctly. An extended piece of forensic detective work enables her to stumble upon the product by accident. The retailer tells her this is a 'cashmere short woollen jacket-style jumper' – clearly, she should have known this.

The product page was organized to help someone looking for a size 10, pink, short, woollen, jacket-style jumper to make an easy purchase. A size 14, blue one becomes a battle of wits, especially when Maeve wants to understand whether it is washable. As she clicks on the add-to-basket button the site then takes her off into a world of additional products, recommended for her in a thoughtful and personalized way; she was unmoved by the Kim Kardashian scent on promotion and thought she understood why she was being recommended to buy a new handbag though didn't want it, but the recommendation for a set of bath towels, a chandelier and erotic soap were just random.

So Maeve, apprehensive about the washability of the cardigan (yes, she was still insisting on calling it that) but confident that Lesley would love it, set off to checkout. This started by insisting that she open an account she will probably never use again and then offered her a comprehensive form to complete enabling the retailer to fill in every field on their expensive and underutilized CRM software. The payment process put her in a circle of death where she missed several hidden required items and every time she put one right she was required to enter nearly every important thing again.

Exhausted, Maeve felt that at least she had avoided wasting her lunchtime at work and could now let the delivery process take the strain. She had hoped for completion too soon. You see, the retailer had chosen a courier that didn't offer any flexibility and wanted her to stay in all day to receive it as they insisted on making it a 'sign-for' parcel. As a result, the parcel isn't delivered and the redelivery options that didn't require her to stay at home were completely inconvenient, including heading for the depot some 24 miles away from her house.

When the cardigan finally arrived, Maeve discovered that it was too small, and to return it required her to take it to a collection point some 8 miles from home. Despite this, within an hour of it being delivered, she was sent an email asking for a product review and another some hours later asking for a review of the courier. She did look for an opportunity to give a short, simple feedback to both, however the 35-question email from the retailer seemed a rather big ask for an item she ultimately didn't want. These emails continued for some weeks afterwards until she finally unsubscribed out of sheer irritation.

That week she went to the shops and bought the cardigan she wanted: it took her 10 minutes and the shop assistant called it a cardigan.

If anecdotal evidence from friends and family over the peak period from Black Friday to the New Year sales is to be believed, this is less of a fairy story and more of a reality show. More significant from an empirical perspective is our experience over the last 12 months, which demonstrates how much value there is still to be captured from doing nothing more than understanding customer frustration and investing in testing alternative experiences to try to address it.

In 2017 across a range of sectors, the stories that customers play back to us suggest a few common themes that continue to frustrate them as they look to buy products and services. Our findings (Good Growth, 2016–17) point at the following issues:

- 45 per cent cite difficulty finding products;
  - 19 per cent due to stock availability;
  - 11 per cent due to a poor product page;
- 30 per cent point to technical issues;
- 11 per cent blame unclear or unattractive delivery terms;
- 10 per cent say they were thwarted by the navigation;
- 9 per cent (and only 9 per cent) say it was price;
- 6 per cent point at a lack of product information.

There are two conclusions to be drawn from this list:

1 That 45 per cent of users fail to buy because they cannot find a desired product represents a significant lost opportunity and also suggests that the current 'best practice' approach to serving thousands of products to users through hundreds of categories and subcategories isn't working. Having worked extensively in fashion, we can confirm that, as far as the vast majority of online customers are concerned, over-segmentation (for example, smart jeans, casual jeans) is a frustration.

2 That we frequently find technical issues to be a major cause of failures suggests that e-commerce retailers may be focusing on technological innovation over the essential activity of maintaining basic site functionality. It's no good having the latest gizmo if the basics don't work.

So, what does good customer experience look like? Generally speaking, it follows customer interest. A good example of this is that if a customer has searched for a specific product, then the result presented should take the customer to the most relevant place in your website, not to a more general page, or even worse, the home page: Amazon is the master of this. If your product or service is more complex or can be customized or there are many variations, then the landing page needs to help the customer start the purchase journey: Apple does this particularly well.

Online shopping has to be intuitive and that means that navigation structures need to be developed from a customer perspective: UK department store John Lewis is a great example. It also means that search delivers. There isn't a silver bullet on search: one of the biggest things is to understand how customers describe things and ensure that these terms are appropriately tagged; the other is to ensure that you handle failed search enquiries effectively. A good example of search handling is found in UK catalogue retailer Argos. Finally, you have to have product pages that are comprehensive and understand the order in which your target customer wants to engage with the detail: a great example of these is upmarket fashion house LK Bennett.

Don't let your CRM system drive the deal. Overly demanding checkout processes (including failing to let customers checkout without you harvesting their data) are a turn-off for many customers, and basket abandonment rates are generally high. Customers want as frictionless a checkout as they can whilst protecting security of payment: the master of this is Amazon. Apps do offer easier and faster payment – but they have downsides too. There are very few apps people are happy to have sucking up battery to run all the time on their smartphone or tablet. There are also few apps that customers use regularly enough to always have the password/user ID to hand or in the front of their memory. Amazon (powered by Prime in particular) and millennial fashion retailer ASOS are examples of apps that work in this regard.

Think about the customer after taking their money. The online customer journey may finish with a nice 'thank you' page and an email, but the total journey doesn't finish until the goods arrive or the service is consumed. Your choice of courier could define whether customers return: if they don't have a customer-oriented approach to delivery management then your customer may never return. Make returns easy – check when you set up return routines that they work for all customers and not just those in large metropolitan areas.

Finally, think about this as a relationship that builds over time and don't act like a needy friend or relative who constantly seeks approval and therefore does nothing but ask you about themselves all the time. There is value in thinking about the engagement of new customers; something that UK online retailer JD Williams does particularly well. Think about how reviews and referrals are handled – eBay has driven its business model through this; and finally, don't ask people endless questions about you and what you want to know about you! Use simple, open feedback surveys that make it clear that you want your customers' feedback, and then act on it and tell them what you've done.

There are some organizations out there claiming that the answer to improving customer experience is personalization. We believe that the keyword is relevance. You cannot personalize for people you don't know. Actually, it's pretty difficult to personalize for people you do know – after all, how many of us have actually bought something recommended to us by Amazon or any other site where we can arrive as a known quantity? The cost of personalization is significant and, unless you have very significant scale, you may well not recoup the investment in the substantial modelling that is required.[32]

Generating a return on personalization investment is further complicated by recurring patterns of customer behaviour. Whilst users may visit multiple times before transacting, the preference of guest checkout, particularly for smaller retailers, restricts the ability to capture user details. In addition, much of personalization relies on the logic that because I bought 'x' last time I want to buy 'y' this time. Or even 'because I told you a year ago I was interested in "a" I am still as interested'. These assumptions come with significant risk – all you know is something from a point in time – you know nothing about any subsequent sales engagement.

In fact, customers are more likely to respond to a simpler nudge based on relevance – the sharing of what others actually bought in addition to the item they have put in their basket. Amazon is reported as attributing 35 per cent of its revenue to its smart algorithms that link what other customers did to your interest.[33]

Growth drivers

The importance of customer experience is a critical enabler of growth. It allows you to service the need of someone who has chosen to engage with your proposition. To deliver it requires you to have that in-depth understanding of the customer in the market. But on its own, customer experience can't drive growth. That comes from doing four things well:

Finding more of the right customers

Knowing how to locate the right customers and investing scarce resources in working hard to optimize marketing spend online ensures that you can maximize the interest in your target segment. Investing somewhere because others are doing the same is always a poor strategy. Be cognizant of the stages at which you may be finding your targets. Generally speaking, if you are invading their space (for example, a display ad on a site they are visiting for other reasons or an ad on a social media site) then you are encouraging consideration, more than likely at a later date than now or even over the next week or so. If you are responding to an active search then you are talking to customers who are more likely to want to buy – this is conversion thinking. The type of keyword used may help you understand how far down the funnel they are. For example, a search for best SUV would suggest someone is at the beginning of the search for the right car so the engagement is much more about introducing your SUV and why it's a great choice. If someone searches for your model they are much closer to that decision and don't need to be resold the car, but engaged in the detail of choices, delivery and where the car can be test driven. This isn't personalization; it's segmentation based on an understanding of customer intention.

Attracting more of the right customers

Data-driven insight should not be confined to the task of optimizing a sales engagement on a website. Lazy agency behaviour and the adoption of simplistic automation to increase margins mean that a great deal of paid digital advertising does not deliver an adequate return. Test and learn strategies are as important in ensuring that money spent attracting interest generates a result in the target group of customers. Ad position and click through rates are vanity measures unless they are tied to transactions (becoming a lead or making a purchase). Campaigns need to be optimized just as much as landing pages and sales funnels. Effective digital marketing is less about getting the creative right first time and more about testing alternative headlines and copy to learn about what creative is most effective at attracting customers, who then go on to convert (even if this is on a return visit).

Persuading them to act

The key here is understanding conversion effectiveness. Of itself, a conversion rate of 2, 3 or 4 per cent (or higher, or lower) tells you very little. Even if you have benchmarks to judge this against they aren't that helpful. They are always historical and don't reflect necessarily the context in which your business is operating. What is much more insightful is understanding how many of the people on your site at any one time have landed with the intention of buying, and of those how many you persuaded to act. You find out the level of intention through smart intention surveying; the actual number comes from your analytics. This is conversion effectiveness. You can put a value on investing in improvement by taking your average basket value and multiplying it by the number of intending purchasers then subtracting the actual number of purchasers. Taking this forward as a key performance indicator (KPI) will help you understand how good your performance really is.

Retaining their loyalty and commitment

Loyalty is a big word. It is something that is given to you and, if you abuse a relationship, it is something that can be quickly taken away. If it is, then it is difficult, if not impossible, to win it back. Despite this, many businesses treat their customer relationship management as a one-way channel to drive additional sales. Many don't even ask for permission to build a relationship but grab the customers' data and start bombarding them with emails. This is not the way to build loyalty. Wearing down the customer to give up and pay attention through attrition is hardly a strategy for a successful relationship that builds over time and creates genuine lifetime value. For one thing, customers are now far more likely to shop around even if they end up choosing to deal with you again; and for another, even if I have once booked an hotel in New York through you, don't keep assuming for the next six months I might want another – that will drive most customers nuts! Think about loyalty as a relationship: enable your customers to define what they want from you. Don't impose your agenda on them. Stop guessing (however smart your algorithm) and start asking.

The final point in this section is about digital marketing. It is really important to separate out brand from the process of enabling customers to find what they want and engage with it. At first reading this may seem an odd thing to say. Surely a brand is what attracts in the first place? That is true if we think of consumers as a whole, but online, and especially by the time they are searching and entering your digital ecosystem they have stopped being consumers and have become shoppers.

Your brand may have a 'tone of voice' but in a physical shop you don't impose this on your shop assistants; indeed, in our experience, the best shop assistants have their own tone of voice and ways of engaging the customer that are unique to them but resonate with the customer. It is this resonance that is so much more important when engaging with people setting out on a shopping mission than your brand guidelines. You are in their space now and if you want them to engage, you'll need to be willing to experiment until you find the words, tone and style that work for them. The outcome of this process may well be that you break your brand guidelines because you are not talking about yourself, but you are in conversation with the customer.

Treat externally generated consumer profiles carefully when thinking about engagement online. Whilst it may be helpful to have these when thinking about consumer and brand marketing, and for some 'lifestyle' propositions they may work well, generally they have a limited utility when it comes to shoppers. First, it is difficult to determine who is on the site unless you are sampling users regularly, as many of the tools that claim to inform you about users can get it very wrong. Secondly, shoppers often buy for other consumers so you are probably talking to a wider spectrum of potential customers than you might think. Finally, whilst you may aspire to a market segment, you may not be selling to it: when we worked for BHS before its collapse, we discovered that their average customer was 10 years older than the one they thought they were selling to!

There are places where brand marketing is important: like television, cinema or print in pre-digital days. Marketing activities that interrupt people in their daily lives need to capture the brand proposition. In digital marketing these are things like social media marketing and display advertising. However, much of the marketing activity that drives growth online is what used to be called 'below the line' activity. You want to talk to customers to trigger their buying responses, and that means understanding what works for them.

Leadership actions

Digital has impacted virtually every sector of the economy and nearly every demographic group of customers (be they charity donors, potential subscribers, leads for complex or large-value transactions completed offline or retail customers). Trends suggest that economic activity transacted online will continue to grow and that as it does the use of smartphones/mobile devices will represent the fastest growing segment. In this context, leaders need to make choices about where and how to allocate both capital and revenue expenditure such that they can maximize returns and grow at least as fast, if not faster, than the competition.

This chapter has looked at the growth imperative. It has argued that from a commercial perspective the key challenge is to make sure that the investment in technology and in the activities associated with sales and marketing online creates a positive return as quickly as possible, not least because technology has an increasingly short shelf-life. In particular, it suggests that the starting point for leaders in thinking about where to allocate resources is the current customer experience and where that is failing to perform to its potential. It has also argued that alongside this there needs to be a clear understanding of what it takes to locate, acquire, engage and retain customers and finally, that in setting the parameters for marketing investment, leaders insist on a strategy that defines the role for brand and the freedom to enable customer engagement that delivers growth.

There are three things that leaders might want to consider as they assess how well positioned they are today to drive growth online:

- Take yourself through the main customer journeys from search through to transaction and completion. Identify what worked/didn't work for you. Get your friends and family to do the same – they are far more likely to tell you the unvarnished truth than those who work for you.

  – Once you've established your data baseline, test it against your e-commerce team. Have they got an insight platform that can attest to your experience or dispute it? Or are they working on assumptions and opinions or part-data?

  – If there's a gap, insist on a full insight platform so the voice of the customer can be clearly heard and used as the catalyst for change.

- Review your online marketing strategy. Is it clear which channels are being used for consideration and which for conversion? What are the KPIs in each channel and is it clear what the return on advertising spend is per channel?

  – Is there clear segmentation thinking about stages in the shopping journey? Are you thinking shopper as opposed to consumer?

  – As you look at the data, is there a clear test and learn programme behind your marketing campaigns?

- Do you have a loyalty scheme/programme? If not, why not?

  – Is it a transmission of endless emails or a relationship building activity with two-way communication?

  – Who is setting the customer agenda – you or the customer?

References

1 https://www.thestreet.com/story/14024114/1/trump-bump-grows-into-subscription-surge.html [accessed 28 March 2018]

2 http://www.thedrum.com/opinion/2017/01/12/who-wants-today-s-newspapers-ft-chief-john-ridding-why-print-still-has-future [accessed 28 March 2018]

3 http://www.nielsen.com/us/en/insights/news/2016/newspapers-deliver-across-the-ages.html [accessed 28 March 2018]

4 https://www.statista.com/statistics/272411/newspaper-advertising-spending-in-the-us/ [accessed 12 May 2018]

5 https://www.statista.com/statistics/274622/print-advertising-expendature-in-the-united-kingdom-uk/ [accessed 12 May 2018]

6 https://goodgrowth.co.uk/wp-content/uploads/2017/03/Can-subscription-save-quality-journalismpdf.pdf [accessed 12 May 2018]

7 https://www.iab.com/wp-content/uploads/2017/12/IAB-Internet-Ad-Revenue-Report-Half-Year-2017-REPORT.pdf [accessed 12 May 2018]

8 https://www.marketingweek.com/2016/01/26/ad-fraud-the-marketing-industrys-7-2bn-problem [accessed 1 September 2017]

9 http://www.thedrum.com/news/2016/07/20financial-times-thinks-programmatic-time-nigh-cost-hour-red-bull-credit-suisse-and [accessed 1 September 2017]

10 https://www.exchangewire.com/blog/2015/09/11/ad-tech-2016-consolidate-commoditise-converge/ [accessed 12 May 2018]

11 https://www.forbes.com/sites/roberthof/2014/08/27/study-mobile-ads-actually-do-work-especially-in-apps/#1ec1666b57aa [accessed 30 March 2018]

12 https://www.emarketer.com/Article/US-Ad-Blocking-Jump-by-Double-Digits-This-Year/1014111 [accessed 30 March 2018]

13 https://www.ft.com/content/cf362186-d840-11e7-a039-c64b1c09b482 [accessed 12 May 2018]

14 *Financial Times*, #Tech FT, 9 March 2017 [accessed 30 March 2018]

15 http://www.managementtoday.co.uk/slow-death-print/article/138895 [accessed 30 March 2018]

16 https://goodgrowth.co.uk/wp-content/uploads/2017/03/Can-subscription-save-quality-journalismpdf.pdf [accessed 12 May 2018]

17 https://www.kayak.co.uk/news/mobile-travel-report-2017/ [accessed 27 January 2018]

18 http://www.phocuswright.com/Travel-Research/Research-Updates/2015/Surprising-Rise-of-Renting-Shared-Space [accessed 27 January 2018]

19 http://wwwmetrics.com/banking.htm [accessed on 27 January 2018]

20 https://www.statista.com/statistics/286273/internet-banking-penetration-in-great-britain/ [accessed 27 January 2018]

21 http://www.chinadaily.com.cn/business/tech/2017-08/01/content_30315259.htm [accessed 27 January 2018]

22 https://www.smartinsights.com/digital-marketing-strategy/online-retail-sales-growth/ [accessed 27 January 2018]

23 https://www.smartinsights.com/digital-marketing-strategy/online-retail-sales-growth/ [accessed 27 January 2017]

24 http://www.retailresearch.org/onlineretailing.php [accessed 27 January 2018]

25 https://www2.deloitte.com/content/dam/Deloitte/uk/Documents/consumer-business/the-changing-face-of-retail-where-did-all-the-shops-go.pdf [accessed 27 January 2018]

26 https://newzoo.com/insights/rankings/top-50-countries-by-smartphone-penetration-and-users/ [accessed 27 January 2018]

27 https://www.retailtouchpoints.com/features/news-briefs/chatbot-acceptance-rises-but-human-backup-still-preferred [accessed 28 January 2017]

28 Sourced from SEMrush, May 2018, by Good Growth Ltd

29 Good Growth Ltd all-client database, December 2017

30 SEMrush [accessed 31 January 2017]

31 Using the ONS figures for UK Population from 2016

32 There is an excellent piece on this by Tim Harford published by the *Financial Times* in 2014 called 'Big data: are we making a big mistake?' that explains the statistics behind this assertion

33 http://time.com/money/4373046/how-amazon-gets-you-to-pay-more/ [accessed 28 January 2018]

.

The importance 04
of innovation in
driving success

Executive summary

At one level it can be argued that everything in digital is innovation; after all, digital transformation requires change, often significant, to ensure that the investment required delivers its promised return. Much of digital failure springs from not changing enough, particularly in failing to make the organizational changes needed to ensure the best chance of success. But this generality hides a universal truth: that innovation without a purpose defined through understanding a human problem will rarely deliver a return. This chapter explores the role of innovation and how this differs from creativity. It identifies some areas where innovation in digital is known to add less value than some of the hype might suggest and defines an approach to innovation that, if applied to digital thinking, could deliver significant success.

Leadership in business is leadership of innovation

There have been several significant developments in leadership thinking over the past 25 years. In the 1990s, the *Harvard Business Review* published a paper by Ronald A Heifetz and Donald L Laurie that introduced the idea of adaptive challenges.[1] They defined these as murky systemic problems with no easy answers, whose answers do not reside in the executive suite. Solving the problems requires the involvement of people throughout the organization. Adaptive work, they argued, was counterintuitive for leaders as, rather than providing solutions, they had to ask tough questions and leverage the collective intelligence of the organization. Fundamentally, it required leaders to challenge the way 'we do business'.

In 2005, Keith Grint developed work done in the 1970s to suggest that we faced three types of problems, each of which required different strategies to resolve them: tame, critical and wicked.[2] Grint defined a wicked problem as complex, rather than just complicated: it is often intractable; there is no obvious solution; moreover, there is no 'stopping' point; it is novel; any apparent 'solution' often generates other 'problems'; and there is no 'right' or 'wrong' answer, but there are better or worse alternatives. In other words, there is a huge degree of uncertainty involved and thus it is associated with leadership. The leader's role with a wicked problem is to ask the right questions rather than provide the right answers, because the answers may not be self-evident and will require a collaborative process to make any kind of progress.

Concurrently with the articles above, insights were published from those interested in the context in which leaders were being asked to perform successfully. Eddie Obeng (1997) presented a picture of a new world where just about everything you ever thought was right, was in fact wrong.[3] He described the impact of digital technology on the pace of change in the social and business environments as living in a world that is changing faster than we can learn. He argued that this pace of change was the driver of the complexity facing organizations today and asked the question: 'Why is it that when we do the same things today that used to work in the past, they no longer work?' His observations were of organizations running into serial failure by 'doing what they have always done' and his conclusions were that organizations needed to develop new ways of approaching both old problems and new ones – primarily starting with key stakeholders (consumers and customers), and using insights into their actions and behaviours to generate solutions where the implementation strategy was 'test and learn' as opposed to the 'big bang' thinking that dominated engineering, IT and other project dominated functions. Obeng introduced four types of projects that he argued should replace the 'one-size fits all'.

At about the same time as Obeng was developing his thinking in the United Kingdom, the US military equivalent descriptor 'VUCA' moved across into more general use. This acronym sums up a world that is volatile, uncertain, complex and ambiguous. Its relevance for leaders is in how they view the conditions under which they make decisions, plan forward, manage risks, foster change and solve problems. The use of VUCA in business organizations is often in a strategic process that helps leaders anticipate the issues that can shape competitive conditions, understand the potential consequences of issues and actions, recognize interdependences, prepare for alternative scenarios and interpret events. This is a US term and gets significantly more focus in North America and, whilst there is no one article or book that can be credited with its coining, it is often used to frame the modern leadership challenge.

Finally, in our previous book (2015) we highlighted the importance of shifting the organization paradigm from leadership driven by theses to leadership driven by hypotheses.[4] We argued that in a 'world that is changing faster than we can learn' where problems are adaptive rather than technical, organization leaders have to build the capability to understand the difference between a thesis and a hypothesis, and build the processes and skills to develop hypotheses collaboratively with their customers. A thesis is a theory put forward as a premise to be maintained or proved, whilst a hypothesis is a proposed explanation made on the basis of limited evidence as a starting point for further investigation.

We argued that the 'old world' model of arguing a thesis to justify investment is no longer tenable – given that there are no longer right answers that are clear and obvious: if test and learn is the best way forward, then organizations have to be able to test against hypotheses that are informed by 'deep data' about customers and the market. These can then be used to test solutions that can be rapidly 'mainstreamed' should they be successful. Organizations that continue to look for theses where all the data and thinking is aimed at justifying a single (and often costly) solution are far less likely to succeed.

In the same book we also introduced the idea of 'mis-organization'. Mis-organization is not mismanagement. This is a malaise of modern organizations that don't understand the need for adaptive responses and try to treat wicked problems using approaches that are only suitable for technical ones. You can spot mis-organization where, despite a well-thought-out strategy, people coalesce around processes, policies and practices that conspire to undermine its ability to achieve its goals. Once spotted, fixing it requires people to change behaviour as well as capabilities to improve performance.

So, if we summarize these themes:

- We are living through a time where social and economic changes are combining with a step change in technology to create an environment that is highly volatile and where it is difficult – if not impossible – to keep pace with markets and customers.

- This volatility makes more issues complex and ambiguous compared to those faced by previous generations of leaders, and has also made the challenge of resolving complex and ambiguous issues even more difficult.

- Management and leadership practice has not caught up with this change – in particular, we are likely to impose project structures that are best suited to technical (or tame) problems to try to address adaptive (or wicked) problems. The result is inevitably failure or, at best, limited success.

- Technical approaches are based around 'management by theses' where we look to justify one solution over all others. Adaptive approaches encourage us to adopt 'management by hypotheses' where we look to explore options, collaborate across the organization and then test and learn from trying and adjusting our solutions. Volatility and ambiguity require an agile and adaptive response rather than one where we take big bets and hope they will pay off.

- Organizations find working in adaptive ways much more challenging than technical ones. They amplify uncertainty and ambiguity, and require leaders to orchestrate many resources and to keep everyone abreast of developments as things change around them.

- Leaders need to watch their organizations carefully for signs of mis-organization and be willing to challenge both performance and behaviour to ensure that they cut through. Mis-organization often happens when teams adopt 'technical' approaches to adaptive problems.

We conclude two things from this: first, that the role of the leader has shifted significantly in a generation from one who knows the answer to one who knows how to get the right resources, financial and human, in the right place at the right time to get to the answer; and second, that the pace of change is such that we can no longer talk about being an effective leader of change but rather how to be an effective leader in change. This means you have to understand how to innovate and just as importantly how to innovate successfully.

Just because you can, doesn't mean you should

Digital technology lets your creativity run riot. It offers virtually unlimited options to brand and product owners and, especially where pockets run deep, big investments can get made because a business has the wherewithal. The vast majority of us, however, are not working in organizations where creativity is valued above all else. We work in environments where scarce resources are invested behind activities that fall into one of four categories:

- They are required to comply with the law – for example, data protection regulations require investment in security, controls and audits.

- They add value through the reduction in operating costs flowing through to improved earnings – for example, investment in improved back-office management systems that reduce the cost to serve.

- They build capacity or capability that enable growth in revenue and/or profitability – for example, the acquisition or development of skills that enable in-house delivery of activities at a cost lower than an outsourced supplier.

- They add value through the generation of more revenues, which in turn flow through to improved earnings – for example, the development of a new website, app or digital marketing campaign.

These resource allocation decisions are more often than not associated with a business case: for compliance, the case is simple – it's a cost of doing business; but for the others we need to establish, as best we can, the value that should be expected from the allocation of resources to a particular priority. The challenge for business leaders is that the further they work their way down the list the less certain the return. Growth is notoriously difficult to predict and, if the finance directors of our acquaintance are to be believed, it is almost always over-estimated compared to the reality post the investment. But this shouldn't be the case in digital. The ability to test cheaply and often quickly, means that business cases should be more robust and risks identified and managed more effectively than in many other channels. Somehow, however, quite possibly because it is digital, organizations make decisions that owe more to belief than to data. Here are two relatively expensive innovations that serve as good examples.

We need an app for that

If you are a retailer, you probably don't. In fact, if you are considering an app as a route to market or as a brand engagement investment you might like to take a closer look at these industry statistics:

- Only about 5 per cent of smartphone users' time is spent on retail apps[5] – yes, that's right, a Forrester survey (2015) discovered that 95 per cent of the time is spent doing things other than shopping.

- In the same survey they report that 60 per cent of us have two or fewer mobile retail apps.

- A 2016 analysis from the United States[6] suggests that time spent engaging online on smartphones is overwhelmingly biased in favour of apps, but that the apps that dominate are those that support social networking, entertainment, travel and search.

- Data from an app measurement company in the United States[7] shows growth in retailer app use being outstripped by those in non-retail apps and suggests that Amazon is way out in front in this, followed a long way back by eBay.

If this doesn't make you think, then here's the killer punch: data from Localytics (2018)[8] suggests that nearly 80 per cent of e-commerce app users who downloaded an app stop using it after three months. The best performing apps in terms of retaining most users are those associated with media and entertainment.

If you believe the latest available data from the United States from companies employing more than 500 people (2014) the average cost of building an app is US $270,000[9] and the range most often cited as an acceptable budget is US $50,000–$100,000. These costs are for development only. Add to this the cost of running the app, maintaining it, updating the content, analysis of the interaction and running related loyalty or engagement programmes, and the total resource level required in the first year probably doubles.

In a recent report looking at the challenge of retail apps by consultancy L2 (2017) it was reported that 44 per cent of luxury retail brands have removed their apps from the app store since 2015[10] and 56 per cent of brands with an app in the store had not updated it for over a year. It would seem that retailer disinterest is in some way directly correlated with consumer churn. We tend to distrust 'tick box' surveys because they get people to respond to a pre-set agenda rather than actually ask them what they think, so treat the following with caution: six out of ten UK citizens surveyed (2017)[11] said that they were unhappy with retail apps, wanting to see better incentives and loyalty schemes and, in the same report, 26 per cent said they wanted to see retailers implement AI tools to offer a more personalized shopping experience. We have to say that in more than six years of talking directly to online customers we have never heard anyone suggest this is what they want, but maybe we've been talking to the wrong people!

A thoughtful piece by Econsultancy blogger Nikki Gilliland (2017)[12] pointed out that, despite the trend in some fashionable marketing circles for 'gamification' of online experiences and brand engagements, much of the success of Amazon's app is due to its no-frills, easy-to-shop experience. She also points out that Amazon, like its next biggest rival eBay, and apps of those like Etsy and ASOS are marketplace sites that are more likely to draw in regular customers because of the range of wants they can satisfy, unlike those of more traditional retail offerings. What makes these apps successful isn't creativity: it's innovation that responds to a real customer problem.

Video sells

There are endless video producer and social marketing sites that keep citing all sorts of incredible statistics about the impact of video on sales conversion. In our experience, miracles are rare and silver bullets near-on impossible to find, and if these claims had any significance then we would be drowning in video when we shop – and to date, we are not. This is quite possibly because the impact that is reported tends to be in social media marketing. For example, according to Brightcove (2016)[13] social video generates 1,200 per cent more shares than text and images combined. But then, our own client database and data provided by external sources all confirm that traffic from social media advertising is consistently the worst performing channel in terms of conversion to sales. Much of the hype on video, therefore, is coming from social media engagement not from commercial websites. In our own client experience, video has made little or no difference to engagement in a purchase journey, let alone conversion. That's not to say that a well-made video, well placed and addressing a key objection or concern, can't make a difference to conversion, or at least the time from consideration to conversion.

Video can play a significant role, particularly in the following circumstances:

- Where the product is new or unfamiliar or where a demonstration of capability or impact can be communicated far more effectively than by text and images. A report from CrazyEgg (2017)[14] shares a case study for a software product where the addition of video increased both on-site engagement and the conversion of visits into trials.

- At early stages in the sales funnel where buyers are in consideration as opposed to conversion mode and where the purchase is of a greater value or has a more personal significance. Our own experience with the Open University showed that, early on in the buying cycle, providing a video created significant engagement online; however, as the closing date for applications approached the interest in engaging with the video fell away significantly, reducing to almost zero. Its role was in the early stage where customers were considering which provider to choose; when that choice was made customers were looking for specific, detailed information far better communicated by text and images.

There is one other area where there is evidence to suggest that video works: in the area of customer support. Software giant Salesforce published a report (2017)[15] that identified that customer experience was the defining line between businesses that were struggling and those that thrived. Your customer experience doesn't end when they pay you: it runs right through delivery and problem solving and service support. Work done by video marketing specialists Vidyard (2017)[16] suggested that video was playing a role in delivering outstanding customer service post purchase in two ways:

- Saying sorry – done well it not only saves a customer, but can create a passionate advocate. A short video (filmed on a smartphone or via a laptop/desktop) can bring an apology to life and make it memorable and personal. The extra effort shows you mean it.

- Helping customers use your product or service – all three of us had to watch the YouTube video on how to insert the micro-SIM into an iPhone. There was no way that a written explanation was easy to give or understand, and a video was an outstanding way to show us exactly what we needed to do. It's just a shame that it wasn't on the Apple website that we found the help we needed! Breaking up text-heavy FAQs/Help areas with customer-oriented 'how to' videos is one way in which you can enhance your customer experience.

All other video activity should, in our view, be seen and judged in the same way as TV and cinema. It can create awareness, it can encourage consideration, it can make you memorable, but direct, measurable, impact on sales is limited. It is fundamentally a marketing decision and should be weighed against other marketing activities.

Innovation versus creativity

What we are exploring in this chapter is the critical role that innovation and innovation thinking plays in the optimization of digital strategy. In so doing, we want to draw a very clear distinction between innovation and creativity. According to *Chambers Dictionary*[17] creativity is being inventive or imaginative; in our words, it is the ability to have ideas in response to how you see the world. Innovation we define as the bridge between ideas and value. It is creativity with a purpose and, in any activity where the purpose is to engage other people, these ideas have to be generated in response to how those people see the world, not you. In the world of digital business, creativity, unless it responds to the customer agenda, is likely to destroy value.

Apps and videos are good examples of areas where creativity risks value destruction; others are things like chatbots, complex functionality in sales engagement and gamification. There are examples of these ideas working well for businesses, but they do so because they were responses to insights about customers and their experiences. But not only that, they were outcomes from a process of experimentation where alternatives were tested to establish the best outcome for customers. Just copying others' ideas is not a fast track to success: wherever possible, test your ideas and measure them against clear commercial KPIs.

There are two other issues to consider when looking to innovate in response to insight derived from customers in the market. First, whatever you develop to put into test must pass the 'authenticity' test. Technology brings transparency and requires businesses to be authentic in what they present to the market, as the reality will rapidly be shared widely, not just by their customers but also by those who choose not to become customers. Being honest, clear and thoughtful with customers in your market works best. It builds and reinforces brand reputation as well as helping to establish trust in the early stages of customer engagement and loyalty post the initial transaction.

The second issue is utility. This is where the biggest risk sits for any creativity-led activity: the potential for ideation to run ahead of the market, rather than respond to it. This does not exclude the role of invention and products or services that deliver a quantum leap forward; rather it reminds us that even the iPad was developed through a process that identified unmet customer needs, even if as customers we could not have described an iPad as the answer to our problem. The customer should lead the ideas process. By that we mean that all ideation in digital business should start with insight into the current customer experience, and that this should encompass those who choose not to engage with your proposition just as much as those who do. Insight, and the process of ideation in response to it, should be a bottom-up process rather than a top-down one.

Designing success

Our proposition is that innovation is the capability to respond to change and exploit it as an opportunity. For an organization to be innovative, it needs a purposeful and organized process that enables it to seek out changes and analyse the opportunities they provide. Once spotted, it needs to search for the most effective response through testing potential solutions and learning from the outcomes to hone and develop further such that they create value. The question that leaders need to answer is how best can they build this capability into 'business as usual', such that they build and maintain high-performing organizations.

Innovation, high performance and a focus on the customer

There is plenty of research available that highlights the traits of successful businesses. In our view, these boil down to the ability to achieve three outcomes:

- **Maintaining organization focus** – this is created through:
  - ensuring that you have established a shared and clearly understood purpose for why the organization exists across all your employees, regardless of level;
  - having a shared understanding right across everyone of what the organization does and how it does it;
  - creating a shared desire to close the gap between today's performance and stretching performance goals.
- **Developing resilient leadership** – businesses succeed in great part due to attracting and building leaders and managers who are willing to:
  - change what they do and how they do it. This sits at the heart of building a culture of innovation;
  - learn and keep learning. This supports the value of experimentation and testing;
  - stand up for the organization's values. Cultures can become toxic very quickly if positive values are allowed to slip. In digital teams, the most toxic culture you can have is one where the customer is excluded from the conversation about where to make changes to improve performance;
  - make change happen. Leaders need processes through which they can make change happen. In digital, these processes need to start and end with the customer.
- **Establishing a resilient organization** – organizations need to be resilient themselves to be able to engage with and respond to change. This comes from establishing:
  - a positive culture that engages everyone;
  - a shared way of working based on a willingness to 'test and learn';
  - a focus on the customer and an instinct to want to respond to their changing needs.

These outcomes all require a capability to respond to change and then exploit it as an opportunity. This is the essence of innovation. Many organizations are now striving to succeed in very fast-changing environments. In these circumstances, the most successful strategies are those that are driven by a deep understanding of the customer, not just at one point in time, but at any point in time. The rise of the 'big data' proposition, of web analytics at point of purchase and other methodologies are all driven by a desire to get as close an understanding of customers in a market as possible. They require structured processes and a discipline if they are to be utilized effectively.

Innovation processes help systematize how to engage with customer insight and how to use it to develop opportunities that will create value. If responding to the demands of customers requires people at every level to innovate this means that:

- Organization leaders will need to know how to encourage, nurture and sustain innovation. The key to this is setting a cultural expectation. Leading for culture is one of the most demanding things we can ask of a leader. It requires a very active engagement at every level, it takes regular reminders and challenge every day and it occasionally requires changing personnel to make the point that the new way of working is a requirement.

- Line managers will need to know how to take ideas and put them through processes that empower colleagues to respond to customer requirements. This means that leaders need to establish an expectation that everyone involved in supporting growth works to a common set of processes, standards and measurements. They also need to stand by the process and demand compliance.

- Employees will know how to fix things for themselves. A strong culture that puts the customer first, and a simple and effective process that insists the organization responds to the customer, enable employees to make confident decisions to improve performance through experimentation.

Building capability in innovation

There are some significant implications for organizations of engaging with innovation. Probably the most important, yet most difficult to change, is that in an increasing number of circumstances, 'one way' of doing things is no longer a viable operating model. It needs to be replaced by 'many ways' – whose commonality is a golden thread of shared values against which people are recruited and developed. This requires a culture that is open to diverse views, willing to test and learn and to learn as much from failure as from success.

Figure 4.1   Using design principles to drive innovation

SOURCE © Good Growth Ltd

As a result, the capabilities required in successful 21st-century organizations will be those that help people live comfortably with ambiguity, explore the wider world, engage with a range of alternatives and stay as close as possible to customers in the market. To innovate successfully in the future, organizations will need to apply these capabilities through a common process to think through, and engage with, potential solutions to business problems. It is the process that will drive a shared answer rather than a shared mental model or set of biases. Organizations that cannot operate effectively without a 'one size fits all' approach will be increasingly limited as the world in which they operate changes at a faster and faster rate.

One powerful approach that embraces these challenges is the application of the principles that are used by designers to respond to human problems and find solutions in products or services (Figure 4.1). Popularized more recently as 'design thinking' by, amongst others, Professor Roger Martin (2009),[18] this argues that people-centred design approaches are likely to deliver solutions that create real value, both financial and social. Developed in detail by the innovation business IDEO, design thinking is a process that contains activities and stages that, whilst they are recognizable elements in looking for ideas, are put together in a different way. It is different from the traditional approach to problem solving, in that it starts by looking at a challenge through a designer lens and builds in learning throughout until a solution emerges that meets three key criteria. These criteria are that any solution is:

- **desirable** – it has to be attractive to the people whose problem you are trying to solve;
- **feasible** – it has to work for the people whose problem you are trying to solve;
- **viable** – it has to be financially viable and deliver a return.

This process has six stages, each of which maps against the classic approach taken by designers to solving human problems. In the context of improving the online customer experience this process works as follows:

- **Commercial challenge** – it starts by defining the challenge that is being solved for the business, not the customer. The art here is not to set the scope so wide that it becomes 'an elephant', nor too small such that the effort expended isn't focused on the wrong problem. Our general rule online is to set the challenge as that of understanding why customers do not buy (or become a lead for non-transacting sites).

- **Observe and enquire** – pull in as much data, quantitative and qualitative, as you can from every stage of the customer journey – understand what is happening and how customers react.

- **Form insights and hypotheses** – we think the best way of describing this is building a hypothesis. An insight isn't necessarily accurate – it's your best-informed understanding taken from your observations. This means that further down the process as you experiment with potential solutions, your understanding may be shown as flawed and a new, better-informed understanding established in its stead. The only confident action that should follow the establishment of a hypothesis, is the testing of that hypothesis with potential solutions. If you move from insight to changes in the journey without testing you are risking destroying value.

- **Prioritize opportunities** – this is the identification of the potential problems to be solved and the identification of those problems that, if solved, would generate the greatest return for the business. This idea of greatest return is important – it may be that an initial review identifies a specific problem as offering the greatest potential value, but the cost of solving this problem is significant and the net return, therefore, less attractive. It is the greatest return we should prioritize.

- **Develop test ideas** – this is where creativity plays a major role. Having identified the problem, we are looking for as many ideas as possible as to how to solve it. This stage demands creativity and then a process by which we apply the desirable, feasible and viable filters to prioritize potential solutions.

- **Test and learn** – having created a priority order against which we will test potential solutions, we then test them against pre-defined criteria to assess success. Normally, these should be commercial (for example, conversion uplift, revenue per user uplift, click through rate improvement, return on advertising spend improvement and so on). Tests that meet or beat the criteria should be implemented for all customers as quickly as possible to ensure the greatest commercial return.

In Chapter 7, we describe how these principles are applied right across the online journey from the earliest stage of locating the right customers through to retaining their loyalty post transaction into four key processes that put innovation at the heart of digital customer experience transformation.

A new process or way of working will not thrive by itself. It needs to do so through the active support and engagement of leaders in the organization. Leaders themselves need to know how to lead and participate in the establishment of the new thinking as well as supporting the creation of new ways of working. This also requires a culture that reinforces the need for an orientation towards the customer. Every managerial unit of an organization should have responsibility for contributing to innovation in the way the company works; in addition, it should strive consciously to advance the art in the particular area in which it is engaged. To do this requires leaders to be supported in:

- making deliberate choices about organizational models;
- focusing on areas where innovation is required, either to keep pace with change or to take advantage of it;
- redefining management systems, including rewards, so that they encourage and recognize both the adoption of the process as well as successful outcomes that drive business growth through customer orientation.

Innovation needs an organization response

Innovation is an organization capability challenge and for it to succeed requires a layered design approach that:

- engages the most senior leaders quickly such that there is clear operational support for change;
- enables a tailoring of any roll-out such that there is a critical mass that can make change happen locally against relevant strategic imperatives;
- trains internal champions in all areas to be able to support local leaders roll out the process and key skills into the organization such that people feel empowered to fix things for themselves.

Whilst there are always dangers with setting a financial target in advance, we believe there is value in creating a direct link between the investment in this capability, and direct and measurable results from applying the new skills and process. One of the most successful ways we have used to build capability is to work on real business projects (we have used digital, offline and all-channel activities as learning vehicles) where there are costs and benefits to be gained through approaching innovation using the methodology above. A good case study on this approach can be found on our website.[19]

Thinking through the product life cycle

Digital is no different from any other business channel in that products and services offered through it, or developed for it, are subject to the same process from launch through to maturity as physical ones. What is different, however, is how a business can think about innovation and the development of product and services when they are being delivered through the digital channel. Over the last three years, we have developed a product testing, launch and development process that allows clients to go to market at a prototype stage and use their digital channel (or create a digital channel) to test propositions, marketing and sales approaches, pricing and so on. This takes our innovation thinking and moves it from working to improve performance of an established product or service into supporting the front-end innovation that shapes new products and services, and the marketing communication that supports them.

This model (Figure 4.2) segments the product life cycle by innovation stages and the relevant digital activities that support each stage. As the product develops and grows so the focus of activity shifts from market-making/market-entry into product differentiation and sales effectiveness and thence into understanding what needs to change, and testing this such that the product can extend effectively rather than decline. In a world that moves faster than we can learn, the one thing that has become increasingly clear is how quickly digital products and services in particular can move through this development cycle. Unless in growth you work hard to understand what customers do not buy and identify where more than the sales and marketing

Figure 4.2   The Digital Product Life Cycle Model

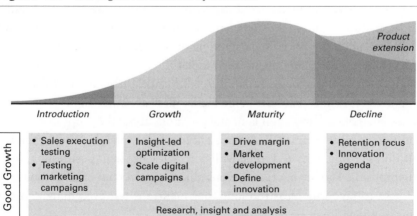

SOURCE © Good Growth Ltd

engagement has to change, decline will have set in and then it becomes much more difficult to put it back into growth mode.

The thinking behind the model reflects the way we think about the stages for the customer journey through e-commerce (see Chapter 7). Product development testing in digital channels is best done by engaging customers at the stage where they are looking for solutions to needs they have already defined. This means that an organization will have already gone through one iteration of the innovation process before moving to market testing. It should have insight on the issue it is trying to address, ideas that could address it, and an evaluation of those ideas such that what is at prototype or beta stage and ready for market testing is considered to be the most likely (or two or three equally likely) to meet that need.

With the most likely solution in a market-ready position, the first activity is to present the proposition to those customers in the market who you believe are the most likely to benefit from it – even if they don't know anything about it. We call this market testing and it involves establishing a market through Google search keyword mapping and then buying interest in the product or service for a limited period of time to build insight from real customers looking for solutions that:

- test and identify the best marketing campaign that can appear in the top three AdWords slots, attract traffic and maximize not just click through but also engagement and ultimately transaction (if that is the goal);

- identify what works in the proposition as currently envisaged and what does not and that may need to be developed further;

- run a testing programme that optimizes how to promote and sell the proposition and builds insight as to why customers in the market do not buy.

Once completed (normally in our experience this needs three to four months to learn sufficient to make confident decisions about next steps), you will then have not just a better understanding of your product or service but also a much better understanding of the market itself and what drives customer engagement and purchase decisions. At this stage, there are normally some important revisions that have to be made: these are often about promotion and sometimes ask more fundamental questions about the proposition, pricing and the target market. It is important to set clear and demanding success measures at this stage and to be willing to kill ideas that, post testing, look unpromising. Too often, organizations talk themselves out of ideas too early, or hold to favourite ideas too long; our mantra is test everything and kill anything that doesn't work quickly.

Once you've made revisions – and possibly re-run the market testing to confirm that you have a proposition that can create value – the process shifts into the growth phase and in the digital channel this demands a ruthless focus on insight-driven performance marketing and conversion optimization. Over time, if you keep building insight (and many businesses fail to do this as a continuous activity) these activities will start to expose where the current proposition is not meeting changing market needs, regardless of how much you change your sales and marketing engagement. This is the emerging innovation agenda that, if used well, can inform a new set of potential ideas and a new programme of experimentation that can identify changes to the proposition that will ensure extension and renewal rather than decline.

From our work in new product development across a range of sectors, we have pulled out the following lessons that leaders might find useful:

- Scope the widest possible market for the proposition. Don't make assumptions about how customers think, look to understand how they think. You only pay for what they respond to and, run properly, you can identify quickly the traffic you are buying that fails to convert and stop buying it.

- Demand innovation in marketing as well as in the proposition. Look for ways of standing out in an interaction that can look vanilla. We have experimented successfully with negative advertising (for example, 'Don't buy until you have looked at this') and with emotional engagement (for example, 'Fed up with… then look here').

- Landing pages in the early stage are critical – they have to talk to customers and their problems before introducing the product. They can be as long as is needed to help the customers understand why your proposition solves their problem. Famously, in introducing the Kindle reader, Amazon used a product page that was over 5.4 metres long.[20]

- Insist on continuous insight generation. This is a general weakness in e-commerce – it's how you will get to spot the point of inflexion when the proposition starts not to meet customer needs as effectively as it has done.

- Test everything that doesn't cost you a fortune and discount failures quickly – don't let pet projects (even your own) absorb scarce resources.

Leadership actions

Innovation in modern business is the lifeblood of growth. It drives not just the development of new products and services but also the processes through which we need to ensure the customer has a voice (indeed, the largest voice) in maximizing the revenue and margin potential of current products and services. The pace of change means that more and more of what leaders face is ambiguous, complex and difficult to address. In such a world, being as close to customers as possible and having genuine insight into the problems they face, and that they are looking for products and services to solve, provides the least risky route to value creation. The principles behind the way designers understand and create solutions for human problems offers a proven framework for leaders to apply in their organizations. At its heart is deep insight into the problem and a willingness to experiment to find the best solution.

This chapter has focused on innovation and the role that it plays in optimizing digital strategy. It has also explored why innovation is not creativity, and how effective innovation is a structured process that brings in and exploits creativity at a stage when it is clear where the organization needs to focus in order to create value. We have argued that innovation is central to the leadership of successful organizations in the context of a world that is 'changing faster than we can learn' and that, in this context, digital itself provides a fast, effective and affordable platform to experiment with early stage innovation in a way that de-risks investment and allows the early testing of ideas and the early killing of those that do not show promise. In thinking about optimizing digital strategy, leaders might like to reflect on these key questions:

- What happens to innovations or innovative ideas in your organization? How are they treated? How far do they get?

- How successful are you at innovating? If you make changes to your digital execution, products or services, how well do they work?

- How successful are your innovations, large or small, at delivering promised returns?

- Is there a process in place through which you evaluate ideas? If there is, does it start with customer insight?

- How much does testing and experimentation play a part in the early stages of innovation?

- How much effort are you putting in to understand the customer in the market to help inform product and service development?

- How much capability is there in the organization today that would allow you to move to adopting an approach linked to the principles in design thinking?

References

1 Heifetz, R and Laurie, D (1997) The work of leadership, *Harvard Business Review*, January

2 Grint, K (2005) *Problems, Problems, Problems: The social construction of 'leadership'*, Tavistock Institute, London

3 Obeng, E (1997) *New Rules for the New World: Cautionary tales for the new world manager*, Wiley, Oxford

4 Bones, C and Hammersley, J (2015) *Leading Digital Strategy*, Kogan Page, London

5 https://digiday.com/marketing/state-retail-mobile-apps-5-charts/ [accessed 13 February 2018]

6 https://www.campaignlive.co.uk/article/mobile-apps-dominate-smartphone-screen-time-fewer-apps-share-bounty/1430347 [accessed 13 February 2018]

7 https://www.recode.net/2017/10/11/16453528/consumers-time-spend-shopping-apps-amazon [accessed 13 February 2018]

8 http://info.localytics.com/blog/mobile-apps-whats-a-good-retention-rate [accessed 13 May 2018]

9 http://resources.kinvey.com/docs/State+of+Enterprise+Mobility+Survey+2014+-+Kinvey.pdf [accessed 13 February 2018]

10 https://www.l2inc.com/research/fashion-us-2017 [accessed 13 February 2018]

11 https://www.campaignlive.co.uk/article/six-ten-brits-unhappy-retail-apps-want-integrated-ar-vr/1421574 [accessed 13 February 2018]

12 https://econsultancy.com/blog/69589-are-retail-brands-ditching-mobile-apps-a-look-at-some-stats-case-studies [accessed 13 February 2018]

13 https://www.slideshare.net/AdelieStudios/adelie-studios-top16videomarketingstatistics2016-56658453/2-Adlie_Studios_Copyright_2016_All [accessed 14 February 2018]

14 https://www.crazyegg.com/blog/videos-boost-conversion-rates/ [accessed 14 February 2018]

15 https://www.salesforce.com/blog/2017/01/second-annual-state-of-service.html [accessed 14 February 2018]

16 https://www.vidyard.com/blog/3-pillars-technical-support-video/# [accessed 14 February 2018]

17 http://chambers.co.uk/search/?query=creativity&title=21st [accessed 14 February 2018]

18 Martin, RL (2009) *The Design of Business: Why design thinking is the next competitive advantage*, HBS Publishing, Boston

19 https://goodgrowth.co.uk/case-studies/dentsu-aegis-network/ [accessed 20 February 2018]

20 http://www.imageworkscreative.com/blog/do-longer-pages-convert-better [accessed 24 February 2018]

The dark side of digital
05

Executive summary

As with so many developments in knowledge and understanding the introduction and exploitation of digital technology comes with a negative as well as a positive. Developing applications using information technology is a relatively low-cost activity compared to, say, the development of graphene or the creation of the atom bomb. Yet, we have seen both the transformational impacts and the devastation that digital can deliver over the past few years. As a leader, you will at some point be confronted by decisions that will require an assessment of the ethics of the options before you. That is true in all aspects of the leadership of any organization, but digital presents particularly tough choices as so much of what you can do relies on interaction with, or building insight into, people through the intermediation of a machine. Innovation comes with responsibilities and often, as in the case of technology, governments and regulators sit behind the curve and have to work hard to catch up. This chapter explores the issues both for individuals and governments and regulators, and at the end lays out a structure through which leaders may wish to evaluate digital decisions.

Are machines disintermediating relationships?

People say that business is based on trust, at least good business is. There is a whole industry that works to build and maintain 'trust' in brands. But is it trust that we are looking for as business leaders or something else? We may be attracted to a brand, but in the process of transacting offline we engage with and eventually trust the person 'behind the counter'. We ask them for their recommendations or for reassurance, particularly if it is something we haven't bought before. If we are unsure about the trustworthiness of a retail assistant, then we take advice from family and friends – people we trust to tell us their experience with the product and on whose advice we can decide whether or not to proceed. Many consumers look for third-party reassurance; however, when this comes from a 'trusted source' what they are doing is using a source that they do not know, but in which they have confidence – for example, a review in *TechRadar*, *T3* or *Wirecutter*.

There is a very significant difference between trust and confidence. Illustrated particularly well through research done by professors Adrian Sargeant and Stephen Lee (2004),[1] the biggest issue is that organizations often confuse the two. As a result, this confusion can end up doing significant damage to business reputations and, as a consequence, performance. Trust is interpersonal – that is, it can only exist between people. In relationships based on trust there is mutual transparency. Confidence is a feeling that is engendered in one party by another, either through regular interactions that deliver as expected (hence 'confidence-building'), or established through quality assurance or compliance mechanisms. These might include guarantees, quality marks, customer feedback scores or adherence to ISO standards. In relationships dependent on confidence you have a one-way transparency – from the supplier to the consumer.

Trust, because it is interpersonal, is fragile. Once broken it takes a very long time to be regained: and often is never regained, at least not fully. This is because trust can only be given by one person to another. When given, it is done so on imperfect information and often without a thorough review, an audit or the taking of significant personal references. It is given on the belief that the other person will operate and behave as expected by the giver – there is no contract or other guiding framework, it is a decision based on a belief. It is a one-way gift, often bestowed with little evidence. If the recipient of your trust breaks it, most often by operating or behaving in an unexpected and negative manner, then the reaction will tend to be emotional and often powerful. Break trust and the damage is significant.

Confidence, on the other hand, is contractual. It offers a clear and often documented expectation that is understood by both parties. It is something that can be protected through careful management of risk and the building of rapid feedback and response mechanisms that can deal effectively with breaches. Confidence is what business needs to survive and thrive, not trust. Business will, from time to time, change how it operates and indeed how it behaves as markets change. What its customers need to accept is that it can change, but that the process of change will be careful and the decisions made will take account of stakeholder views and be taken with a view to maintaining, if not improving further customer confidence – after all, who would take a decision that is likely to damage customer perceptions?

But this happens – look at the decision taken by Snap, owners of Snapchat, in early 2018 to change its customer interface and the consequent impact on its share price. A refusal to engage initially with customer concerns led to an online petition with more than 1.2 million signatures as at the end of February 2018[2] and a share price fall that took US \$1.5 billion off the value of the firm in one day.[3] This is an example of the tension in a great number of 'big tech' propositions between the need to generate revenues to justify the share price and what non-paying customers value about a simple app that they enjoy using to share moments with their friends. It is very difficult if you start without a requirement to transact to put a value on the asset that you are then required to monetize in order to realize value for your investors – in this case, users of the app.

This very public demonstration of a customer confidence issue illustrates a serious potential pitfall, though often in smaller ways, in digital business. In an online transaction, machines disintermediate between suppliers and their customers. They don't just become a barrier but they can also become a barricade, behind which the supplier can often hide and ignore the customer and at which the customer can throw missiles; or even worse, just dismiss it and walk away to find another more engaging supplier of the product or service they are after. This bunker mentality can be quickly reinforced by teams who find themselves under significant performance pressure and try to find solutions to performance by changing the customer experience with no reference to the customer, paying or otherwise.

However you do it (and we have a model at the end of this chapter that you may find useful), the key to building and sustaining confidence in your business with current and new customers is to reach through the technology and ensure you are directly in touch, engaged and listening all of the time when you want to make significant changes:

- Test your ideas thoroughly and measure your test not just in quantitative terms but also in terms of what you have learned from the customer about the change in the experience.

- Make sure you cover all your stakeholders in testing major change.

- Make your contract explicit: don't hide it in terms and conditions that no one reads.

- Make sure you have fast and agile recovery processes so that if you fail the customer then you can put it right so well that the customer is not just satisfied, but will be likely to communicate that satisfaction to others.

The one thing you have to remember is that customers will not put their trust in your website – they can't, it's not a person. You can help them build confidence in transacting through it, or in the information it contains, by working hard to ensure you have the highest possible standards in terms of accuracy and veracity, that you use visuals that give an honest picture, that it is clear how people can contact you if they have concerns and, if you are not offering a phone service, explain why and give assurances about response times. Don't claim to be trusted, just show that you do what you say you will do and there are highly responsive processes in place for the very few occasions on which things go wrong. If you want a good example of confidence building, look no further than eBay.

Can we have confidence in business to do the right thing?

This is a different question from customer confidence in the supplier of a product or service. This is a leadership question and touches on the values and ethical standards you choose to adopt. Why are we asking this question here? Because, unlike many other channels, the ability in digital to handle and manipulate data, sometimes very personal data, about people that you don't know can put business leaders in an invidious position where data manipulation can cross the line into people manipulation. Particularly since the US presidential elections in 2016 and the UK referendum on EU membership in 2017, there is an active questioning of the activities of organizations online by elected representatives and media regulators in many major markets. Whilst this may, for now, be aimed at activity on social media, it won't be long before much of the marketing and communications activity online starts to come in for significant scrutiny.

Before you start to assert that it wouldn't happen in your organization, just consider the actions taken by employees of Volkswagen (VW). In September 2015, the Environmental Protection Agency in the United States found that many VW cars being sold in America had a 'defeat device' – or software – in diesel engines that could detect when they were being tested, changing the performance accordingly to improve results.[4] As the details emerged the BBC reported that this covered about 11 million cars worldwide, including 8 million in Europe. VW disputes liability in the European Union where the emission standards were not as stringent.

A report in the *Financial Times* (2018)[5] revealed that in a legal submission to a German Court the company asserted that its executives were unaware of a conscious effort to deceive emissions tests going back to 2006 and were unaware of a 16-month cover-up in which employees lied to regulators and offered false information to explain 'irregularities' between laboratory tests and real-world emissions. This organizational failure, according to *Forbes* (2018),[6] has so far cost US $25 billion in fines, penalties and restitution in the United States. It also resulted in the arrest, prosecution and jailing of a senior manager in the United States who admitted that he had been part of a cover-up.

The more organizations trust individuals with specialized high-level technical knowledge to achieve demanding goals, the more risk that is accepted by the organization and the more the organization relies on the values and ethical standards of those involved in detail. This is because, regardless of the degree of compliance established across an organization, unless every decision comes up for a review at a senior level (which is impossible in all but the smallest enterprises), the day-to-day actions of individuals are likely to determine the long-term reputation of the business and the degree of confidence in which the brand is held.

This risk is compounded even more by two things: the immaturity of the digital function itself, which means that there are no clear professional standards, and the professional and commercial immaturity of many of the people who work in the field. Digital workers are often both narrowly expert and do not have a great deal of experience post the end of their formal education. The challenge for leaders, therefore, is to think carefully not just in terms of data protection and handling policies and, in the European Union, GDPR compliance, but also to lay out a set of ethical expectations. These will help those working in the field, particularly at the leading edge of digital applications and programming, to think through the decisions they make at a technical and operational level against the context of a number of key criteria, all of which need to be aligned to building and retaining not just customer confidence but also the confidence of society at large and those elected to set the legal and regulatory frameworks within which we operate.

Is 'big tech' out of control?

This issue of the confidence of society as a whole looms large over the digital industry as a whole and, in particular, the dominant players such as Amazon, Apple, Google (and their parent company Alphabet), Facebook, Snap, Uber,

Airbnb, Alibaba, WeChat, Waymo and those competing to grow to this size and influence. There is a rising tide of concern over the corporate governance, values, business ethics practices and financial polices (particularly tax affairs) of these companies, with comparisons being made to the 'robber barons' of the 19th-century corporate United States.[7] Famously so described by 19th-century writer Matthew Josephson in his eponymous book, these people built the modern industrial state that powered the United States to global dominance in the second half of the 20th century. They also amassed huge fortunes for themselves using a raft of dubious techniques, including fraud, stock dilution, the bribing of corrupt politicians, the creation of secret cartels and the ruthless exploitation of poorly paid, non-unionized workers. In the end, their abuses and excesses led to a legislative backlash in the form of the 1890 Sherman Anti-Trust Act, the first US statute to limit cartels and monopolies.

Step back from the context of the historical tale and some similarities emerge in our current age. These have surfaced in articles in *The Guardian*,[8] been given coverage by Forbes,[9] carried by CBS News[10] and covered by Reuters.[11] The use of share classes that reduce the impact and influence shareholders can have over management by some tech companies have led to accusations in *The Economist* of a trend towards corporate autocracy.[12]

This concern about the rise of a corporate autocracy was articulated by George Soros at the 2018 World Economic Forum in Davos.[13] His observation centred on the power of a very few large digital firms to shape attention. 'The power to shape people's attention is increasingly concentrated in the hands of a few companies… it takes a real effort to assert and defend what John Stuart Mill called "the freedom of mind". There is a possibility that once lost, people who grow up in the digital age will have difficulty in regaining it.' His concern was that there was little vested interest in effective self-regulation, suggesting that what he called 'internet monopolies' have neither the will nor the inclination to protect society against the consequences of their actions.

This sense of the development of a small group of incredibly powerful organizations would not normally be an issue for a business book, if it wasn't for the impact that a small core of them are having on business practices and performance worldwide. In 2017, Google and Facebook attracted more than 60 per cent of digital advertising spend in the United States.[14] In the same year, at least one prediction suggested that Amazon would be responsible for nearly 44 per cent of all US e-commerce sales and close to 4 per cent of all retail sales.[15] This scale of earnings and the fact that, unlike in virtually every other industrial sector, these companies are not paying for their raw material (data they collect for free from every interaction on their digital real estate), together with clever management of their tax affairs, have generated significant cash holdings that dwarf many traditional companies.

This scale comes from significantly enhanced profitability compared with traditional manufacturers of good and services and has enabled investments by a number of digital companies into the next generation of technology applications. These applications have the potential to transform the economic and social landscape in which business operates. Some, indeed, might argue that they are already doing so. An increasing amount of what is deployed at scale in digital channels is based on machine learning or 'artificial intelligence' (AI). Combine this with the application of engineering and you have the basis for robotics that could wipe out whole classes of jobs, unless there is careful and considered engagement by government and regulators into how societies can engage with change and enable a smooth transition into an economy not based entirely on human economic output.

The development of the 'Internet of Things' or digital communication-enabled connectivity will not just deliver enhanced home security or car safety, but it could also easily be used to track children, record conversations, prompt unnecessary consumption and invade privacy to such an extent that by accident (and some might argue stealth) we expose the totality of our lives to others for commercial, social and political exploitation. The connectivity of everything to a smartphone also gives rise to social and psychological concerns about how we engage with technology. In 2017 and 2018, we experienced a parade of tech luminaries, including the founding president of Facebook, warning about the sophisticated machinery of engagement and persuasion being built into smartphone apps. They talked about distraction, productivity, how social networks alter our emotional lives and relationships, and what they're doing to children.[16]

In a piece in the *Financial Times* (2017)[17] Rana Foroohar argued that 'big tech' was making vast gains at the expense of the individual consumer. Her analysis suggests that the current position taken by the US anti-trust authorities has failed to understand the way Google, Amazon and Facebook in particular make their money. As they offer up their services for free they meet the core of the 19th-century definition of 'non-monopoly' behaviour – the artificial sustaining of a higher price – as they do not charge for their services but are platforms that are free to use. But, they are still an anti-trust issue as we may not use dollars to pay for these services; however, we are paying in data and it is the collection and use of that data that should be a cause for concern. This is because the acquisition of billions of data points enables the large digital companies to 'tilt the playing field' in favour of themselves. Their data manipulation can become people manipulation as they plant suggestions in front of consumers that, if adopted, make them even more profitable. Like others, including a 2018 report from a combination of authors from Stanford, Columbia and Microsoft,[18] she argues that the time has come to consider treating data as raw materials and pay the owners of those materials for their use. This would radically change the dynamics of digital and, in our view, probably for the better. It would reduce the profits of the digital giants reducing the temptation to abuse their market power and it would also help in rebalancing the economy as we move towards a world dominated by AI, where the nature of work itself may well present an existential challenge to developed economies.

The power of digital technology to transform our world, for good or evil, is beyond our imagination. Allowed to develop with the interest of only platform owners to set a compass, the risk of a dystopian future is far greater than one where every stakeholder plays a part in framing the direction of travel. To date in 2018 little, if any, of this is regulated anywhere in the world. It is not even yet properly understood by governments and regulators or by business leaders. The power it can unleash, however, has been rapidly understood by those with extreme views, those wanting to cause dissent, disharmony and discord, and those who want to make money at any cost.

Facebook's 87 million problems make the point

In early 2018, the Cambridge Analytica/Facebook data story broke in the United States and the United Kingdom. By mid 2018, the initial story had grown into a global issue where the personal data belonging to around 87 million people, some of whom were not even on Facebook, seem to have been extracted and then manipulated by a third party for a combination of commercial and political gain.[19] By the time you are reading this, we are sure that the story will have moved on again, so this section is not aimed at the specifics of the issue, but at the principles that it illustrates, many of which have been raised so far in this chapter.

Business model dilemma

One of the differences in this case versus that of Volkswagen earlier, is that we are not talking about aberrant behaviour in an organization that is transparent with its 'customers' in how it makes its money from them. From the day it first looked for revenue, Facebook had to maximize the harvesting of data and its understanding of how to attract human attention in order to monetize its members. As soon as you look to do this, such a business model then drives a culture that looks to understand more and more so messages can be targeted better and more advertising revenue attracted as a result. So, it developed an ever-improving ability to acquire and utilize data from large populations of people such that it could sell advertising services to third parties.

The business model brings with it another complication in that Facebook does not know the vast majority of the third parties with whom it contracts; and, contractually, takes no ethical or moral responsibility for the messages that these third parties send through to its users. The problem is at the core of what started as a low-scale, low-cost operation to bring people closer together, and has developed an ambition to be the global platform through which people connect; to achieve that ambition someone has to pay.

Cultural dilemma

The second issue is one of culture. Perhaps naively, Facebook (and indeed others who operate a 'free service') set out to be a place of 'free speech' and unregulated interaction. This builds a corporate culture of laissez-faire thinking where resources are aimed at growing users, because the data these users bring with them can be monetized, and this then brings a virtuous circle of growth as investors continue to support the company in the expectation of handsome long-term returns. This culture, in its turn, therefore develops a mindset where intervention is a 'bad thing'. The consequence of this company-wide perspective ensures that from the very top downwards there is behaviour that seeks to minimize the risks associated with the business model, rejects divergent voices as 'spoilers' of the 'free market' in ideas and refuses to take seriously the need to intervene.

Whether it be Islamic terrorism, extreme political views or downright fake news, the issue and its importance has been regularly downplayed and the organization, in the words of its COO Sheryl Sandberg, reported in the *Financial Times*, its leaders were slow to react.[20] Looking at the coverage of the affair, it is possible to argue that at the heart of Facebook's culture is a lack of care for its users and an excess of concern for those who pay to access them. If so, this is a significant cultural challenge.

Advertiser dilemma

Finally, advertisers, and more importantly their agencies, cannot escape from any long-term scrutiny and the searchlight will, at some point, be trained on them. On one hand, if there is a universal truth in marketing, then in any age, marketing money has followed the customer and as customers have moved to consume media and live their lives online, so advertisers have invested behind them to ensure that they are still capturing customers' attention. On the other hand, the move to digital changed the methodology and offered the opportunity for much greater exploitation of data than any previous route to market, and advertisers piled in when perhaps they should have taken a more judicious and measured approach such that they understood exactly what was being done in their names.

At one level, creating content that is relevant for a particular segment of customers and getting it placed in front of them where they are, just sounds like a smarter version of traditional media buying. This is, after all, a highly measurable activity and, as a result, unlike TV or press spending, the effectiveness of this investment can be established far more robustly. And, don't the users of these 'free services' understand the contract they have entered into? At another level, however, what is the impact on the reputation of a brand if it is found to be utilizing the approaches that sound similar to those used by Cambridge Analytica? In TV and in the press, there are regulatory frameworks and structures that are there to protect consumers and, as a consequence, protect brands as well. Operating in the advertising equivalent of the Wild West comes with much higher risks – as the many businesses who have pulled away from advertising on YouTube have already discovered.

In the European Union, this lack of a regulatory framework has been addressed in part by the agreement of a more demanding set of regulations to protect the use of personal data: the General Data Protection Regulation (GDPR). This puts more control into the hands of consumers over access to and the use of their data, and has forced platform providers of all sizes to develop easier-to-understand terms and conditions of use. It doesn't, however, address the issues of accountability for published material or for ensuring advertising standards against criteria such as those applied by the UK Advertising Standards Authority.

If there is any lesson to be learned by the rest of us from all of the examples raised above, it is to think very hard about two things: what is being done in our names that might look as though we are manipulating people through activities undertaken by those we employ to work in these channels; and where are we putting our brands that on closer inspection may be supporting behaviours and beliefs that are at odds with our espoused values?

Is business at the heart of the problem?

What funds the good, the bad and the ugly are adverts. Intriguingly, not adverts from the extremists, the exploiters and the perverted, but from businesses: to be blunt, probably your business. Quoted in an opinion piece in *The New York Times* by Farhad Manjoo (2018)[21] was the CEO of the Interactive Advertising Bureau, one of the digital trade associations. His proposition was that the initial business model of choice in online media, where consumer engagement was free and advertising would generate the revenues, was far more influential than anyone imagined. He argued that there was a pressing need for the industry to accept its civic responsibility for its effect, but also said that the pace of change in technology was outstripping the ability of companies to understand what was actually happening.

As business invests more and more in machine-learning-based activity that penetrates deeply into the personal lives of people who are active online in order to target with laser-like precision, so it needs to accept its responsibilities for engaging with and benefiting from the digital advertising industry. Over the last few years, there has been a chorus of rising discontent from major advertisers about fake views, inappropriate advert placement and poor value for money. We believe that business should not limit itself to an economic debate. It needs to accept that its investment in digital advertising has created an ecosystem that exploits individuals' data, often given up unwittingly, or even unwillingly, through having to comply with all-or-nothing terms and conditions.

The use that a business makes of this access, the decisions it makes as to how it chooses to engage with and exploit that data, and how it chooses to manage the very fine line that divides data manipulation from the manipulation of people's emotions and opinions, are important ethical considerations. In our experience, regrettably, they rarely appear at the top of the risks and concerns for e-commerce teams. The business also needs to think far more holistically about plans to adopt and engage with some of the new digital technologies that are on offer to drive growth. AI will displace people, sometimes with very positive benefits, but those people need to acquire new skills and find new roles – and not on zero-hour contracts in the gig economy. Connectivity will offer revenue and margin gains from doing things that could result in significant intrusions on privacy. Putting transparency at the front of customer engagement will help people to make their own choices about exactly what they are or are not prepared to share. Finally, whilst all-or-nothing terms and conditions are financially attractive, it's not just GDPR in the European Union that should make you think carefully about the respect with which you treat data.

If you are a leader in a technology company just remember that algorithms are written by human beings. That means that you can set stringent ethical standards on what you are setting out to do and how what you produce can be used. If you don't, then there is no way you can avoid accepting a high probability that one day someone will use your work to do evil.

How might business respond?

There is no doubt that digital technology brings significant benefits, not just commercial ones but also to the wider community. The issue for organizations is to think through the implications of their adoption and use of digital technology, and what they may mean in terms of reputation and customer and wider stakeholder confidence. We believe that leaders need to establish a clear and coherent process against which they should assess the ethical standing of their current practices and future plans. By this we mean that, just as in areas such as pricing, product quality, labelling and local trading standards, the use of data in digital technology needs to meet standards that have been reviewed and adopted at a senior level in the organization. Not only that, but also, we think there is a strong argument for reporting transparently on adherence to whatever standards are adopted. Just as, for example, hospitals in some countries are required to publish statistics on the rate of acquired infection and post-operative deaths.

Business ethics is a tricky topic, not least in that business practices differ across geographies and the degree of tolerance for particular practices varies across jurisdictions. That should not be an excuse for lowest common denominator behaviour but an opportunity to adopt the appropriate standards that protect reputation and build or reinforce customer confidence as well as being a foundation for commercial success. We are not talking here about a long list of restrictions that constrain innovation and commercial decision-making. Rather we are suggesting a set of clear, easy to judge principles that if adhered to help build confidence. They build confidence not because they exist, but because behind them you are willing to put compliance processes in place and hold your business to account. At a basic level, they will need to adhere to regulation standards on personal data (for example, GDPR across the European Union) – that is a cost of doing business.

But there are also simple commitments that we know drive improved commercial outcomes. For example, from our testing on e-commerce sites we know that pledging not to share customer data with third parties, and not to deluge customers with digital communication, increases sign-up rates significantly; and, we also know that email communications, well handled, deliver some of the highest conversion rates.

Here's a simple framework to work through. It is based on research conducted globally by the Reputation Institute[22] and the John Madejski Centre at Henley Business School[23] who, between them, have created two of the defining approaches to understanding the drivers of corporate reputation. The Reputation Institute model, the Harris-Fombrun Reputation Quotient, identifies six drivers, of which three stand out as most significant: the quality of the product or service; social responsibility; and the workplace experience. The Henley work has been based around the SPIRIT model. This argues that what drives perceptions is organization behaviour, particularly as measured by stakeholders. Taking these two as our starting point we have built a simple ethical framework for use by leaders responsible for digital transformation and execution (Figure 5.1). What we are doing is setting a framework for the governance of digital activity (governance being a key element in Harris-Fombrun) and recognizing the importance of behaviour choices as drivers of reputation in the eyes of stakeholders (the underpinning of the SPIRIT model).

Figure 5.1 The Good Growth Digital Ethical Framework

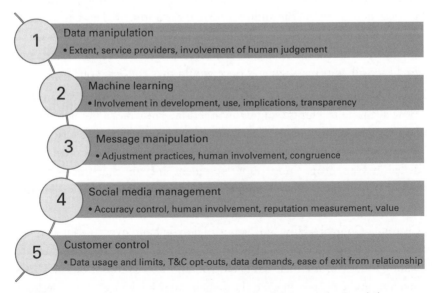

1. **Data manipulation**
   • Extent, service providers, involvement of human judgement

2. **Machine learning**
   • Involvement in development, use, implications, transparency

3. **Message manipulation**
   • Adjustment practices, human involvement, congruence

4. **Social media management**
   • Accuracy control, human involvement, reputation measurement, value

5. **Customer control**
   • Data usage and limits, T&C opt-outs, data demands, ease of exit from relationship

SOURCE Based on research from Henley Business School and The Reputation Foundation

Our thinking moves away from any notion of right or wrong – that is for moral philosophers – it focuses instead on the ethical dilemmas that form the core of debate inside all organizations, for profit or not-for-profit. It is designed to flush out the choices that may be hidden or even unquestioned by those making them and get the organization to confront them, make them explicit and establish principles against which the business can judge its performance in terms of customer and wider stakeholder confidence. It assumes compliance with data and advertising standards in your markets; it is less interested in the what and more concerned with the how. The choices we have defined as:

1 **Data Manipulation** – What is the extent of your data manipulation? What services do you use and how do they work? How much human judgement is involved in the decisions about what you do with data? Are you confident this covers all the key issues? What are the risks if all of this were to be exposed to your customers?

2 **Machine Learning** – Are you involved directly or indirectly in developing and/or using machine-learning applications? What are the implications for customers, employees, suppliers and any others stakeholders in what you are doing? How transparent are these implications? What are you doing now to think through amelioration strategies for any adverse impacts? Have you costed these into your business case?

3 **Message Manipulation** – What strategies and practices exist that adjust or change marketing and sales messages about you, your products or services depending on the audience? Are these automated and, if so, what degree of human interaction comes into play in assessing suitability and alignment with core proposition and/or corporate values? If an audience could see all your messaging at once would that concern you?

4 **Social Media Management** – How are you engaging with social media? How accurate is your messaging/interaction? How much human interaction is there in this activity? Is it sufficient? How are you measuring your impact in terms of brand and company reputation and customer confidence in your proposition? How confident are you that this is adding value? If you shut it down would there be a perceptible difference in your commercial performance? Or your brand performance?

5 **Customer Control** – How much control do you hand over to your customers to shape their engagement with you and the degree to which they are willing to let you use their data? Do you allow them to opt out of T&Cs that automatically give you a right to their data? Do you let them checkout

as a guest and not retain their data past the end of any 'free return' or other required period? If they unsubscribe do you keep trying to persuade them to stay? Or do you just ignore it until they make a real fuss? How difficult do you make it for people to contact a person in your business?

Note: We have thought about this in the context of a reasonably simple e-commerce operation. In each category, there may be more context-specific questions that you may wish to add. Ensure that everyone involved agrees what the questions are before you workshop the answers and the conclusions.

In considering these issues we suggest a workshop approach involving a wide range of stakeholders from those involved in the detail of activity through to those responsible to the board for its execution. Broadly, we suggest a process that operates as follows:

- Agree the questions in each of the major 'buckets'. Decide if, for your organization, you need a further 'bucket' and if so what would be in it.

- Get everyone involved together for each 'bucket' and work through their area to identify for every activity the answer to the questions.

- At the end of the discussion for each 'bucket' look at your answers and reflect on:
  - Are there any that clash with published values? Why?
  - Are there any with which we as a group are uncomfortable? Why?
  - Are there any of the above that, if our customers saw this analysis, we think they would have concerns? Why?
  - If not our customers, who would be concerned?
  - What is the gap we need to close to dismiss these concerns or reduce them such that we are confident that, if challenged, we can defend them successfully?
  - What will we do to close the gap, by when and who will do it?

- If there is a disagreement refer the issue upwards for guidance – this will help everyone involved understand how the leaders of the organization want the business to work.

- If there is a significant cost to change or a potential commercial implication then refer the issue upwards for a decision, sharing all the facts as transparently as you can.

- Assuming you can resolve your 'gaps', you can codify what you think is an acceptable set of principles, against which you can measure your compliance on a time basis that works for your business.

- Finally, you need to agree how you want to report these and whether you are willing to share this transparently with key stakeholders. This is probably a decision to be taken at the most senior level.

And what should be the public policy response?

As we mentioned earlier, this is a business book, not one on public policy, but from a business perspective we think there are some public policy principles that would help competition, remove unfair advantage and set the tramlines within which business and civil society can collaborate to ensure a successful transition through what is clearly the third Industrial Revolution (the first being mechanization, the second, automation and the third, digitalization). These principles are:

- Whilst we should embrace, exploit and engage with digital technology, there are strong arguments for governments and supra-national bodies to engage all sections of civil society in establishing proper regulation of the application of digital technology to protect social cohesion. Without this, there is a risk that big tech and big data become Big Brother, and the control of the direction of travel and the degree of change in the production and ownership of wealth shifts so radically that societies come under significant strain.

- Big tech needs better regulation as an industry. It can be a force for bad as well as good. Under-regulated, we get fake news, manipulation of people and groups, opacity and a willingness to take the money but not the responsibility for how the money is generated. Content platforms should be regulated just like other media channels. Treating them as publishers may be tricky but ensuring everyone who publishes is named in full, and easily identifiable, should be a minimum. This doesn't stop freedom of expression or the right to say what the majority disputes – but it does make it clear that if you publish it, you can be held accountable for it.

- Big tech is too big. Both in the United States and in other jurisdictions, politicians should consider whether there is now such a threat to competition that the largest of these organizations should be forced to split into their constituent parts. In a very well-argued blog, Ben Thompson (2017) asserted that Facebook should not have been allowed to buy TBH by the US authorities. He did so on the basis that the 'wave through' granted by US and UK regulators to the acquisition of Instagram was based on a flawed understanding of the business model. His piece goes on to conclude:

The issue is straightforward: networks are the monopoly makers of the internet era. To build one is extremely difficult, but, once built, nearly impregnable. The only possible antidote is *another* network that draws away the one scarce resource: attention. To that end, when it comes to the internet, the single most effective tool in antitrust regulation is keeping social networks in separate competitive companies. That the FTC and Office of Fair Trading failed to do so in the case of Instagram and WhatsApp is to the detriment of everyone.[24]

- As the business models become clearer and the digital giants struggle to control what appears on their platforms but continue to monetize their dominance, it is, in our view, time for the regulators to reconsider their early insouciance and look again, before it is too late to take action. In 2018, the former CEO of Walmart Bill Simon told the US Congress that, in his view, Amazon should be broken up.[25] He argued that the e-commerce giant has operated its retail segment at a loss for decades, subsidizing the retail portion of its business with profits from other areas, such as web services. His assertion was that it was 'anti-competitive, it's predatory, and it's not right'. He went on to say that 'It'll hurt small retailers, and it'll hurt speciality chains'.

- Finally, there needs to be a reform of business taxation to recognize that digital businesses make their money in very different ways from those that were assumed when taxation regimes were established. The point was taken up on the same CNBC report, above, by Gerald Storch, former Vice Chairman of Target and founder of Target.com. He referenced a 1992 Supreme Court ruling that said states couldn't collect sales taxes gathered by mail-order catalogue companies unless the businesses had a physical presence in a state. Storch's point was that half of all online product searches begin and end on Amazon, and that the playing field in retail should be more level, something it has not been in the past. The same argument applies right across the European Union, with regulators and the Commission starting to plan for an alternative tax regime based on sales in-country. In addition, in the United Kingdom local business taxes have been seen as significantly advantaging non-high-street businesses such as Amazon.

Leadership actions

Confidence in business continues to track at all-time lows[26] and the media interest in the dark side of digital does not look like receding any time soon. This will inevitably spread distrust and dent confidence in platforms, websites and the brands that stand behind them. Research shows that social media platforms are some of the least trusted sources of news (but news on social media from friends is highly rated – hence, the manipulation of people by those trying to influence the debate).[27] Responsible behaviour that shows respect to customers and acts in as transparent a way as possible will help insulate your business from the general malaise. The big challenge for business leaders is to ensure that their organizations have clearly understood ethical frameworks in place, and hold not just their own teams to account but those of the agencies and professional services businesses with whom they work to deliver their digital futures.

This chapter sits at this stage in the book because we believe it sets up a fundamental strategic challenge for all digital leaders – how to ensure that their business delivers an optimized digital strategy in a way that is sustainable and, when exposed or tested in the court of public opinion, can stand out as one in which all stakeholders can have confidence. What has gone before explores failure and the need to innovate; what follows is how to execute successfully. This is the bridge. It reminds you that whatever you do, however exciting the technology and its possibilities, you have a wider responsibility to all your stakeholders to do the right thing by them. That's good business.

There is only one action that we are asking you to take away from this chapter – consider completing an ethical framework exercise. However confident you are in your business values and those of your colleagues, don't assume anything. Probe hard, shine a torch in places that don't get looked at very often. Check. It might be the way you save a great deal of damage further down the track.

References

1 Sargeant, A and Lee, S (2004) Trust and relationship commitment in the United Kingdom voluntary sector: Determinants of donor behaviour, *Psychology & Marketing*, **21** (8), pp 613–35, July

2 https://beta.techcrunch.com/2018/02/21/snapchat-responds-to-the-change-org-petition-complaining-about-the-apps-redesign/ [accessed 6 March 2018]

3 https://www.theverge.com/2018/2/22/17040332/snap-stock-price-kylie-jenner-tweet-snapchat-1-billion-market-loss [accessed 6 March 2018]

4 http://www.bbc.co.uk/news/business-34324772 [accessed 7 March 2018]

5 https://www.ft.com/content/f77a6280-1d71-11e8-956a-43db76e69936 [accessed 7 March 2018]

6 http://fortune.com/2018/02/06/volkswagen-vw-emissions-scandal-penalties/ [accessed 7 March 2018]

7 https://www.theguardian.com/technology/2012/jul/01/new-tech-moguls-robber-barons [accessed 7 March 2018]

8 https://www.pastemagazine.com/articles/2017/12/7-examples-how-amazon-treats-their-90000-warehouse.html [accessed 7 March 2018]

9 https://www.forbes.com/sites/ianaltman/2015/10/27/what-amazon-is-doing-to-small-businesses/#43b98df952d4 [accessed 7 March 2018]

10 https://www.cbsnews.com/news/apple-admits-to-slowing-older-phones-because-of-battery-issues/ [accessed 7 March 2018]

11 https://www.reuters.com/article/us-uber-corruption/what-is-at-stake-for-uber-in-u-s-bribery-probe-idUSKCN1BW0HH [accessed 7 March 2018]

12 https://www.economist.com/news/business/21716654-snaps-refusal-hand-out-any-voting-shares-part-wider-trend-towards-corporate [accessed 7 March 2018]

13 http://www.bbc.co.uk/news/business-42826915 [accessed 8 March 2018]

14 https://www.emarketer.com/Article/Google-Facebook-Tighten-Grip-on-US-Digital-Ad-Market/1016494 [accessed 7 March 2018]

15 https://www.recode.net/2017/10/24/16534100/amazon-market-share-ebay-walmart-apple-ecommerce-sales-2017 [accessed 7 March 2018]

16 https://www.axios.com/sean-parker-unloads-on-facebook-god-only-knows-what-its-doing-to-our-childrens-brains-1513306792-f855e7b4-4e99-4d60-8d51-2775559c2671.html [accessed 8 March 2018]

17 Foroohar, R (2017) Big Tech's power remains unchallenged [Video] *Financial Times*

18 https://www.theguardian.com/technology/2017/oct/05/smartphone-addiction-silicon-valley-dystopia [accessed 8 March 2018]

19 https://www.theatlantic.com/magazine/archive/2017/09/has-the-smartphone-destroyed-a-generation/534198/ [accessed 8 March 2018]

20 https://www.ft.com/content/9e973ba4-3903-11e8-8eee-e06bde01c544?emailId=5ac78da54dc78f0004235e36&segmentId=3934ec55-f741-7a04-feb0-1ddf01985dc2 [accessed 7 April 2018]

21 https://www.nytimes.com/2018/01/31/technology/internet-advertising-business. html [accessed 8 March 2018]

22 https://www.instituteforpr.org//wp-content/uploads/Reputation_2005.pdf [accessed 8 March 2018]

23 MacMillan K *et al* (2004) Giving your organisation SPIRIT, *Journal of General Management*, 30 (2), pp 15–42

24 https://stratechery.com/2017/why-facebook-shouldnt-be-allowed-to-buy-tbh/ [accessed 8 March 2018]

25 https://www.cnbc.com/2018/03/29/former-walmart-us-ceo-congress-consider-splitting-up-amazon.html?recirc=taboolainternal [accessed 7 April 2018]

26 https://www.edelman.com/trust-barometer [accessed 8 March 2018]

27 https://uk.reuters.com/article/uk-media-fakenews/fake-news-hurts-trust-in-media-mainstream-outlets-fare-better-poll-idUKKBN1D002O [accessed 9 March 2018]

Emerging digital 06
business models

Executive summary

As digital has developed so have business models as organizations look to exploit the opportunities offered by data. Digital offers significant additional opportunity for older businesses on top of those models through which they operated offline. For producers, it offers the opportunity of engaging directly with consumers rather than indirectly through retail distributors; for retailers, it offers the opportunity to offer product ranges that do not have to be fulfilled through their own supply and distribution network; for content owners, it enables direct distribution and the opportunity to earn from subscribers, advertisers and producers; and for services, it offers a whole new approach to their delivery. At a strategic level, the choices come with implications for the organization of the production, supply and delivery of the proposition; at an executional level, the implications are for the how, not the what, and this is where the risks of failure are significant. This chapter explores the primary models and lays out the key executional considerations for leaders.

A map of e-commerce

In our previous book,[1] we introduced a model of e-commerce as a place where the battle for customer attention primarily took place, between competing propositions in response to a search query or jostling for attention in an email inbox. Once the attention has been gained, the challenge is to generate a successful transaction. A significant amount of e-commerce still happens this way, but as the channel has developed so has the range of places where potential customers are engaged and established customer relationships developed. Figure 6.1 shows the flow through the channel.

As we have referenced before, apps are a fraction of the total traffic on the web for all bar a handful of retailers,[2] but they are used effectively as tools through which to engage loyal and/or frequent shoppers and, in some

Figure 6.1 The e-commerce flow

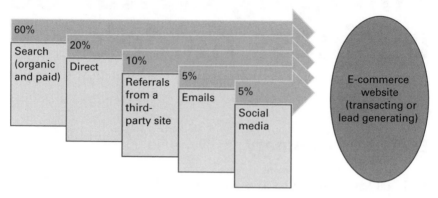

other sectors, are the preferred method of engagement with the customer (for example, ride-hailing apps, hotel or travel aggregators and car parking services). According to our all-client database, direct traffic (that is, where a customer has a proposition bookmarked or enters the website directly into the search bar) accounts for roughly 20 per cent of traffic, whilst email generates about 5 per cent. The other significant sources for traffic are affiliates (that is, third-party referrers of traffic who are rewarded should that referral generate a transaction) who seem to account for between 5 and 15 per cent depending on the sector, and social media (1–5 per cent). This means that search (organic and paid) accounts for about 60 per cent of traffic on an average e-commerce website.

Locating and engaging customers

The location and attraction of customer interest is still a highly competitive activity, so much so that it has spread significantly over the last three years into a plethora of social and media channels where people spend the majority of their time online. It has also generated a significant increase in affiliate activity, particularly through media owners where many product and service reviews now offer links directly to the transaction page. If we look at Facebook as an example, in 2012 its total revenue from advertising was around US $4.3 billion; in 2017, it was reported as being 10 times greater at nearly US $40 billion.[3] This represents approximately 98 per cent of total revenue. According to PwC, affiliate marketing and lead generation attracted nearly £1.6 billion of advertiser investment in 2016 in the United Kingdom alone, with the research suggesting that this investment generated over £19 billion in sales.[4]

We believe that, in the context of all these choices and the large variation in commercial outcomes, it is useful for leaders to demand clarity from their e-commerce teams about the positioning of digital marketing investment and how the impact will be measured. In our view, there is a continuum of engagement online from activity that looks very similar to that for TV/radio, outdoors and much of print (addressed at consumers at large or against a specific demographic definition to raise awareness of the brand, such that when the time arises they would consider purchasing the product or service) to promotional activity close to the point of purchase that offline you would see in some print leaflets though the mail, and in-store/in-venue promotional activity (the encouragement of people shopping to opt for your brand or service at a stage when they have the intention to transact).

We talked earlier about the need to identify whether investment is for consideration or conversion and how best to measure the returns from each, such that it is possible to measure comparative performance. Currently, businesses are regaled with data from differing platforms and providers, all trying to position themselves as a 'value for money' investment and all using the data points that best sustain their proposition. What leaders want to know is the comparative effectiveness of their resource allocation decisions. Our observation is that it isn't in any provider's interests to enable that to happen transparently, so it is important that a business focuses on a single unifying set of measures that enable comparative assessment as best as possible. An example of data that doesn't provide information is the continuing use of impressions as a data point. Whilst many agencies and marketing professionals still quote impressions as a measure of effectiveness, all it does is tell you how many people might have caught a glimpse of an advert (and the way impressions are counted it will most likely be only a fleeting glimpse at that). It tells you nothing about the advert's effectiveness or impact.

Conversion

For activities that focus on conversion, it is relatively straightforward to identify impact and engagement: through using return on advertising spend (ROAS) as a simple and effective comparison. This is calculated as a percentage derived from the revenue generated as a direct result of the spend in the marketing channel, as per this example:

Spend in PPC £10,000; Sales from PPC £500; ROAS = £500/£10,000 = 5 per cent

There is a complication that leaders should not let divert them from the objective of comparative performance assessment: how to attribute sales when a customer journey may have involved engagement with several advertisements, either in the same channel or across several channels. This is often described as a debate as to whether one should attribute the sale to the advert clicked first or that clicked last. Google has recently created a range of attribution models to help assess effectiveness within its own ecosystem. Simply put, these are:

- **Last click** – This is still the approach used in most AdWords campaigns and it gives all the credit to the last clicked ad and corresponding keyword that led to a conversion.

- **First click** – First click is the exact opposite. First click attribution gives all the credit to the first clicked ad and corresponding keyword.

- **Linear** – In this model, all clicks that lead to the conversion are given the same amount of credit.

- **Time decay** – If your business has a longer conversion cycle then time decay allows a weighted attribution, meaning clicks that happened closer to the conversion are given more weight than clicks that happened further away from the conversion.

- **Position-based** – This attributes value to the position of click on a time-line with the business choosing the value to attribute to each position.

- **Data-driven** – Data-driven attribution models automatically give conversion credit based on past data performance.

Our instinct, unless there is a good business reason, is to adopt a position-based logic for investment in the Google ecosystem that allocates 50 per cent of the value to the first click and then 25 per cent to the second, 12.5 per cent to the third and so on to the last click. The most challenging thing for a proposition to do is to prompt consideration. This is particularly so for an unknown brand. Even amongst known brands, attracting the first engagement from a customer is a big challenge. The quality of that advert, and its associated landing page, to retain the interest of a browsing shopper must be high to ensure that the shopper continues to retain your product or service as a possible purchase. Giving additional credit, therefore, to the first engagement seems to be sensible. However, even with this approach, it is nigh on impossible to track the impact of any activity in the non-Google ecosystem on a customer's decision to transact. This takes us back to looking at ROAS as the comparative measure for any marketing investment aimed at converting customer interest into a sale.

Consideration

One of the mantras that leaders will keep hearing about digital is that 'everything is measurable' and, to an extent, that is correct – everything associated with an action is measurable, even if, like impressions, the measure isn't particularly helpful. For activities aimed at consideration, however, the measurability challenge is just as challenging online as it is offline. There are some advantages – impressions is a better measure than 'readers' for a print media product and 'likes' on social media can tell you who has engaged to some degree – but the basic measurement of whether or not people are aware of, and have positive attitudes about, your product or service is no more easy than assessing the impact of activity on TV or in the cinema. Classic marketing measurement approaches can apply and as they cut cross channels, can help with assessing comparative impact. These include:

Brand awareness

Although the effectiveness of measuring brand awareness in order to calculate marketing ROI is questionable, understanding both the level of brand penetration in a given market and gaining insight into how customers became aware of your brand can help marketers to assess changes in brand awareness over time. Tactics for quantifying brand awareness include:

- Surveys – surveying can be used to either ask a random selection of people if they can recall your brand or product, or to ask existing customers how they heard about you. Polling audiences to measure brand awareness requires a level of brand reputation to be effective, with surveys typically asking questions such as 'name three companies that provide X' or 'what products/services does X offer?' Movements in the ability to recall or recognize a brand is the metric that you would use as a measure to see movement over time.

- Website traffic – an analysis of the volume in direct traffic over time can help brands to understand changes in brand awareness. Though attribution of direct traffic against a particular marketing activity is difficult to quantify, rises in direct traffic can provide an indication of increased brand awareness.

- Search data – measuring the movement in branded search impressions using Google Search Console is a simple way for brands of all sizes to view how many people are searching for your brand online. A deeper look into which branded search terms are increasing in impressions will also help to assess the performance of different elements of a marketing strategy. Likewise, the direct traffic volume gives an indication, though not necessarily an accurate one, of changes in the volume of customers visiting your website directly, so acts as another signal of overall brand awareness and visitor intent.

Brand mentions and sentiment

Social listening can be used to analyse existing conversations about your brand on the web, in particular on social media, to measure both volume of mentions and sentiment of the conversations. This method somewhat overcomes the existence of bias that may occur in customer surveys, where the respondents may not provide honest answers. All of these metrics can be used to form benchmarks to track a baseline of performance for your brand and monitor changes in activity over time. Social listening measurements include:

- Mentions – measuring the number of times your brand is mentioned online, both within and outside of your owned channels, provides an indication of the level of conversation happening around your brand. This can be monitored over time to identify changes and seasonality.

- Reach – this will indicate the potential audience of the brand mentions, based on the size of audience achieved from the activity.

- Share of voice – there are a number of tools for estimating the share of voice or mentions within a specific market, many of which have significant fees associated with their use. This measurement is more concerned with understanding the opportunity for brand reach rather than actual awareness, but can play a role in understanding brand performance against competitors within a competitive marketplace.

Brand trust, reviews and recommendations

Measuring the number of customers who recommend your brand or service is a useful way of quantifying the level of trust and visibility you have, which can be leveraged within the consideration phase. There is no single metric for understanding the level of brand recommendations or level of trust online, but using a combination of the following measurements can help build a picture over time alongside any efforts to increase loyalty later in the customer life cycle:

- Backlinks – though not effective as a singular metric, the number of links to your site from external sources is a measurement of brand endorsement so should be monitored alongside branded search volume and referral traffic.

- Online reviews – measuring both the number and sentiment of online reviews as well as any trust mark score, for example Google reviews or a third-party review provider, can be useful in understanding the overall impact of the brand.

- Referrals – accurately measuring word-of-mouth referrals is difficult, although customer surveys within the conversion funnel may help to provide an indication of the volume of customer referral activity. More advanced referral marketing solutions such as MentionMe can more accurately measure, incentivize and attribute customer referrals, which will, in turn, have an effect on the brand visibility at the consideration stage.

Resource allocation

In our work, what has emerged in this part of the e-commerce business model is the critical importance of being able to scope and experiment to identify the optimal mix across channels that delivers the best possible outcome in both consideration and conversion. This is complex econometric modelling and it requires careful thought and a high level of technical capability. The payback, however, can be significant and, where margins are under threat and agency fees are linked to a percentage of spend, investing in a deeper understanding of mix can deliver benefits to both top and bottom lines. We call this the Resource Allocation in Marketing Model (RAMM™) and, as you can see in Figure 6.2, it pulls together three key elements.

Figure 6.2　The Resource Allocation in Marketing Model™

Overall, the RAMM™ gives leaders a way of measuring brand health and modelling the impact of changes to marketing strategy and activity, such that they can then test and learn about the impact of every aspect of marketing activity on their business performance. Marketing in the 21st century is increasingly focused on measurability and impact. Leaders need to be able to make effective judgements and doing this requires the right measures, not any measures. The challenge in this aspect of e-commerce is not to confuse data with information.

Selling and retaining customers

What customers want

The challenge online is not just to win a transaction but to build a relationship such that not only can you build repeat transactions, but also build a network of advocates who engage their friends and acquaintances through recommendations such that they become a trusted provider. There is a plethora of statistics about customer behaviour and what encourages people to buy and stay loyal, much of it contradictory and all of it used to justify a vast array of differing solutions, technologies and customer retention schemes. Cutting through the latest research and looking for repeating themes across different reports can explain much about the direction of travel in e-commerce sales engagement models:

- People buy when they have a recommendation: Accenture[5] reported in 2017 that over 40 per cent of US consumers would select a brand or retailer if recommended by friends or family, and over half who responded to the survey said they would recommend. A MarketingSherpa report[6] in 2017 suggested that 61 per cent of shoppers would recommend if they were satisfied by the experience of a brand or retailer.

- Service is a significant driver, regardless of demographic: a 2017 ICSC report[7] suggested that 74 per cent of Millennials would switch to a different retailer if they had poor customer service. But shoppers will give brands/retailers with an historic good record a second chance: MarketingSherpa reported that 82 per cent of satisfied customers will 'likely' or 'very likely' keep shopping with a company and give it another chance if something goes wrong.

- Protection of privacy matters: Accenture reported that 85 per cent of US consumers are loyal to brands that safeguard and protect the privacy of their personal information, whilst a 2017 global survey by e-commerce platform provider SAP/Hybris[8] suggested that 79 per cent of consumers will leave a brand if their personal data is used without their knowledge.

- Variety and experience drives engagement: CapGemini's 2017 customer experience survey[9] reported that of the organizations surveyed, only three out of ten match customer expectations but eight in ten consumers are willing to pay more for a better customer experience. Interestingly, they found that 75 per cent of organizations believe themselves to be customer-centric but only 30 per cent of consumers agree. According to Accenture, 41 per cent of US consumers give their loyalty to organizations that present them with new experiences, products and services.

- Price, or at least 'value for money' matters, regardless of the demographic: ICSC reported that 92 per cent of loyal customers rank price and value as the top driver for loyalty to specific retailers, followed by product/quality at 79 per cent and variety/selection at 71 per cent.

Even these three recurring themes from a series of customer and consumer surveys in 2017 have to be treated with some degree of caution. They are asking for opinions, not tracking actual behaviour. Opinion polling comes with an increasingly large health warning, as we find more and more examples that suggest what people say and what they do are not always congruent. However, if we take them as indicative of direction then there are some obvious themes that are clearly influencing e-commerce practice:

- Variety, novelty and extension into shoulder services to retain customer engagement and to encourage return visits. This is about building a reputation for meeting the widest possible share of customer needs and is driving business models that look to extend range without extending working capital requirements.

- Price is a driver of customer choice and whilst there are many who would pay more for an enhanced experience, there are many who would not want to pay any more than anyone else for the same experience. In this regard, online enables highly transparent price comparison. This need for reassurance on maximizing value drives business models that work to offer assurance about price through trawling the market for comparable deals for the same product.

- Value for money, as opposed to price per se, is often the most cited issue we find with products and services offered online. Most of the time the issue is the failure to explain properly and clearly the value proposition, but it demonstrates the sensitivity of the online shopper to this issue.

Value for money concern is the driver behind business models that look to present and curate choice across a whole market, such that customers can make an informed decision about the purchases they want to make and the level of expenditure they are willing to commit in any transaction. Here, the model looks to share the range of choice available at every price point.

- Customer service and the creation of longer-term, loyalty-based relationships sits behind a fast-growing business model that puts a service relationship at the heart of the transaction, as opposed to one that focuses on product value or value for money. Here, the response is to enter into a service contract that delivers value in itself alongside the value delivered through the core proposition. This is no longer the preserve of the loyalty card, but also extends to a range of service and added value propositions.

How business is responding

In response to these trends, four core business models have emerged. They are not necessarily exclusive, but they require leadership understanding of the choices that need to be made and the potential trade-offs that follow as a consequence.

Marketplace

Whilst for many years the preserve of Amazon and eBay, marketplaces are now a much more common business model across many retail sectors and not only exist as 'marketplace' platforms but also within single retail propositions. The principle of a marketplace is straightforward – it offers an online platform for a range of competing and non-competing propositions that can be found in one place and transacted through one portal. The advantage of a pure marketplace portal to business owners is that they never have to hold any stock nor take accountability for the fulfilment (and return) of orders made. The advantage to customers is that it reduces the amount of 'shopping around' in order to get an understanding of the range of offers for the areas in which they are looking.

Marketplaces operate on a revenue-sharing business model. Sell through a marketplace and the owner of the marketplace earns revenue by charging a commission on each purchase made. Peer-to-peer marketplaces are those where the platform is completely independent of allegiance to a specific retailer. They are particularly appealing to small and medium-sized producers and retailers who cannot necessarily compete with the big brands in their field, but will benefit from the advertising muscle that comes from participating in a third-party platform – part of the commission on sale will go towards funding online marketing. In peer-to-peer marketplaces, whilst eBay is the prime example and is used not just by individuals but also by businesses, another good example is Etsy, which focuses on art, handmade and vintage items, and one-off products mainly in home and fashion.

Food delivery has seen a significant rise in peer-to-peer marketplaces with platforms such as Just Eat, Deliveroo, Grubhub and Foodpanda. Another sector that has seen the rise of this type of platform includes car rentals such as Turo, a peer-to-peer, car-sharing platform that in 2018 boasted thousands of cars in more than 4,700 cities and 300+ airports across the United States, Canada, Germany and the United Kingdom.[10] Other platforms include Zipcar and Drivy. In financial services too, platforms such as Kickstarter and Crowdfunder have introduced crowdfunding, where businesses can access funds direct from those with capital looking to invest, rather than through the agency of a bank or investment fund. More recently, the idea has spread from start-ups and businesses looking for working capital into non-profits and individual projects.

Working independently has become more common across many developed economies and enables access to talent across several markets, not just the talent pool around your locality. What started as a way of finding technical talent (especially development talent in IT), has now expanded into a range of professional roles and marketplaces for finding targeted talent at a reasonable cost. Freelancer, Fiverr and Fourerr, for example, make money by charging fees on every successful completed project and with a significant number of registered users, these websites also manage to earn from on-page advertisements. To give an idea of scale, Freelancer, the leading peer-to-peer marketplace for digital technology professionals, had 27 million users as of April 2018.[11]

Home-renting online has exploded with the growth of Airbnb, creating an opportunity to globalize what had been a fragmented local industry. Whilst Airbnb was the first, others have stepped in to offer property owners a range of solutions to monetize their homes. These include FlipKey, HomeAway and GuestToGuest. In a related field, home and personal services had for years been the preserve of Yellow Pages and local directories. Whilst these provided a listing service they didn't add value to both trader and customer by enabling online booking or access to quality assurance through ratings or other customer feedback. This is rapidly changing; for example, Angie's List, a US-based marketplace for local services, claimed in 2018 to have more than 10 million verified reviews of service providers and that around 6 million households check their site every day.[12] It is one of the biggest online market-places for local services ranging from home improvement to health to auto and other professional services. Other popular online local marketplaces are Thumbtack, Zaask, Rated People and TaskRabbit (now owned by IKEA).

In all of these markets there are mechanisms that regulate behaviour and quality assure transactions. All offer some kind of sanctions regime on either buyers or sellers for failure to adhere to the rules governing the transaction or for falling significantly short of the advertised proposition or agreed price. Products can be returned and money refunded for poor services. All, too, offer some kind of mediation or dispute resolution. These elements are critical to sustain confidence in the market and to encourage new buyers and sellers to engage with the platform.

The other form of marketplace is retailer-led. This is where a retailer offers third-party goods or services in addition to its own. At its apex is the Amazon model, where the retailer not only offers additional products but also competes with third-party providers of the same product, and in some lines offers pre-used alternatives alongside brand new ones. In 2014, research from Warwick University[13] reported that Amazon sold over 2 billion third-party items through its marketplace platform. Also operating this model are global players such as Flipkart and Alibaba. Increasingly however, this model is being extended and utilized by big brand retailers to extend their range and reach as the look to attract and retain customers and fight off the threat of the ever-increasing range extensions of Amazon, Flipkart and Alibaba. In May 2018, in a move clearly aimed at responding to the growth of Amazon, Walmart launched a takeover bid for Flipkart.

Target, Sears, Wayfair, Best Buy and Walmart in the United States, and players such as ASOS, Tesco, Next and GAME in the United Kingdom, all offer marketplace propositions. In response there are businesses that support producers in integrating and maximizing their reach across all these different offerings. For the seller, there are attractions and detractions: whilst all of these retailers attract significant visitor numbers every month, the business models they employ, like that of Amazon, ensures that there is a significant commission to be paid for goods sold in this way. For the retailer, whilst there are attractions in range extension at little or no real cost or increase in stock, partner programmes in marketplace are challenging to run and resource hungry. They really only work if there is a critical mass of choice and if both partners and customers believe they are getting value from participating.

The choice as to whether to offer a marketplace is an important one for a retailer and can be framed around what we call the 'five pillars' of market-place, as shown in Figure 6.3.

Figure 6.3 The five pillars of marketplace

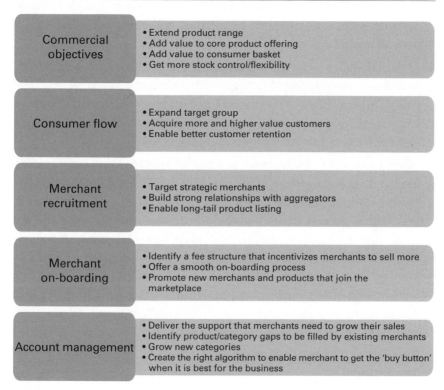

Commercial objectives	• Extend product range • Add value to core product offering • Add value to consumer basket • Get more stock control/flexibility
Consumer flow	• Expand target group • Acquire more and higher value customers • Enable better customer retention
Merchant recruitment	• Target strategic merchants • Build strong relationships with aggregators • Enable long-tail product listing
Merchant on-boarding	• Identify a fee structure that incentivizes merchants to sell more • Offer a smooth on-boarding process • Promote new merchants and products that join the marketplace
Account management	• Deliver the support that merchants need to grow their sales • Identify product/category gaps to be filled by existing merchants • Grow new categories • Create the right algorithm to enable merchant to get the 'buy button' when it is best for the business

SOURCE © Good Growth Ltd

Having spent a significant time working on strategy and execution for one of the leading marketplaces in the UK high street, we developed this framework to support the channel leaders think through the five key elements that go into framing the choice as to whether and how to get into a marketplace:

1 Be clear on the commercial objectives and make sure that you can deliver, ideally on all of those in the model above in your execution. Stock control/ flexibility and range extension are critical as is one of more customer value or higher value baskets.

2 Think about how this will help to attract more customers and retain greater loyalty with more repeat purchases. This should frame the types of partners you are looking to attract.

3 Make sure your business has a really good understanding of the market(s) that you are moving into, and the segmentation and price points within which it operates. This enables you to ensure that your targeting strategy delivers your commercial and customer objectives. Long-tail thinking is really important here; by this, we mean understanding how your partner (merchant) choice will enable you to cover the greatest possible range of customer interest as measured by the 'long tail' of keyword queries in a particular market segment.

4 Make sure that you have a considered and active programme of partner (merchant) on-boarding. Marketplace failure comes, as in most things digital, from a failure to execute well and on-boarding, as with people, is a critical element of getting a successful outcome for both parties. Make sure the fee structure works for both parties – don't be greedy.

5 Have an account development strategy at an individual and category level and, most important of all, make an active and considered choice about how to allocate the 'buy button'. The decision as to who gets the 'buy button' in answer to a search query from outside or inside the site is the biggest 'single' decision you will make in a marketplace. It is obvious if you have a single supplier, but if you have competing products in a category or, even more tricky, if the retail owner of the site also has a competing offer then this becomes an important call. Whatever you decide, make sure it is transparent to all concerned; and, in our view, never play games with your partners to your own advantage.

Aggregation

Aggregation is a business model that makes its money from offering customers value by gathering together competing propositions in one place and converting that interest into a sale from which they generate a fee. Its success in travel and tourism was significant, initially through the aggregation and sale of un-booked rooms at short notice (lastminute.com) and then into full service platforms such as Expedia, Hotels.com and Booking.com. The latest statistics available (2017)[14] suggest that around US $567 billion was transacted online in travel bookings through these and other sites worldwide. Aggregation has moved not just into all parts of the travel economy (car rental, flights, holidays, for example) but also into financial services, real estate and, most recently, take-out food.

For many business leaders, aggregation is thought of as an unwelcome and often margin-eroding activity that can drive prices down. Customers, on the other hand, often believe that these players help them get a complete understanding of a market and the choices within it, perhaps not always appreciating that some of the benefit of any saving in price goes to the aggregator by way of a fee. However, the impression that these 'price comparison' sites drive down prices is not necessarily correct. Research by David Ronayne

(2015 and revised in 2018)[15] suggests that perversely, where aggregation exists, even if there are competing aggregators, the impact of the aggregator fee negates any potential benefit of price competition for the customer. In other words, whilst the aggregator benefits, the customer in the market may be no better off compared to one who had just gone direct to a provider of goods or services. This may go some way to explaining why hotels, train companies and airlines increasingly advertise that the only way to guarantee the 'best' price is to book direct.

Participation in aggregation, therefore, is a choice that leaders in some sectors (such as hotels) may find increasingly difficult to avoid as it is the first 'port of call' for consumers shopping for particular goods or services: the Ronayne research reports that in the United Kingdom, aggregators for utilities and financial services have been particularly successful, with the UK Competition and Markets Authority estimating that 85 per cent of consumers have used such a site. As a consequence, the revenue of the four largest aggregators in the United Kingdom is growing fast: a conservative estimate of their total 2016 revenue was £800 million.[16] However, leaders may want to look carefully at strategies that can protect margin through programmes that build loyalty and encourage customers to engage directly with their brand.

In 2017, the UK Competition and Markets Authority launched an investigation into the business practices of aggregator sites in the travel industry, focused on whether or not customers were getting a good deal, particularly the manner in which hotels were presented. Commission paid by hotels is usually at least 15 per cent, but they can pay extra and be given a higher profile in the results. Press reports quoted one aggregator as telling hotel owners that: 'We'll provide an estimate of the predicted increase in page views that you can expect for the additional commission.'[17] In addition, it will also review the sales engagement strategy of asserting that many other people are looking at the same hotel or that there are few rooms left, or that a particular rate is available only for a short time. The report in *The Independent* (2017) highlighted that sometimes two claims, such as 'in high demand!' and 'last-minute price drop', can be used for the same property, even though they are mutually contradictory: if a room really is in high demand, there is unlikely to be any need to cut the price.[18] Finally, the CMA will look at the extent to which sites include all costs in the price they first show customers or whether people are later faced with unexpected fees, such as taxes or booking fees.

Aggregators make their money from buying customer interest and putting themselves between the customer and the provider of the goods or services in which that customer has expressed an interest, and taking a fee/

commission payment from providers after a transaction has occurred. In some sectors, for example travel, they have replaced a physical distribution system (travel agents), on others they have imposed themselves in the space between the customer in the market and the provider. They are not necessarily secure: a report by the London School of Economics (2016)[19] suggested that they may be challenged increasingly by the power of the gatekeepers whom they currently utilize to engage customer interest. Google and Facebook are increasingly looking to generate income from their powerful customer data holdings, and through the introduction of services such as Google Shopping they are getting closer to being able to compete with the more established aggregators. As we have demonstrated in Chapter 5, they have the funds to compete aggressively.

Intermediation

Intermediation is, in essence, meta-aggregation. It is the aggregation of all price comparison data for a particular product or service into a single point to meet a specific customer need. Fast-growing examples of this trend are in the travel industry, with offers such as Trivago, bought in 2012 by online travel agent Expedia, and Kayak, owned by their big rival, the Booking Group. More recently, TripAdvisor has also moved into this sector. This generally serves the most price-sensitive sections of the market and suffers from the same challenges as the aggregation model above. Outside areas like travel, where there is an obvious hierarchy of aggregation, intermediation can be less obvious. For example, some marketplace owners can act as an intermediator as well as an aggregator, where they offer their own plus third-party propositions where the third party is itself a marketplace. Intermediation firms earn most of their revenue from referral fees[20] with the product owner paying for the referral to the aggregator site and then also paying the aggregator its commission on top. Like the aggregators, they are at greatest risk from Google and Facebook deciding to deliver this service direct.

This is one business model that is far more difficult to adopt as a choice. Apart from the obvious challenges of a significant investment in technology, it requires a market where there is a distribution model for goods and services that already has an accepted role for third parties. The challenge for leaders whose goods and services are sucked into this model through being on aggregation sites is to ensure that their pricing policies across the various distribution channels they use don't expose them to a significant erosion in margin. In hotels, some of the larger chains have seen intermediators as an opportunity to go direct to market and avoid the aggregator channel and the consequent impact on margins of a direct commission. For example, a search for a hotel room in London's Hyde Park on Trivago[21] showed the Mercure chain offering a direct booking option at the same price as all the aggregators and being the first listed option. It could be inferred that Mercure may well have decided that paying to be the preferred deal here is a better commercial decision than giving the business to an aggregator.

Subscription

The final major business model is subscription – a proposition that generates a regular income from customers over an extended period. At its simplest, it is the model that sits behind traditional propositions such as membership clubs, gyms and so on, and a significant proportion of media businesses from traditional newspapers such as *The Wall Street Journal* and *The Times* of London through to the new generation of video-on-demand businesses such as Netflix. It has some significant advantages over traditional transactional models, not least a longer-term assured income stream and the ability over the period to develop a relationship with the customer that can build loyalty. Software publishers initially used this thinking to create their licence model where, in consumer markets after buying the initial product, updates and continuing support were subject to further fees every time there was a new version release. In business-to-business sales, annual licences were charged for mass use of software operated from a central server.

As the internet developed and business software moved through from a corporate server-base to one that can operate on a remote or 'cloud' base, this model has been the basis of the rise in 'software as a service' (SaaS) businesses. Their model is that customers pay a monthly fee to get access to this software in the same way that clubs provide services in receipt for subscriptions to a member. The main difference between SaaS businesses and software companies is that SaaS is hosted in the cloud. This removed the need for a licence to activate the software and any infrastructure to host it. Instead, the SaaS company hosts their 'membership'. This has significant attractions to business customers who do not want to invest significant sums of capital in creating an IT infrastructure and, as a result, incur the long-term costs of maintaining it and changing it to respond to changes in their markets.

These SaaS solutions often become core to their business customers. Businesses such as SalesForce, which provides sales and customer relationship software, and Zendesk, which provides software to enable customer service teams to deliver their support, become essential tools of the job. That makes the decision to change one with significant risks and helps build in longevity into the contract. This makes them highly profitable. There are many ways for a SaaS business to earn money but typically the bulk of a SaaS business is going to be its recurring membership revenue. As every customer is technically only renting software on a monthly basis, instead of outright owning it with a one-time purchase, this means every month the SaaS provider earns another bit of profit from the customer. It is this recurring income model that generates the very high company valuations seen in this sector.

SaaS models have also introduced another business opportunity – that of the solutions partner. Solutions partners are normally third-party firms who work alongside SaaS customers to ensure that they get the maximum value out of their purchase. Often these engagements are for an initial set-up period where customization, familiarization and training are an important part of ensuring customers get the best possible return for their subscription fees.

Whilst most leaders will make choices to adopt SaaS solutions in key parts of their business, few will be building these types of products. However, the principle behind this proposition is being exported into non-digital businesses and this is an area of opportunity. One of the most obvious examples is Amazon Prime, where customers are encouraged to pay a monthly fee for a bundle of services including video on demand and, in many urban areas, same-day delivery for products bought directly from them. UK grocers Tesco, Sainsbury's and Morrisons all have subscription offers targeted at enhancing their home delivery propositions. In the United States, Target announced in 2018[22] that it was launching a baby clothing subscription product on top of its other subscription offers.

This is an extension of subscription thinking that can be seen in other sectors. Called Cat & Jack, Target's box adds to the company's existing beauty box service and extends a strategy that looks to combine convenience and discovery to grow revenues and to sustain its loyal customer base. The model underpinning this initiative is one that is becoming more common: the curation of products to offer customers a combination of the 'latest' – sometimes, like the baby box, before the clothes hit the physical stores, the convenience of home delivery and the experience of 'discovery' through a carefully curated set of articles – sometimes against pre-set criteria and at other times totally entrusted to the retailer. A good example of the exercise of choice in discovery is the London Sock Company, which offers customers the option of defining the products they want to receive over the year or 'being surprised' and engaging with products they may not have chosen for themselves. US examples of this rise of the fashion box include Trunk Club from Nordstrom and Trendy Butler.

For leaders of retailers and producers in particular, subscription services offer a choice that ensures there is a steady monthly revenue coming from customers and an opportunity to build loyalty relationships. However, the more they move from a service solution (such as faster delivery) to a product one, the more challenges they are setting themselves over and above their core business. These include refreshing and renewing product offers, managing potentially non-core activity where capability may be an issue, and building sufficient scale without the cost of customer acquisition moving the subscription offer into negative margin. Subscription propositions need to offer value to the customer as well as to the business. In our experience, we believe they work best when they meet the following criteria:

- They are a logical extension of the core business that will appeal to a significant segment of the current customer population.

- They can be linked to a current value proposition, for example a loyalty programme where customers have already crossed over the barrier of providing more of their data than the minimum.

- They do not require a significant monthly outlay for the 'entry-level' service (and there are opportunities to enhance the experience for those customers who want to).

Trust and loyalty

At the heart of any customer relationship are two complementary concepts: trust (or confidence/organization trust as we defined it in Chapter 5) and loyalty. In digital we are removing the personal from what are intensely interpersonal concepts and in doing so we have to work twice as hard to establish any kind of effective relationship. In addition, there is also a considerable body of research and survey material available that suggests customers are far less ready to trust an unknown or unfamiliar proposition, and far fewer of them are willing to be loyal at any cost.

Deciding whether or not to engage with a product or service proposition is nearly three times more likely to be influenced by a known person or respected authority (yourself, someone close to you or a trusted independent expert) than it is through receiving a marketing email.[23] Research by AC Nielsen (2015)[24] reinforces this 'personal' impact. It also suggests that even Millennials would trust marketing messages in more traditional formats such as TV, over those found in social media and more broadly online. Key points from their 60-country survey give some shape to the challenges business faces as it thinks about how to engage customers:

- Of online respondents, 85 per cent said they trusted the recommendations of friends and family.

- Of those surveyed, 66 per cent indicated that they trusted consumer opinions posted online and more than half of global respondents (56 per cent) trusted emails they signed up for.

- The ratings for social media and online marketing were below 50 per cent, but despite this they can still drive customers to take action – possibly because they had seen or heard other reassurances, though this isn't clear from the survey report.

- There was very little difference in the level of trust in online between Millennials and older demographic groups – they were slightly higher but still nearly 50 per cent did not trust what was presented to them. Like other demographics, they showed a greater willingness to trust friends and family most and other marketing channels such as TV.

One final point: the lack of trust can drive customers away. In a recent (Accenture, 2017)[25] report 43 per cent of consumers switched providers because they lost trust in the company and 38 per cent said their loyalty to brands is more driven by trust (for example, personal data security) today.

Research undertaken in 2016 by Webloyalty[26] in the United Kingdom and Ireland explored many aspects of the customer experience and its impact on loyalty. Five points of note that help to frame the extent of the challenge:

- Over 50 per cent of UK consumers used more shops in the fashion, grocery and homeware retail sectors than they did in 2011.

- The single largest driver of dissatisfaction was poor customer service – over 70 per cent of consumers cited this.

- Increasing time pressure means that consumers have less time for everyday shopping, which makes convenience the key factor. Over 50 per cent said that convenience was a big driver in their shopping choices.

- Compared with the 1970s there has been an explosion of choice – for example, more than 40 years ago the average shopper would be able to pick from 49 different styles of lamp; today, the choice is heading towards 10,000.

- Many more consumers would move their regular supplier of telecoms/broadband, financial services and utilities rather than change their grocery store, although this was perceived to be nearly twice as easy.

Whilst we have used a few sources to illustrate the point, the story the data tells is repeated often in research from many other sources. This is an environment where there is a far greater array of choice than at any other time in our economic development, and with the advent of digital technology that choice is available to far more people than at any time in history. This combination of choice and availability does two things: it disrupts traditional or established relationships, particularly where the choice becomes limited or stale; and it creates an enhanced set of expectations for the customer experience. As a consequence, it becomes harder to persuade customers to engage with a particular proposition – primarily from paralysis of choice – and to retain their interest after transaction – primarily because of a failure to deliver the best possible customer experience both during and post the initial transaction.

What leaders have to consider, therefore, is how best to create a virtuous circle of customer engagement by recognizing the link between loyalty and trust, and thinking through the stages of the engagement process as a continuous process. We describe this as the Customer Continuum and it is shown in Figure 6.4.

Figure 6.4 The Customer Continuum

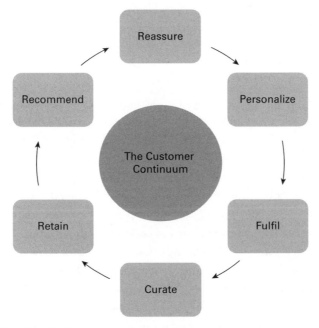

SOURCE © Good Growth Ltd

Our model has six stages:

- Reassure – make it easy to engage by removing the barriers associated with unfamiliarity. Look for third-party and social proofs, but even more importantly establish a way for your customers to become advocates to their friends and family in a way that benefits them and those to whom they recommend you. A great example is the incentive of a shared benefit (you get 10 per cent off your next order and they get the same off their first one, for example).

- Personalize – segment as quickly as you can in the sales engagement and, if it's complex, offer quick escape routes into direct human contact. If people disengage, find human, personal and engaging ways of enticing them back – don't do the equivalent of digital shouting and send endless impersonal emails; find clever, personalized ways of re-engaging.

- Fulfil – transact as quickly as possible and fulfil the commitment not just through good email communication but making sure that your delivery partner is as committed as you are to meeting expectations.

- Curate – aftercare is as important as the persuasion that goes into closing the sale. Don't ask for a review the minute the parcel arrives or the moment they have left the venue; don't bombard people with random and generalized emails – build a relationship. Think of how to do that and work with your most loyal customers to learn how best to do it. Look for reviews of both product and service – identify a preferred solution and use this actively in your engagement. Don't forget Google+, however, particularly if you are a less well-known brand in your market.

- Retain – loyalty programmes and structures continue to be an important part of a customer-centric ecosystem. Loyalty programmes are soaring. A study by Accenture in the United States (2017)[27] found that 77 per cent of consumers participate in a retail loyalty programme, 46 per cent have joined a hotel programme, and 40 per cent are part of an airline programme. In another study (Wantedness, 2017) 88 per cent of US consumers said they wanted to engage with brands that are setting new standards in meeting their expectations.[28] In addition, 56 per cent said they felt more loyal to brands that 'get me' and show a deep understanding of their priorities and preferences, and 89 per cent are loyal to brands that share their values. Why is this important? Well, after building a relationship, customer spend grows alongside trust. Eventually, loyal customers spend 67 per cent more than new ones (Link, 2017).[29]

- Recommend – once established as loyal (the definition of which changes hugely across different sectors) ask them to recommend friends and family. There are some highly effective technology platforms out there that you can use to enable this – we have partnered effectively with MentionMe as an example. This model can be increasingly seen in marketing programmes across a number of sectors in the United Kingdom. Grocers such as Aldi, with a mutual 10 per cent discount offer, and banks such as Nationwide, with their offer of a £100 deposit in both accounts, are good examples.

Leadership actions

Understanding the drivers of e-commerce and the business model choices that sit behind them is an important requirement for business leaders in all functions. The structure of the market has changed, but not significantly. Search (and mainly search through Google) remains the dominant driver for the vast majority of businesses. As marketing investment shifts into social media so more customers arrive from this source. In this situation, where change will continue, understanding the impact of marketing spend, in particular the return on investment, becomes increasingly important. But it remains stubbornly challenging owing to the way providers handle data, agencies report their activity and internal teams prioritize KPIs. This means that leaders need to be assertive and define in what way and how they want performance to be reported. More than this, they need to invest in thinking far more strategically about resource allocation in marketing to ensure that they are maximizing the impact of their total investment.

What is also clear is that there are business model choices that can be made – active and reactive; and these are significant decisions that have the potential to alter performance radically. Marketplace is a potentially attractive business model if it is structured and well-thought-through; aggregation and intermediation can be effective distribution channels but require careful decisions on pricing; subscription is a fast-growing trend that offers plenty of opportunities, but again high-quality execution plans and consideration of the operational implications are required to ensure that this creates value, rather than destroys it. Behind all these models lies the challenge of establishing trust and building loyalty.

This chapter has dealt with the business model choices that sit behind e-commerce and how these can be informed by a ruthless focus on return on investment in marketing, and a carefully structured approach to the executional issues behind the chosen business model. There are seven things that leaders might want to consider as they assess how effective their business model choices are:

- Marketing
  - Understand where your traffic is coming from and how it performs – ask for a comparative ROAS analysis by channel where you are paying to attract customers; ask whether the investment is for consideration or conversion and how effectiveness is currently measured.
  - Look at how attribution is handled in your current reporting – if it isn't a 'position-based' approach ask for the logic and ask for a position-based alternative assessment to see if this might change decisions about resource allocation.
  - If your marketing spend is significant then consider the relevance of a RAMM® approach where you can model, refine assumptions through testing and create a platform for better informed choices to drive enhanced returns.

- Business model
  - If you are operating one or more of these models then take stock of your commercial model and operational execution. If you are operating a marketplace use the marketplace 'five pillars' to sense check.
  - If your team is evaluating any of these options make sure they are looking at the operational as well as commercial challenges. In all cases, sales on their own add little or no value unless they come with a positive margin that can run through to the bottom line.

- Customer engagement
  - Run through the Customer Continuum and ask for each stage: are we doing this? If yes, how are we measuring performance in each? If not, give your operation a score out of 10, where 10 is outstanding and 1 is poor. If you are not doing something at each stage, why not?
  - Having established the baseline, set an aspiration and ask the team for a plan to get there – they may find the sections on trust marketing and loyalty marketing in the next chapter useful in thinking through what to do and how to drive this.

References

1 Bones, C and Hammersley, J (2015) *Leading Digital Strategy*, Kogan Page, London

2 https://www.business.com/articles/mobile-apps-vs-mobile-web-do-you-have-to-choose/ [accessed 19 March 2018]

3 https://www.statista.com/statistics/271258/facebooks-advertising-revenue-worldwide/ [accessed 19 March 2018]

4 https://performancein.com/news/2017/04/12/uk-online-performance-marketing-spend-hits-1578-billion-2016/ [accessed 19 March 2018]

5 https://www.accenture.com/us-en/insight-customer-loyalty-gcpr [accessed 30 March 2018]

6 https://marketingsherpa.com/freestuff/customer-first-study [accessed 31 March 2018]

7 https://www.businesswire.com/news/home/20170815005733/en/Prices-Raise-Customer-Loyalty [accessed 31 March 2018]

8 https://www.hybris.com/en/gmc55-the-global-2017-sap-hybris-consumer-insights-report [accessed 31 March 2018]

9 https://www.capgemini.com/resources/the-disconnected-customer-what-digital-customer-experience-leaders-teach-us-about [accessed 31 March 2018]

10 https://turo.com/ [accessed 2 April 2018]

11 https://www.freelancer.com/ [accessed 2 April 2018]

12 https://www.angieslist.com/ [accessed 2 April 2018]

13 https://warwick.ac.uk/fac/soc/economics/research/workingpapers/2015/twerp_1056b_ronayne.pdf [accessed 5 April 2018]

14 https://www.statista.com/statistics/238852/online-travel-bookings-worldwide/ [accessed 3 April 2018]

15 https://warwick.ac.uk/fac/soc/economics/research/workingpapers/2015/twerp_1056b_ronayne.pdf [accessed 5 April 2018]

16 https://warwick.ac.uk/fac/soc/economics/research/workingpapers/2015/twerp_1056b_ronayne.pdf [accessed 5 April 2018]

17 https://www.independent.co.uk/travel/news-and-advice/hotel-booking-websites-investigation-selling-practices-bookingcom-expedia-agoda-hotelscom-trivago-a8022551.html [accessed 5 April 2018]

18 https://www.independent.co.uk/travel/news-and-advice/hotel-booking-websites-investigation-selling-practices-bookingcom-expedia-agoda-hotelscom-trivago-a8022551.html [accessed 5 April 2018]

19 http://www.lse.ac.uk/businessAndConsultancy/LSEConsulting/pdf/Amadeus-The-Future-of-Travel-Distribution.pdf [accessed 5 April 2018]

20 https://www.quora.com/How-does-trivago-make-money [accessed 5 April 2018]

21 On 5 April 2018

22 https://www.retaildive.com/news/target-debuts-cat-jack-baby-box-subscription-service/517677/ [accessed 5 April 2018]

23 https://webloyaltycorporatecontent.s3.amazonaws.com/the-unfaithful-consumer-report-webloyalty_1457431881.pdf [accessed 5 April 2018]

24 http://www.nielsen.com/eu/en/press-room/2015/recommendations-from-friends-remain-most-credible-form-of-advertising.html [accessed 5 April 2018]

25 https://www.accenture.com/t20170216T035010Z__w__/us-en/_acnmedia/PDF-43/Accenture-Strategy-GCPR-Customer-Loyalty.pdf#zoom=50 [accessed 6 April 2018]

26 https://webloyaltycorporatecontent.s3.amazonaws.com/the-unfaithful-consumer-report-webloyalty_1457431881.pdf [accessed 5 April 2018]

27 https://www.accenture.com/t20170216T035010Z__w__/us-en/_acnmedia/PDF-43/Accenture-Strategy-GCPR-Customer-Loyalty.pdf#zoom=50 [accessed 6 April 2018]

28 https://www.wantedness.com/ [accessed 6 April 2018]

29 https://www.slideshare.net/margaretlink/the-ultimate-guide-to-customer-loyalty-in-2017?qid=e7e8506b-32a3-4865-8ce1-ff4664e2f79d&v=&b=&from_search=2 [accessed 6 April 2018]

The e-commerce 07 system

Executive summary

Understanding your business model and how it translates to digital is essential, but it is the effectiveness of the underlying e-commerce execution that will ultimately define the degree of commercial success or failure. In our experience, poorly planned and executed activity will at best limit potential commercial performance and at worst cripple the enterprise. On the flip side, getting it right will improve efficiency, reduce costs, increase customer satisfaction and loyalty and generate improved returns. This chapter introduces the proposition that e-commerce is an integrated system, not a linear process. This thinking supports leaders to think strategically about the online journey and shows how this can be used to map, evaluate and drive performance. It describes each of the key stages of the entire customer life cycle, from locating and acquiring customers, through to their engagement and retention. It builds on the Customer Continuum introduced in the previous chapter and shows how loyalty can increase the rate of new customer acquisition. Finally, it exposes why failing to think about the customer as a whole can prohibit performance gains that can only be achieved by addressing the wants and needs of the customer in a more holistic way.

The whole is greater than the sum of its parts

Standard e-commerce thinking talks about a customer journey and how to drive customers through each stage. This has led to an increasing fragmentation of digital disciplines and, as a result, the retention of a bevy of unrelated agencies by many e-commerce teams to deal with each stage. We prefer to focus on customer experience, regardless of where they are in any digital journey and to see that experience as an integrated system. Thinking of it in this way can help to explain why some digital experiences are positive and others negative – they have managed to establish a virtuous circle or conversely, have found themselves in a vicious one. As in any system, establishing a virtuous circle drives positive outcomes and enables growth; a vicious circle delivers a downward spiral fuelled at every stage by adverse effects.

By understanding the activities and key performance levers of each stage and how they influence the next, business leaders can drive the performance of the entire customer experience and make informed choices regarding the execution of their digital strategy. By thinking of their digital engagement as a system, we can create a framework that can be used to reveal how each key stage is contributing towards overall commercial performance and, ultimately, lifetime customer value (LCV). This particular metric is key to establishing and sustaining a virtuous circle (and it never ceases to amaze us how few businesses have a grasp on this). Put simply:

> **Lifetime customer value (LCV) = average order value (£) / (1 – repeat purchase rate) – cost to acquire**

For example, in a scenario in which average order value is £100 and there is a 20 per cent chance of a user who purchases coming back to purchase again, with a £10 cost to acquire the user in the first place, the lifetime customer value is £115:

> **LCV = {£100 / (1–0.2)} – £10**

Whilst other approaches to calculating LCV may be, arguably, more accurate (for example, in accounting for customer retention rate and a discount rate) in our experience, many retailers in particular struggle to quantify such values and so cannot report customer lifetime value using these methods. The methodology detailed here is straightforward and can be reported using data sourced from a web analytics platform such as Google Analytics.

The aim in digital business is to maximize lifetime customer value in relation to the costs of customer acquisition. By focusing on this, as opposed to more myopic metrics such as site conversion rate (very typical) and total traffic volumes (even more typical), businesses are able to identify their most profitable customer segments, optimize the economics of customer acquisition strategies and leverage the loyalty of current customers to help find new ones. What concerns us is that as digital becomes increasingly ubiquitous and organizations invest more and more into technology, how few of them think about their e-commerce operation and customer experience as an integrated system (let alone how to measure, evaluate and improve it). This can lead to a number of issues and ultimately suboptimal commercial performance:

- **Quantity over quality:** Traffic strategy and activity that focuses on quantity at the expense of quality, flooding the website with poor-quality traffic that costs the business time and money, drives down revenue per user, decreases quality scores and can skew optimization activity towards a single and less profitable customer segment.

- **Relevance:** Acquiring new customers through paid advertising, only to channel them onto a web page that is irrelevant to their intentions or needs, leading to abandonment and subsequent knock-on impact on commercial metrics.

- **One size fits all:** Optimizing websites for the masses (in itself not a bad thing) but then failing to recognize key customer segments and responding to their specific or unique needs. For example, in our experience it is often the loyal and returning customer who is overlooked.

- **Beyond the buy button:** Optimizing right up to the 'buy button' or point of engagement, but then a failure to consider any form of optimization or improvement of customer engagement following this.

- **Leveraging loyalty:** Missing the opportunity of using existing and loyal customers to become brand advocates and use trust marketing to build the customer base.

Not working to an effective operating model is the single biggest barrier to digital performance. Regular surveys highlight a significant gap between aspirations and outcomes for digital investments. As we referenced at the beginning of the book, the most regularly quoted reasons for failure are those associated with the organization. We believe this comes from failing to see the integrated nature of the digital system and therefore adopting classical and increasingly irrelevant organizational models to operate the chosen model. A classic choice is the separation of online merchandising, sales and marketing. This automatically fragments the organization and militates against a 'whole system' view. Our own experience of helping organizations overcome these issues leads us to conclude that the primary obstacles can be broadly grouped into three themes:

- **Technology:** This relates to fragmented tools and data silos that capture and report on customer activity throughout the e-commerce ecosystem. Because there is a tendency for organizations to think about a journey as opposed to a system, the way they disaggregate technology and reporting conspires to make it difficult to get visibility of the full customer experience and understand customer behaviours and needs.

- **People and process:** This issue extends into people and process, where it is also typical to find a separate team and/or agency commissioned to drive the performance of a single stage of a journey. The focus of contracts, performance systems and self-interest in maximizing one element often creates an end result that delivers a limited ability and even less motivation to take accountability for the full experience.

- **Leadership and culture:** This is often exacerbated through leaders who find themselves at a disadvantage as each fragment is reported differently using different metrics. As an emerging discipline where there is less detailed understanding in the leadership of traditional organizations, digital is at risk of developing an 'expert-led' culture where the detail of business and operating models is abdicated to experts rather than delegated and critically reviewed, as would be the case in any other area.

E-commerce as an integrated system

The e-commerce system

Our framework (Figure 7.1) describes a continuous loop of activity with four distinct stages, each with its own set of activities, KPIs and supporting processes. The output of each stage feeds the next and, if well planned and managed as an integrated whole, will enable the development of a system operating in a virtuous circle that drives growth through the establishment of increasing lifetime customer value.

At the heart of the system is a customer-centric organization and culture and we discuss this in depth in Chapter 8, as it is the single biggest critical enabler of a system that works. Customer experience is delivered through four connected stages:

- **Locate** – this is the process of identifying and defining the right customer for the product or service on offer. It represents the initial touch point for potential new customers and marks the first step in an ongoing process

Figure 7.1   The e-commerce system

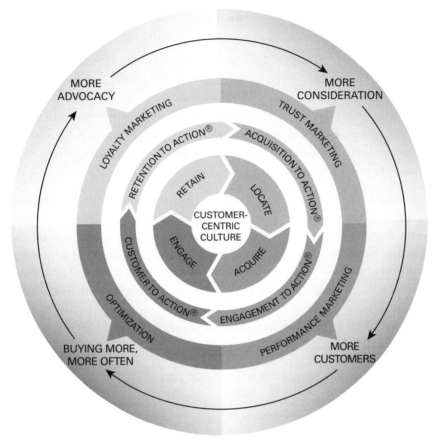

of building data-led insight into the customer. Questions addressed at this stage include: Who is the target customer, where are they, what are their needs and how can we build their trust?

- **Acquire** – this is concerned with serving the most effective content for each customer segment such that it generates a relevant visit. It is the process of defining the activity and making the resource allocation choices behind this. This is achieved through a combination of owned, earned and paid media activity.

- **Engage** – this is focused on ensuring that customers experience a website that addresses their needs such that what results is a positive engagement with the proposition in the desired manner. At the heart of this is the process of establishing the barriers to transaction through the developing of customer insight. Once the process identifies possible reasons, it drives a continuous programme of testing alternative executions to identify the best approach to reducing or removing the barriers.

- **Retain** – the development of long-term relationships with target customers that encourage loyalty, brand advocacy and repeat transactions. This is driven by a process that builds data and insight that enables customers to be engaged through understanding their needs and preferences. Once relationships are cemented, the process looks to encourage recommendation and referral such that it becomes easier for the business to locate and acquire new customers.

For each of these stages we have developed processes that connect to support the delivery of the whole system and these are described in some detail later on in the chapter. At this stage however, for it to be a whole system, the activities in each have to connect in a way that is integrated and adds value to the whole customer experience.

The system connections that transform customer experience

The successful delivery of each stage is only part of the picture. Whilst each represents a key element of the online experience, focus must also be paid to the interfaces between them. This is what turns a 'customer journey' paradigm into a customer experience system one. The most significant of these interfaces are:

Matching consideration to conversion

Information relating to the location, drivers and behaviours of target customer groups established in the first stage are essential inputs into any effective acquisition strategy: the focus of the second. When this connection is compromised, businesses execute acquisition strategies that are inadequately targeted and use suboptimal channels for reaching and engaging with their target customer set. Getting this interface right ensures that you match target customer wants and needs with your proposition through the appropriate channel and campaign strategy.

CASE STUDY   TIME Inc.

By understanding the customer demographic for UKCE, a major UK cycling events company and part of TIME Inc., we were able to identify that their proposition had particular appeal to groups of friends who share an interest in cycling. Focusing on the group rather than the individual informed a number of key acquisition choices, including the decision to branch out beyond AdWords and introduce paid activity in social media.

In this particular example, social media played a significant role in advertising events and encouraging people to share content with their friends and peers, increasing year-on-year ticket sales by around 46 per cent during peak trading whilst simultaneously increasing the return on advertising spend. By introducing new channels to build awareness and audiences for the product in markets where people want to share events, we were successful in driving significant improvement gains with reduced advertising costs.

Relevancy

Having acquired initial interest, there are many reasons why that interest fails to convert into a transaction and being able to operate effectively across the interface between acquire and engage can transform performance. In this case there are two key considerations: relevancy and remarketing – How to make the first experience of the website as relevant to the acquired customer as possible? If this fails, how can the business re-engage with customers after they have left a website without converting?

Landing pages that are tightly aligned with a user's search query convert better than landing pages that aren't. The logic being that a tailored landing page is more likely to provide the content or information a customer is looking for. Conversely, direct users to an irrelevant page such as a broader category page, or even worse a home page, and they are likely to simply leave to search again and as a result check out the competition. Poor relevancy will also cause Google (who want to provide its users with the best search results possible) to banish your ads to lower positions – unless you pay through the nose. This is because, in simple terms, Google awards the top spot in its paid results to the website with a) the highest bid, and b) the most relevant landing page. This has an important implication for any e-commerce system: the website that is best at monetizing clicks (converting to a lead or a sale) will float to the top of the ad rankings and stay there until someone can push it off with a higher bid. This is because relevant search results keep searchers coming back to Google, so it automatically elevates web pages with better engagement and conversion metrics to appear higher in the results.

We introduced the landing page ratio metric earlier and we developed it for the reason that there is no point sending customers who respond to lawnmower adverts to a page that doesn't feature lawnmowers. If you have a high ratio then your e-commerce team is working hard to align the messaging on your web page with the interest users expressed when they clicked your ad. If it's much less than 80 per cent you still have a lot of untapped revenue that can be liberated by creating more targeted experiences for users. By using conversation rate optimization practices outlined later in this chapter, the performance of landing pages can be further optimized by capturing customer insight data and then using this systematically to test changes to the execution of the page in a quest to find an optimum solution that drives the greatest volume of conversions.

We have flagged the issues with personalization and it often comes up as a potential solution to this issue. Making a landing page or website experience relevant and targeted for a segment of customers is good; making it bespoke to a particular individual sounds even better. The problem is that you can't personalize something if you don't really know anything about that person. Personalization needs permission, and if you don't know that person then you are very unlikely to get this.

In the case of an existing customer or registered user, then you may have a better chance of success as important information relating to a customer's preferences and purchase history can provide helpful clues, but for the rest it's at best ignored or at worst will drive your customers away because it's not relevant to them. When was the last time you visited a website and spontaneously decided to splash out and buy something from the random array of products presented to you under the 'you may also like' heading? Probably not that often.

Even if customers visit, they may not transact. The response in e-commerce terms is remarketing. This is a form of online advertising that enables businesses to reconnect with visitors to their website who may not have made an immediate purchase or enquiry by promoting their product or service on other sites on which the visitor lands. It takes the logic of the landing page and uses the activities of visitors to the website to create and position a relevant and targeted ad as they browse elsewhere around the internet. Now for the health warning: no amount of remarketing (and the associated spend) is going to entice a visitor back to a website if a) the wrong customer was targeted to the website in the first instance, and b) the website landing page materially failed to address the target customer's needs.

This is a great example of the value of thinking about e-commerce as a whole system, rather than a series of disaggregated activities. Good remarketing activity should be off the back of a robust acquisition strategy and optimized website, and segmented down to a suitable narrow spectrum and continuously tested so that a high ad relevancy and low cost per click can be achieved. The ability to segment and become super-targeted with remarketing campaigns relies upon a robust source of customer insight data. Spread your bets too wide or fail to test, and you will pay the price with lower ad relevancy and corresponding higher cost per click for your efforts.

Beyond the buy button

A good website encourages as many visitors as possible to transact. By this we mean buy or become a lead. But what happens after the transaction? 'Whole system' thinking encourages leaders to think about engagement beyond the buy button. The focus here is on building a longer-term trusted relationship wherever possible. The value of this is often twofold: it is usually easier to sell to an existing customer rather than a new one, and you can also capitalize on your trusted relationships with the existing customer base to help find new customers to join the club. Simple but effective techniques include email capture and encouraging some form of account creation or site registration. This provides a route to communicate directly with your existing customers through email marketing and other direct channels. But here is the rub: how often have you been presented with clear and compelling benefits of signing up or registering with a website? Our guess is rarely. Much as in all of the proceeding stages, businesses need to work hard to communicate the relevancy and benefits of a proposition, including why a customer should sign up or create an account.

The same rules apply for how existing customers are engaged with email marketing. Similar techniques used to build insight for purposes of improving website performance can be adapted to build deep and meaningful insight into how customers do and don't engage with your email marketing content. Different email executions and offers can then be tested and measured against open rates, click through rates and ultimately conversion rate to sale.

The majority of online retailers, within both traditional e-commerce and media, are highly active with regard to capturing email registration, either through the use of registration pop-ups and paywalls for media subscription or mandatory registration during transaction for e-commerce. However, in our experience this level of enthusiasm rarely percolates to the emails themselves. Whilst email marketing is often viewed as a 'best practice' activity, it is less thought of as a strategic avenue to building a relationship with the recipient and ultimately driving revenue growth. Our client benchmark database reports email activity as generally performing better than many other channels. As a result, it gets less attention and internal practice typically aligns to common 'best practice' methodologies regardless of industry. This generally involves weekly or monthly emails detailing a new offer or sale period. In our experience, many of these do not even link the user to the correct product or landing page. The other use of emails is in basket abandonment, where a follow-up email is sent to a customer who has left a product unpurchased at the checkout stage. These may generate immediate revenue but rarely encourage repeat purchasing. Our most common observation to clients is that high frequency, generic, marketing emails, which simply pester recipients asking them to buy every day but never providing a reason to, may generate some sales but are more than likely to be driving many more recipients away.

CASE STUDY   *The Economist*

As with broader conversion rate optimization, email optimization must begin with the customer. This process identifies the key barriers to email effectiveness through creation of an effective customer insight platform, which encapsulates the entire email channel, not only the effectiveness of the email campaigns themselves, but also the on-site execution of email landing pages and the upstream execution for capturing email registration itself. In our experience, the major barriers to email effectiveness are the lack of effective user engagement, typified by a sales engagement that confuses what should be a relatively simple proposition or the lack of a simple provision for users to manage their relationship: either having to sign up for every email at once, or unsubscribe from all of them. These barriers to effectiveness are often compounded by the lack of an overall email strategy where, as a result, email campaigns are viewed in isolation rather than as a cohesive whole and there is minimal cross selling between email campaigns (for example, weekly updates, new product offers, recommendations and so on).

By working with the client team at *The Economist* we were able to use a combination of customer surveys, email-click maps and analytics to understand customer engagement with email marketing campaigns. This insight was, in turn, used to develop and test both new eNewsletter propositions (for example, daily versus weekly) and executions (with images and without) to measure the impact on open rates, click through and ongoing site engagement. Using this combination of insight to drive experimentation enabled the team to identify the most appropriate frequency and execution of newsletter for unique customer segments in order to drive engagement with the website.

Closing the loop

This final interface brings us all the way back around to the beginning – from retain back to locate. This is achieved by encouraging loyal and engaged customers to become brand ambassadors through advocacy, reviews and referrals to help locate and acquire new customers. Normally, in digital organizations there is very little connectivity between those responsible for the acquisition of new customers and those responsible for what might be called 'customer relationship marketing'. Yet current customers could be a significant channel of communication through to new ones. To do this well needs data points from every stage of the system to create as full a picture as possible of current customers, the experience they have been through and the value that they give back to the business.

This picture provides insight into the motivations of the current customer base and the needs that have been satisfied as they move from looking for products or services, though engaging with your proposition, to closing on a transaction and consuming the outcome. Understanding this provides several opportunities to engage the current customer base in helping you extend it:

- reviews and endorsements, not just on product/service but also on the whole experience;
- loyalty programs aimed at more than just buying more referral programmes that extend the reach of your marketing into current customer friends and family;
- advocate programmes (particularly effective in B2B) that not just encourage but incentivize selling into new customers by current and past ones.

This is the key interface that distinguishes 'whole system' thinking from the more mainstream model of activities along a linear customer journey. It closes the loop and in so doing sets the seal on a virtuous circle that, when it works well across all four interfaces, can drive superior growth.

Dissecting the system – the growth drivers

In Chapter 6 we covered how personal relationships play an increasingly large part in selling where human interaction is lacking. Put this into an environment where trust in brands is in decline and consumers are increasingly cynical of advertising, and businesses must work harder than ever before to build sufficient confidence in their proposition so that customers will engage with their brand. You can have the best product or service in the market but if prospects do not trust your brand they will not buy from you. *Marketing Week* (2017) [1] reported research that 70 per cent of consumers now do not trust advertising and nearly half of them distrust brands.

Trust marketing

Trust marketing is the establishment of a powerful and authentic reputation for delivering:

- on your proposition promise – all the time and every time;
- for all your customers – old and new;
- and for wider stakeholders in the community.

Smart organizations look to maximize confidence in the market through investing in activities that reinforce their status as a 'trusted' player. The activities they often adopt to achieve this include:

- Peer referral – providing a service or experience to customers worthy of referral to others. This is increasingly powerful in a digital landscape where the general backdrop is one of increasing distrust and suspicion.
- Differentiation – whilst it is easy to replicate execution it is far harder to replicate motivation and culture. Being clear about what makes you different (and being willing to lose some sales as a result in order to gain many more) and standing out in a noisy marketplace can help differentiate from the 'me too' competitor set.
- Authenticity – a trustworthy brand needs to be authentic at all times. Authentic brands are those that express themselves consistently across the entire customer journey and in so doing improve brand reputation and increase customer loyalty as a result.

However, building market confidence is more than just a growth opportunity; it is also a critical activity for future proofing a business. Brands that fail to build a sense of trust in the market will miss out, not just on sales but also on the insight that comes from a willingness to share data (increasingly important in a post GDPR Europe) and the opportunities to grow through a better understanding. For example, personalization requires permission, but customers are increasingly selective over with whom they will share data. Brands who achieve this are already at a distinct advantage over those who don't.

We have developed a process for establishing an effective trust marketing strategy. We call it Acquisition to Action® and it is shown in Figure 7.2.

The process start point is to address the need for consistency of values between the external (brand) experience, the internal (organization) one and the role they play in strategy. Having established alignment it moves decision-taking through the proposition and performance focus before driving choices in both loyalty and advocacy. The stages are:

- **Brand values** – we all hope to have a clear set of brand values, underpinned by an aligned strategy and organizational culture. The ability to deliver on intent breaks down the moment that any of these fundamentals become misaligned. Brand values that are contradicted by the goals

Figure 7.2   Acquisition to Action®

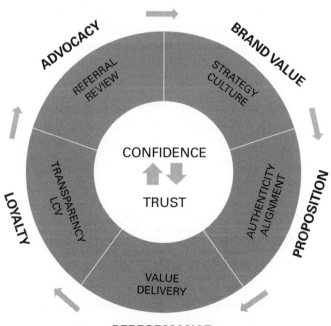

or culture of an organization are more likely to have an inverse impact on customer confidence. The outcome of this stage is a clear brand and organization values map that identifies areas of potential misalignment and gaps, and provides a lens through which business and marketing strategies can be reviewed to ensure alignment.

- **Proposition** – authentic propositions are those that meet the marketing in every way possible throughout every aspect of the customer experience. Just meeting your promises is no longer enough. In simple terms, each and every touch point should seek to clarify and reinforce what it is you are selling and, through this consistency, customers begin to understand and build confidence in what the brand represents. The outcome here should be a clear understanding of the alignment between strategy, brand and product/service and the identification of any issues that need to be resolved.

- **Performance** – measuring the value of confidence in the market in a brand and associated products or services is an important decision. This process moves businesses away from consumer brand trust barometers into measures that are much more focused on their customers and those who directly interact with their proposition.

- **Loyalty** – getting all of this right builds loyalty in the existing customer base to help drive lifetime customer value and brand advocacy. Transparent reviews and referrals from loyal and engaged customers can be used to drive new customer acquisition, reinforce brand values in the market, and open up a channel of two-way communication that can be used to further improve, refine and scope the proposition for the future.

- **Advocacy** – this is the acme of market confidence: a brand where the normal outcome of the customer experience is the creation of active proponents who sell the proposition to friends and family. It is a more active and engaged status than the writing of a review; it is the creation of advocates and champions who are energized and confident to get out there and promote the brand.

None of what is covered above is particularly revolutionary on its own; putting it together into an integrated process and looking for real-time customer measures that can be tracked as a proxy for 'trust' is. We have built this process as many brands are failing to maximize their potential in their market due to a siloed and 'channel first' approach to marketing. Trust often falls foul of the need to drive more immediate commercial gains, and the metrics surrounding a channel-first marketing approach encourage a set of activities and behaviours that can actually put this at risk.

Businesses can start the process of building an integrated approach through an audit that defines a strategy and implements changes that are measured, reported and then further optimized. The audit stage encompasses a range of lenses. It looks for the alignment and consistency of values to proposition an activity. Workshops with key stakeholders are a great starting point to build clarity and challenge assumption regarding brand and product positioning. These can be used to explore and map out what the brand aspiration and values are, and what the business thinks of customer perceptions. To get a wider view this is then triangulated with search, social media and online reviews health checks.

The outcome of the process is the optimization of four key touch points that influence customer trust, namely search, social media, reviews and referral (Figure 7.3).

The best social connections are those that are based on trust and purpose, not just promotion (which is cheap loyalty). These customers are more likely to understand why the brand they are engaging with exists and what it stands for.

Connections on this basis drive relevant audience engagement to the website. In terms of search engagement, these connections are also based on relevant queries leading to tightly aligned landing pages and web estate. Get this right and companies are not only rewarded with quality traffic, but site ranking is rewarded from trust signals, further boosting search rankings. Pulling these activities together into a single process can drive not just growth on its own but also act in conjunction with the other parts of the system to create a significant strategic advantage.

Performance marketing

Increasingly, customer attention is acquired through payment in search, display and remarketing. Most organizations look to maximize their returns on this investment by focusing on efficiency and effectiveness. The most successful understand the importance of judgement in this and are moving away from dubious automated programmatic solutions to a model where they can protect their brand as well as build their business. There are many reasons for the shift away from blanket investments in large automated programmes, not least being the dissatisfaction with the veracity of outcomes reported, as we highlighted in Chapter 2. In our experience, however, this is one of the areas most likely to drift into a vicious circle most quickly without a rigorous focus on performance optimization.

Figure 7.3 Trust marketing

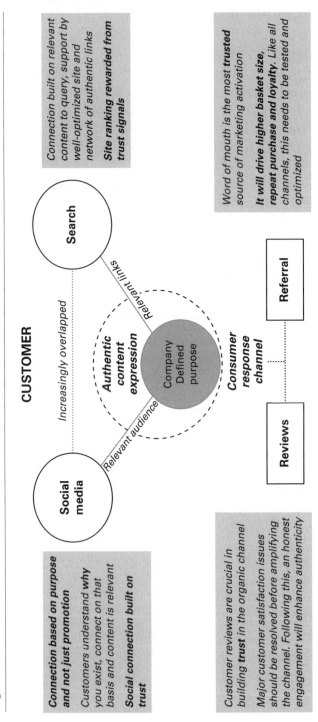

Our approach has been to develop a process called Engagement to Action.® This drives a performance focus across every element of paid digital marketing and is driven through the application of continuous test and learn. The process is shown in Figure 7.4.

We have chosen to call this part of the system 'performance marketing' as one of the distinguishing features of online marketing activity is that there are very clear measures in place to track performance, usually based on a sale, lead, click or presentation to a customer in the market – measured as an impression.

It should all be about performance, yet many agencies still stubbornly persist in holding onto traditional measures of impact and effectiveness from the days when measurability was not focused on outcomes, but rather inputs. Impressions and likes are not outcomes; shares do not sell anything by themselves. This element of the system is all about getting the best possible 'bang' for your 'buck' and is firmly focused on investment that drives conversion (as opposed to trust marketing, which is focused on consideration).

The process works on a similar set of principles to Customer to Action®:

Commercial objectives

Identifying commercial objectives within the performance marketing element of a digital strategy ensures that everyone involved in delivering against these metrics has a shared awareness of how their impact will be measured. This applies for external agencies as much as internal team members. With digital marketing, you can see a snapshot of your ROI at any given instant, so relevant metrics for measuring performance and setting KPIs include: click through rate (CTR), cost per acquisition (CPA), conversion rate and cost per click (CPC), which will help report on cost per lead or per sign-up, cost per sale and most importantly, return on advertising spend (ROAS – see Chapter 6). Once a clear objective has been defined and agreed, a framework for ongoing reporting against the most relevant performance indicators can be created. Only when this is in place can a test and learn approach to marketing spend be effectively followed.

Insight generation

An important but often overlooked element of defining the approach for accruing traffic and ultimately sales is ensuring that there is enough insight

Figure 7.4 Engagement to Action®

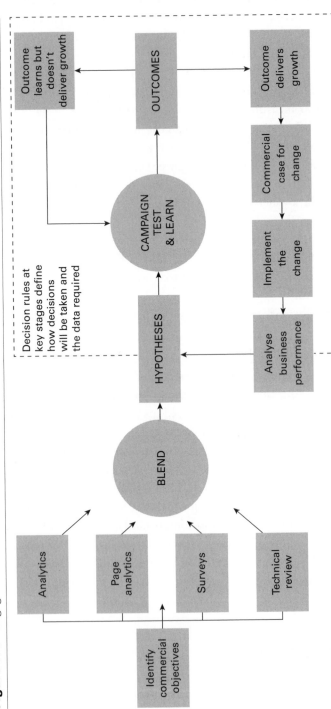

Figure 7.5 The activity flow in Engagement to Action®

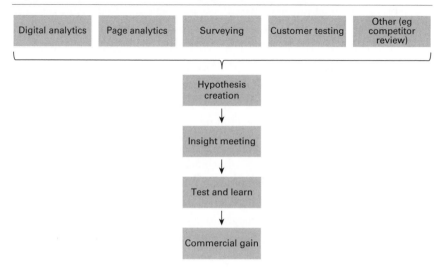

to really understand customers and how to locate, convert and retain them. As shown in Figure 7.5, insight should mix both qualitative and quantitative data sources to build a detailed understanding of your existing and prospective customers and what information they want and need in order to transact.

A detailed customer analysis for informing digital marketing activity should, in its simplest form, cover the following:

- **Analytics** – using tools such as Google Analytics we can map the customer journey and build funnels for core site behaviours, including of course the journey to transact, and use this to build up a comprehensive understanding of the role that each channel plays in accruing and converting users. This analysis will help attribute value to each type of activity and provide a basis for early test and learn planning. The other role of analytics in this phase of activity is to look at the performance of key pages in accruing traffic organically, and how this traffic is mapped to the customer buying journey, to understand its intent. Once we have a view on the performance of the channels at driving activity at each stage in the customer life cycle and measure the intent behind each type, we can more accurately assign value to each source and, where appropriate at a campaign level, more effectively manage marketing spend. We can also understand what content may be missing from the site in order to attract and convert customers more effectively in the future.

- **Page analytics** – once we understand the core on-site behaviours from analysing customer journeys, we can use page analytics to measure on-page engagement. Using tools to review heat maps, combined with measured events through Google Tag Manager, will help to understand not just where customers are navigating, but what they are engaging with. This will help us to understand the core behaviours that trigger an on-site conversion and, alongside measurements such as bounce rate and exit rate, inform decisions on the best pages to optimize as landing pages for paid traffic activity.

- **Surveys** – surveying customers both on-site and through a targeted email campaign with open questions that encourage a free-form response is one of the best ways of understanding where your customers are spending their time online and where they would like to engage with you. The output will be a deeper insight into the opportunity of performance marketing to capture this audience and engage with them outside of your own website, and inform future test and learn activity.

- **Technical review** – conducting a technical audit on your website will highlight opportunities for organic search improvements alongside the content and page performance review mentioned above. Techniques to review the site's accessibility and crawlability using tools such as Moz can help highlight priority tasks for development teams, alongside reviews of overall site performance across device types.

- **Competitor analysis** – when initiating a performance marketing strategy, one of the most important factors to consider is the competitive landscape in which you are operating. This is not an exercise in emulating someone else's approach or targeting, but supporting smart decision-making around best use of available budget by generating learnings that may help inform when, where and how to attract customers. Google intentionally provides such insight in its AdWords platform to help measure your competitiveness on certain terms; however, this should be used alongside performance data from your own campaign metrics to evaluate when bid increases should be made. Likewise, measuring organic search performance rankings against the competition may help in identifying and prioritizing tasks; however, a well-performing website and a customer-first approach to content creation should negate the requirement for a copycat approach to improving performance.

Hypothesis creation

An important distinction in effective leaders who ensure they are continually testing and learning when managing marketing spend is their ability to create and test hypotheses and use the learnings to inform future decision-making, and not theorize the solutions. In an environment fluctuated with new technology and automated processes, it is easy for budget holders to be tempted into a solution-driven mindset; however, that solution should be born from a combination of insight-led testing to quantify the expected impact, ensuring that each hypothesis is accurately tested using appropriate methodologies and metrics. This involves a creative approach to budget allocation, and the ability to manage this effectively will define the quality of the future marketer. This activity underpins optimization and loyalty marketing as well as performance marketing.

Campaign test and learn

Although frequently labelled 'test and learn' as an approach to optimizing marketing activity, few organizations or agencies have a defined approach for effectively monitoring and measuring ad spend or resource costs against a defined objective. A lack of transparency around the management of paid spend, coupled with the difficulties in measuring and attributing value to organic channels, has resulted in inefficient and overcomplicated processes. The real value, however, comes from ensuring that all activity has measurable, documented learning, so that we are testing to learn and not testing to win. With this in mind, budget holders should of course allocate budgets according to the best-performing channels and campaigns, but should not see wastage in small amounts of budget allocated to testing potential new channels or executions provided that such learnings are acted upon. The process of test and learn in driving marketing performance is cyclical, so each test should provide insight that informs the next within a given strategy so that the hypothesis can be fully tested.

Documenting each hypothesis and the associated test results is a learned skill and one that will play an increasingly important role in providing transparency in terms of effort versus output across customer accrual activity. This relates to the importance of creating a defined commercial objective and the ability to accurately measure all activity against it, as well as provide an overall ROAS metric to quantify the impact of paid media management. Channels or activity that can't be effectively measured should be de-prioritized, ensuring an overall focus on the defined commercial objective.

Conversion rate optimization

Conventional wisdom is that the greater the volume of traffic to a website, the greater the potential revenue opportunity. This only holds true if you are successfully converting clicks to conversions. Where a business is buying traffic volume or finds itself in a bidding war against the competition, then its ability to systematically and consistently convert new and existing customers becomes a critical moderator for the return on advertising spend.

As a result, driving performance of digital real estate sits at the heart of an effective e-commerce execution. Conversion rate optimization (CRO) is the process of maximizing returns on landing pages, the sales funnel and the transaction stages. We covered this in detail in our previous book,[2] but for the record here the process we have developed to drive maximum impact is Customer to Action®. It is shown in Figure 7.6. This book, therefore, will not go into the detail of the process, but will highlight the critical elements that differentiate a business with a virtuous circle from that stuck in a vicious one.

Insight generation

Insight generation builds an evidence-based understanding of what customers are trying to do online and where and why they fail. This is a data-driven activity that triangulates a rich blend of quantitative and qualitative data sources to help build a 360-degree picture of the target customer. It aims to remove the speculation, assumptions and opinions relating to who the customers are and what they want, need and do. This shouldn't be approached as a standalone or discrete activity (which all too often it is) but instead as a continuous pursuit of 'always on' customer insight and intelligence that captures evolving needs of the target customer as trends change, channels shift and other macro-economic or competitive activity impacts customer buying behaviour. Hypotheses are built by blending and triangulating the customer data to suggest customer and performance trends.

Figure 7.7 provides a brief overview of the key sources and what, properly executed, they provide. Our previous book will give leaders much more insight into the detail of how to execute each effectively.

- **Web analytics** – these are sourced from software wrapped around your website and are used to measure the flow, exit and actions of users throughout the website. They can be linked to e-commerce revenue and provide a very detailed account of activity across the website.

- **Online surveys** – these are usually served through separate software packages installed on the website. The most effective surveys do not poll but ask up to half a dozen (maximum) open-ended, free text format questions.

- **Page analytics** – these are software packages that are often referred to as 'heat mapping tools'. They are used to show a visual representation of interest, engagement, distraction and redundancy on any given web page.

Figure 7.6 Customer to Action®

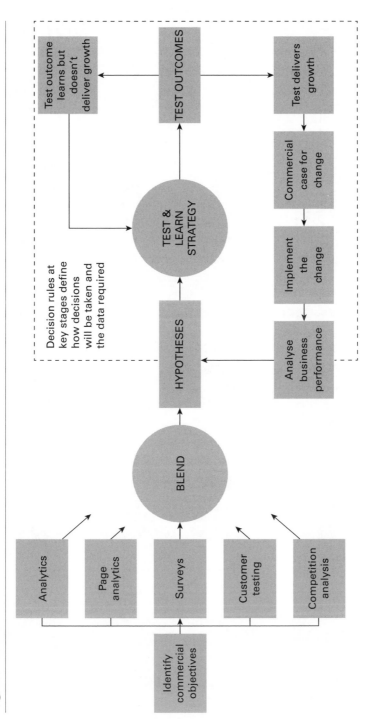

SOURCE © Good Growth Ltd

Figure 7.7 The building blocks of customer insight

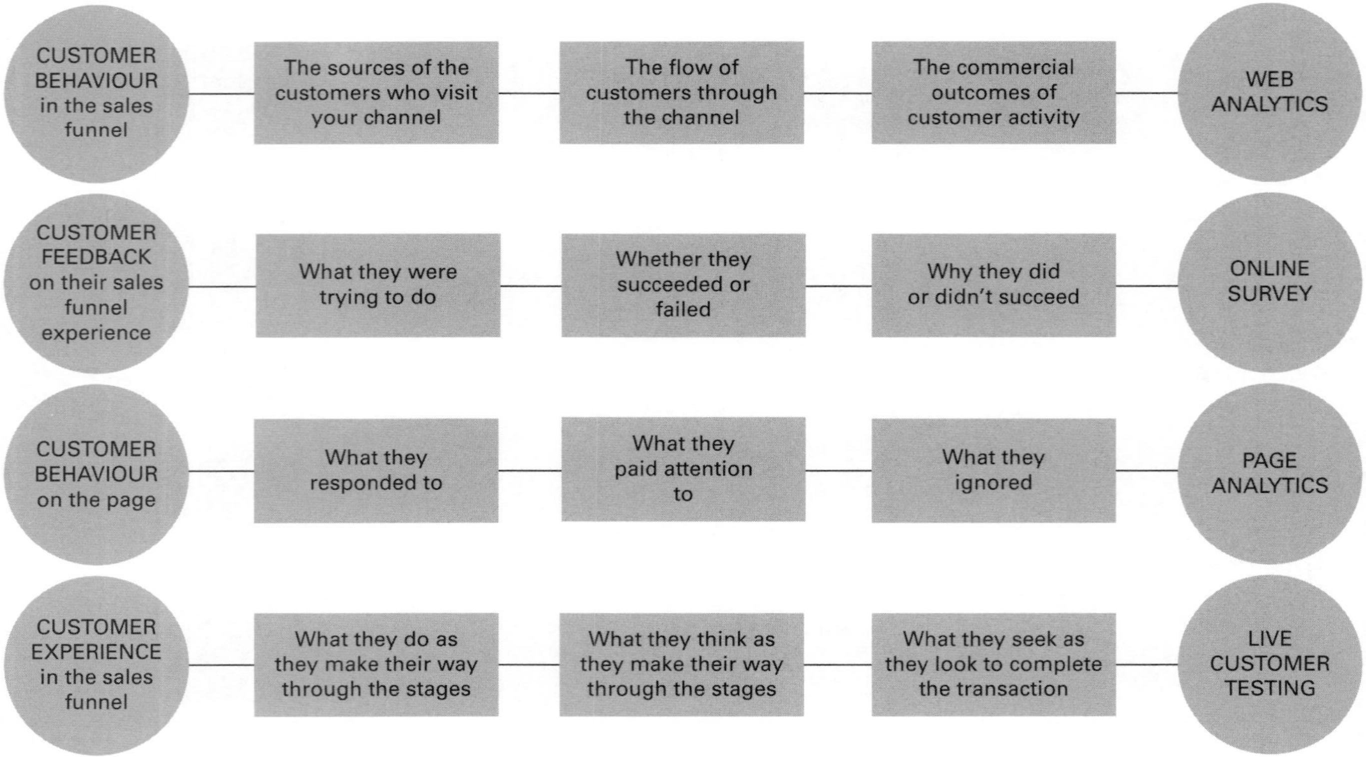

CUSTOMER BEHAVIOUR in the sales funnel
The sources of the customers who visit your channel
The flow of customers through the channel
The commercial outcomes of customer activity
WEB ANALYTICS
CUSTOMER FEEDBACK on their sales funnel experience
What they were trying to do
Whether they succeeded or failed
Why they did or didn't succeed
ONLINE SURVEY
CUSTOMER BEHAVIOUR on the page
What they responded to
What they paid attention to
What they ignored
PAGE ANALYTICS
CUSTOMER EXPERIENCE in the sales funnel
What they do as they make their way through the stages
What they think as they make their way through the stages
What they seek as they look to complete the transaction
LIVE CUSTOMER TESTING

SOURCE © Good Growth Ltd

- **Live testing** – traditional user testing as currently practised has a relatively limited use for CRO as it normally recruits 'testers' often in artificial conditions. Live testing uses real customers online and records their journey and experience through the sales funnel visually and verbally in real time. The benefit being that a business gets feedback from customers who are already committed to considering their proposition for a purchase.

Hypothesis creation

Hypothesis creation is the process of framing and describing themes that emerge from the insight in a way that enables the business to act. It is arguably one of the most critical digital capabilities leaders need to build in their businesses and, in our experience, it is the one most businesses lack. A hypothesis can be understood as an idea or explanation based on some insight and understanding that can then be tested through study or experimentation. It is more than a wild guess, but less than a well-established theory. A well-constructed hypothesis can point to supporting data for each point made and seeks to explain the issue rather than offer up a direct solution. This is a critical element of any process of optimization and is often forgotten in the rush to find a solution: you have to establish an agreed and shared understanding of the facts before trying to solve the problem.

Conversion intent

Conversion intent is an insight methodology developed by Good Growth that places the customer at the heart of performance reporting. This is achieved by reporting conversion rate within the scope of the customer, rather than the business. For example, e-commerce retailers typically convert at 5 per cent but, in our experience, 15 per cent of users are on the site to buy. This understanding of the customer allows us to report **Conversion Rate Effectiveness (CRE)**, a measure of how well you perform against how well you should perform, which in this case would be 33 per cent (5 per cent / 15 per cent * 100).

In terms of informing digital strategy, CRE is a critical measure and a good early indicator for focus; broadly speaking, a CRE of less than 50 per cent suggests an opportunity within optimization and one that is greater than 50 per cent suggests an opportunity within traffic acquisition.

This approach can be developed into propensity modelling using acquired behavioural data – a far better data set on which to assess propensity than quantitative data sets. Our methodology by comparison is far simpler than quantitative modelling but provides granular, actionable insight to inform a digital strategy through a focus on segmenting users into one of three categories:

- users who are on the site to buy – 'I will make a purchase';
- users who may buy if they find the right product – 'I'm just looking but may purchase if I find the right product';
- users who are not going to buy – 'I'm only browsing and do not intend to purchase'.

Understanding the customer in this way enables leaders to develop user propensity pyramids. These describe, visually, the estimated volume of users in each of the segments described above and provide an overall view of the 'shape' of the customer base. For example, as can be seen in Figure 7.8, within e-commerce the pyramid often follows an inverse-hourglass pattern.

Propensity pyramids can be used in a multitude of ways by leaders to set the shape of or focus for their e-commerce teams. A top-heavy pyramid may suggest an issue/opportunity relating to feeding the business with new customers. A bottom-heavy pyramid may suggest an issue/opportunity relating to traffic quality, intent and the performance of the website to address their needs. From a CRO perspective the following insights can be also developed:

- 'I will make a purchase' – users on the site to make a purchase require no sales engagement, simply an effective transactional engagement.

Figure 7.8   A common propensity pyramid

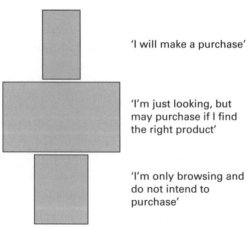

'I will make a purchase'

'I'm just looking, but may purchase if I find the right product'

'I'm only browsing and do not intend to purchase'

SOURCE © Good Growth Ltd

- 'I'm just looking, but may purchase if I find the right product' – these users are open to buying but are not convinced; it is these users who are targeted via optimization activity.

- 'I'm only browsing and do not intend to purchase' – these users cannot be converted; instead the focus should be on engaging them with the brand and driving micro-conversions such as account registration, email sign-up and so on.

Segmentation

We have already touched upon personalization, which in effect is a type of hyper-segmentation, right down to the individual. Segmentation is the most effective approach available in optimization where there is no direct and individual knowledge of the people landing on a website. Segmentation data and thinking come from the work done on locating and acquiring customers, and CRO can be used to exploit this by targeting specific segments in order to quantify the impact of different journeys, executions and sales copy on different target groups. Most 'off the shelf' split testing platforms will include some element of targeting ability, and the best enable you to integrate with tools such as Google Analytics where you can set up far more complex customer attributes and targeting conditions to work with more refined or nuanced customer segments.

Another neat trick is to use the principle of self-segmentation where the visitor defines his or her own segment. As an example, in the case of a global office space provider we introduced a welcome overlay on entry to its website that included a set of simple choices that are used by customers to select the size of business they represent. Doing this proved our hypotheses that knowing whether a customer was an entrepreneur, start-up, SME or global enterprise had a significant influence on engagement. Segmentation strategies are often focused on demographic, geographic or behaviour differences. The tests that these drive can include executional variations (layout and copy) and tests of alternative journeys through the sales funnel, based on assumed degrees of propensity to purchase as shown in Figure 7.9.

Running a testing strategy based on segmentation requires the supporting insight and hypotheses. This means that leaders must ensure that there are segmented sets of their customer insight data available. The same insight data discussed above can be sliced and diced to show these alternative views. Website analytics are relatively straightforward to segment by device and source, but can also be configured for user segments. Surveys and live customer interviews are also easy to tag and filter based on certain types of

Figure 7.9 Segmented testing based on assumed propensity to purchase

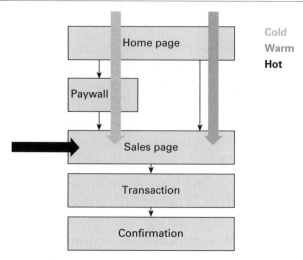

segmentation analysis, for example new versus returning visitors. To do this and add value there are three basic requirements:

- Back-end functionality must enable the identification of users by their segments and deliver different executions or journeys depending upon this criterion.

- Segments must be identifiable within the analytics and testing platform.

- The focus should be prioritized to ensure that user segments are representative of a large enough proportion of total site traffic such that any improvement will translate into a measurable uplift in performance.

Test and learn versus test and test

We cover testing in detail in our previous book (2015),[3] but it is worth repeating here that a successful testing programme is based on the following golden rules:

- Test insight not opinion.

- Establish the success criteria before the test starts.

- Any outcome is a good outcome – a test that fails can tell you as much as a test that succeeds.

- Prioritize your activity based on a combination of potential impact versus speed to implement (a simple high, medium and low matrix will usually suffice).

The differentiator between a vicious and a virtuous circle, however, is whether or not your business is testing for testing's sake – what we call 'test and test'; or whether there is a clear and defined process where the outcomes from each test are reviewed and fed back into the hypotheses. This is then developed further and, from this insight, additional iterative tests are carried out that are focused on driving performance improvement. We call this 'test and learn'. Optimization, in our experience, is rather like drilling for oil. Conversion intent is our equivalent of a geological map – it confirms the existence of wealth that can be extracted; test and learn is the equivalent of drilling test bore holes – it's looking for a rich seam that can be tapped to ensure significant value can be generated. Once found, iterations can then be developed that ensure the well of potential value is optimized fully.

Loyalty marketing

Loyalty is not a scheme. Nor is it a set of disaggregated activities. It is a mindset. It is almost a universal truth that selling more to a current customer is a far easier and cheaper undertaking than trying to sell to a new one. Retaining customer loyalty and building long-term relationships delivers growth at the greatest margin. Companies that operate their e-commerce as an integrated system and which understand that lifetime value should drive the thinking will have this as a focus for investment and effort to create value over time.

Loyalty marketing, therefore, is the maximizing of returns on known customer data, and to help leaders deliver this we have developed a process called Retention to Action®, which is shown in Figure 7.10.

We introduced the Customer Continuum in Chapter 6 and whilst trust marketing and its associated process covers the first two stages (Reassure and Personalize) and part of the third (Fulfil), this process covers the after sales aspects of Fulfil and the execution of the remaining stages: Curate, Retain and Recommend. The key stages are:

- **First sale success** – this covers the aspects associated with the delivery of a seamless service experience from payment, through delivery to conclusion of the sale process and the establishment of an early stage relationship. Vicious circles start here as organizations fail to engage with their distribution arrangements at anything other than a cost or efficiency level. There is a huge difference in using a courier that gives your customers the option to select delivery arrangements, organize to have parcels left and to send messages to the driver about say, entry codes, to one that offers parcel tracking but when you call their call centre says the driver can't be reached as contact numbers are not held centrally.

Figure 7.10 Retention to Action®

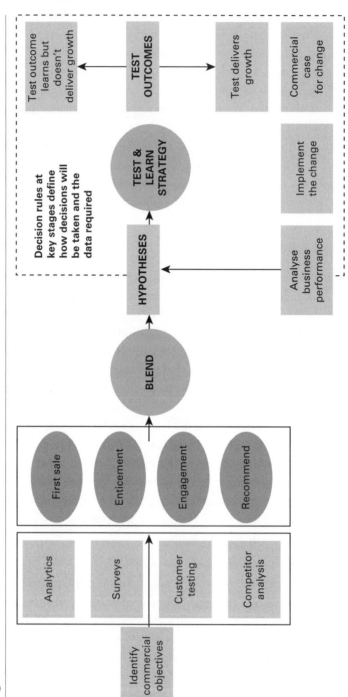

In addition, have you thought about how the product arrives at the door? Is it stuffed full of useless leaflets from other providers, only there to help you reduce the cost of delivery? Requiring your customer to recycle unwanted packing, particularly those incredibly irritating polystyrene pieces, is not a great experience for anyone.

- **Enticement** – this is about effective curation of the engagement experience. It includes thinking through the initial offer and the customer experience in these dimensions:
  - reward programmes;
  - reviews;
  - email marketing;
  - post sale self-service (where applicable).

  Vicious circle watch-out! This is an early friendship not a lifelong partnership and at this stage you may have generated some interest but you are not the recipient of long-term commitment. This means, for example, that there is a high probability that drowning your new friend in heavy selling emails isn't going to do much to endear yourselves to him or her. Nor is asking for a product review on the day it arrived.

- **Engagement** – this focuses on building and deepening the relationship. This is where we can think about encouraging more data sharing to help personalize the experience to enhance repeat purchases and self-service, build a belief that feedback is encouraged, and respond to and encourage rewards scheme engagement that leads people to think about referral.

- **Recommend** – by this stage the relationship should be committed and one where the customer is willing and able to become an advocate and can be enrolled to become a willing participant in a referral programme.

The success of the process comes from thinking in an integrated fashion right the way round the system and having a clear view of the data that you eventually want in a committed, long-term, value creating relationship. As in any relationship, however, asking for everything on the first date is rarely a fruitful strategy.

Leadership actions

This chapter has argued that e-commerce is an integrated system that, at its best, operates as an integrated loop aimed at creating the best possible customer experience at every touch point. The issue facing leaders is to identify where their system is in a vicious circle. These come primarily either from having a poor process or no process in each of the four stages, or from disaggregation of the stages such that one is failing to work in harmony with another. The aim is to establish a virtuous circle where the whole works so effectively that it drives an increase in lifetime customer value. What drives the system are disciplined and effectively managed processes that don't just operate on their own but in a coordinated way such that the interlinkages are effective.

These processes drive four sets of activities that have to be managed as a whole (and are often not, leaving them open to being driven as competing activities, often driven by competing agencies with competing agendas). In these activities are some very important ideas and concepts that should have a leadership focus as they are growth drivers that differentiate superior performance: trust marketing as a whole is a different and powerful way of looking at SEO and social media marketing; campaign test and learn turns marketing from a creativity challenge into an innovation process; conversion intent and user pyramids help focus CRO onto problems that, if fixed, can lead to growth; segment testing shows how differentiation can deliver better results and Retention to Action® is an integrated way of thinking about loyalty and the development of a staged engagement that drives advocacy in the market.

This chapter focused on the executional detail that leaders need to master if they are to cut through the noise in the execution of strategy and optimize the return on the resources involved. As a start they may want to consider the following:

- Map what you do and do not do today against the system. Where are the gaps? Are they deliberate or do they suggest that you are not taking advantage of all the levers available to you to drive growth?

- Work out where the vicious circles exist. Where is value being lost and what is driving this? Lack of a strong process? Unfocused or routine activities that don't add value? Competing agencies disaggregating the effort?

- Ask for an assessment of LCV. If you can't get it ask why, and then work out what you need to achieve our simple model calculation. Once you have got this, look at performance over the last few years if you can. Which way are you heading?

- How well do you pull together your earned media (social, referrals, reviews) and how focused are you about your brand reputation amongst customers in the market?

- Finally, look at your post-transaction experience and activity. Are you killing customers with emails? Do you make it easy for them to self-serve? How good is your delivery service – do they make it easy for the customer or difficult? Overall, how far are you from delivering the best possible customer experience in this area?

References

1 https://www.marketingweek.com/2017/06/29/arrogance-brand-purpose-distrust-ads/ [accessed 9 April 2018]

2 Bones, C and Hammersley, J (2015) *Leading Digital Strategy*, Kogan Page, London

3 Bones, C and Hammersley, J (2015) *Leading Digital Strategy*, Kogan Page, London

Building a customer-centric culture

08

Executive summary

Throughout this book we have talked about the importance of organizational alignment. It is the single biggest barrier to successful optimization of digital strategy and yet, in our experience, it is the area that gets the least amount of attention. Plenty of focus is given to talent and technology but, perhaps surprisingly, they are not on their own an assurance of growth. Without the right operating model and a culture that enables it to work effectively, talent and technology will not deliver the optimal outcome. In fact, in the e-commerce system the most likely trigger points for vicious circles come from a failure of the 'talent' to implement or operate the 'technology' effectively. Digital is a people business and people need frameworks to be at their best. Frameworks have to define the processes through which the organization will work to deliver, the standards by which it will judge performance and the behaviours it expects to be demonstrated by its employees. This chapter explores what defines an effective e-commerce organization and how leaders can think strategically about organization alignment and performance.

Organizational alignment

We started this book by talking about strategic failure and there is one model (Figure 8.1) we want to share at the start of this chapter that we use to encourage leadership teams to focus on strategic optimization.

What this represents is the direct link between why the enterprise exists, its strategy, the business model it adopts to deliver the strategy and what we call the operating model – the organizational framework and the required

Figure 8.1   Organizational alignment

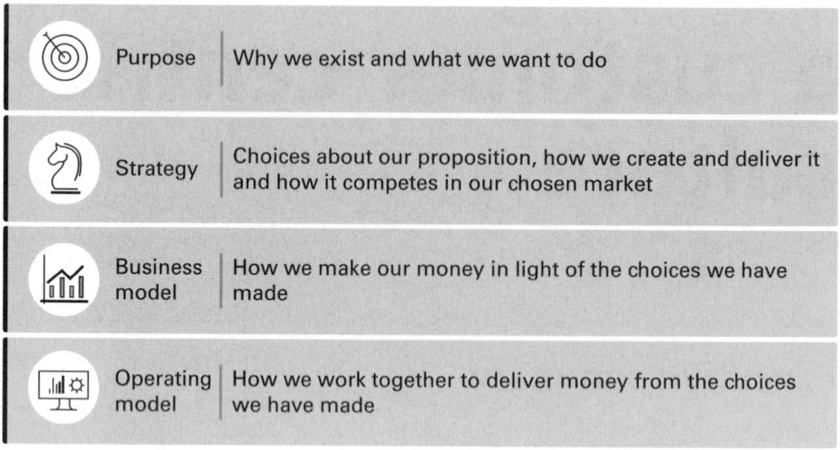

⊚	Purpose	Why we exist and what we want to do
♞	Strategy	Choices about our proposition, how we create and deliver it and how it competes in our chosen market
📊	Business model	How we make our money in light of the choices we have made
📊⚙	Operating model	How we work together to deliver money from the choices we have made

SOURCE © Good Growth Ltd

capabilities, capacity and culture that enable it to function effectively. Most organizations are able to articulate purpose, strategy and their business model. Far fewer can boast of a clearly understood and effective operating model, particularly when it comes to their digital activities. This disconnect sits at the heart of so much of the digital failure we discussed earlier in the book. Unclear or incomplete operating models absorb additional resources, financial and human, to put right what goes wrong on a regular basis. Business as usual becomes dysfunctional, accountabilities unclear and roles ill-defined. Organizations become adept at firefighting, but lose the ability to think, reflect, plan and address the important (as opposed to the urgent). Often at this stage, organizational silos begin to form to focus on the 'today' and cross-functional communication becomes increasingly ineffective. Thus, the critical linkages fail and the vicious circle begins to bite.

An operating model lays out how things get done. There are many examples of 'off the shelf' templates: two of the more comprehensive are EFQM[1] and Baldrige.[2] These take a similar approach to that we have applied to e-commerce, using systems thinking to define a series of interrelationships that, when working effectively together, can ensure that the organization delivers the strategy and stays loyal to its purpose and values. Defined well, an operating model can deliver a significant change in strategy and, in the process, refine itself to operate effectively after the change. What follows explores the elements of an effective operating model and then how to benchmark and think through the appropriate steps to close any key gaps.

Digital organization effectiveness

Effective organizations in any environment work because they establish transparently understood ways of working. These are defined through:

- a clearly articulated purpose;
- goals and their associated measures of success;
- core processes that align activity to outcomes;
- thoughtful role definition that supports these core processes;
- a positive culture that is managed actively by leaders to sustain agreed values.

Core purpose

In our previous book[3] we argued that people work best in organizations where there is a clear and commonly understood reason for that organization to exist and with which they can easily identify in their daily routine. In *Built to Last*, Jim Collins and Jerry Porras (2002)[4] explain through examples across a number of sectors the importance of what they have defined as 'a core ideology' to the consistently effective performance of some of the world's leading firms. This provides an organization with a common purpose to which, they argue, every employee can commit and that helps guide decisions about priorities, resource allocation and people development.

Importantly, it is not a vision nor is it a mission statement: it explains why the organization exists. It reminds employees why they come to work and what collectively they are trying to achieve. It is absolutely not a goal nor a measurable outcome nor something to do with creating shareowner value: it is a motivating reason to stay and to try your best to ensure your work is done well. It is a core requirement, we believe, to build commitment and a prerequisite for creating an engaged workforce. It is also a powerful attractor of people. Interestingly, interviewed about the leadership lessons from his research for his book *Good to Great* (2014) Collins made this observation:

> There is a direct relationship between the absence of celebrity and the presence of good-to-great results. Why? First, when you have a celebrity, the company turns into 'the one genius with 1,000 helpers'. It creates a sense that the whole thing is really about the CEO. At a deeper level, we found that for leaders to make something great, their ambition has to be for the greatness of the work and the company, rather than for themselves.[5]

It is this sense of the 'whole team' that is so important for success in the way organizations are constructed and their priorities communicated. If this is true for the 'whole' organization, then it is equally true for that part of it associated with delivering digital and especially any part focused on driving sales. The more fragmented an organization becomes, the more likely it is to lose this unifying principle. For an e-commerce team there has to be an add-on to the organization-wide core purpose and we believe this has to be: 'to deliver an outstanding customer experience'. Focus on the customer, and the money will follow.

Goals and measures of success

Goals are important and measures are mission critical. Leaders need to establish a performance dashboard that calibrates the outcome of the five elements of the e-commerce system. Figure 8.2 maps the dashboard to the system.

These dashboard measures help leaders to understand the health of the total system and indicate where things need attention. They are a mix of lead measures (indicators of future financial performance) and lag measures (outcomes that might explain financial performance) and cover not just activity but also organization effectiveness. Table 8.1 defines the measure, suggests the measurement interval, identifies interrelationships and offers warning-light triggers where leadership attention may be required.

Figure 8.2 The e-commerce system dashboard measures

Element \ Measure	Trust marketing	Performance marketing	Optimization	Loyalty	Organization
Outcome	Lifetime customer value				
Goal	Reputation index New customer acquisition	ROAS	Revenue per user Conversion rate effectiveness	Referral rate	Employee engagement
Process	Social engagement Referral response	Cost per acquisition	Testing ROI Testing strike rate	Review rate	Process effectiveness
Activity	(Un) prompted awareness Referral conversion rate	Lost impression share Click through rate Impressions	Conversion rate Landing page ratio Ave order value Purchases per purchaser	Review score Loyalty Engagement Self-service effectiveness Customer churn	Values alignment Capability alignment

Table 8.1 The e-commerce leadership dashboard – activity measures

Measure	Definition	Measurement interval	Interrelation	Warning-light trigger
Lifetime customer value	The lifetime value of the average customer	Monthly using a moving average over time approach (MAT)	• ROAS • Reputation index • Revenue per user • Referral rate • Retention rate	Declining moving average over time
TRUST MARKETING®				
Reputation index	An agreed way of measuring brand reputation and attractiveness from online interactions	Monthly using a moving average over time approach (MAT)	• Referral rate • Review rate • Review scores	Declining moving average over time
Social engagement	An active interaction with paid or owned content: normally a share, comment or click through	Monthly unless you are investing heavily in paid marketing in social, in which case weekly	• Likes • Followers • Reputation index	When interactions fall below benchmarks for your industry
Referral response rate	The percentage of people who respond to a referral recommendation	Monthly using a moving average over time approach (MAT)	• Likes • Followers • Review rate • Review scores • Reputation index	Fewer than x% and/or a declining moving average over time

(Continued)

Table 8.1 (Continued)

Measure	Definition	Measurement interval	Interrelation	Warning-light trigger
Referral conversion rate	The percentage of people who reach the website via a referral who purchase or engage with the primary proposition	Monthly using a moving average over time approach (MAT)	• Likes • Followers • Review rate • Review scores • Reputation index • Referral response rate	Fewer than x% and/or a declining moving average over time
Likes	The number of likes by social channel of paid or owned content	Monthly unless you are investing heavily in paid marketing in social, in which case weekly	• Followers • Reputation index	Poor engagement and/or increasingly negative feedback
(Un)Prompted awareness	The percentage of the target market that is aware of the brand, both when prompted and unprompted	Quarterly using survey methodologies	• Likes • Followers • Review rate • Review scores • Reputation index	Fewer than x% and/or a declining trend over time
PERFORMANCE MARKETING				
ROAS	The return on advertising spend, measured as a percentage	Monthly unless you are investing heavily in paid marketing, in which case weekly	• Click through rate • Impressions • Lost impression share • Cost per click	Less than 100% and/or a declining trend in performance

Metric	Description	Frequency	Related metrics	Notes
Cost per acquisition	The amount of marketing investment in a particular channel (eg AdWords) divided by the number of customers who transact successfully from that channel	Weekly or monthly, depending on scale of investment	• Click through rate • Conversion rate	This should be measured against a target established by a business case
Lost impression share	The number of impressions you were eligible to receive but, owing to a number of reasons, did not receive	Weekly or monthly, depending on scale of investment	• Lost impression share (budget) • Lost impression share (rank)	>5% suggests inefficiency
Click through rate	The percentage of people who see an advert and click on it	Weekly or monthly, depending on campaign		Requires a target to be measured against; below this should be a flagged issue
Impressions	When an ad is fetched from a platform and is considered 'countable'	Weekly or monthly, depending on campaign	• Viewable impressions (for display advertising)	See Lost Impression Share

OPTIMIZATION

Metric	Description	Frequency	Related metrics	Notes
Revenue per user	The amount of revenue generated per user	Monthly using a moving average over time approach (MAT)	• Conversion rate • Average order value	A declining moving average over time
Conversion rate effectiveness	The percentage of users who buy compared with the percentage of users who intend to buy	Quarterly	• User purpose of visit	Less than 25%

(Continued)

Table 8.1 (Continued)

Measure	Definition	Measurement interval	Interrelation	Warning-light trigger
Testing ROI	The additional revenue generated from testing compared with spend on testing	Quarterly	• Testing velocity • Testing efficacy and win rate • Average order value	Less than 100% or declining trend over time
Testing effectiveness strike rate	The number of tests that win, either commercially or executionally	Quarterly	• Testing velocity • Test complexity	Less than 30% commercial win rate
Conversion rate	The number of users who buy compared with total site traffic	Monthly using a moving average over time approach (MAT)	• Traffic • User purpose of visit • Device split • Conversion rate effectiveness	Declining trend over time
Landing page ratio	The ratio of landing pages to keywords	Quarterly	• Traffic • Digital marketing spend	Less than x%
Average order value	The average value of a conversion	Monthly using a moving average over time approach (MAT)	• Conversion rate • Basket size	Declining trend over time
Purchases per purchaser	The ratio of transactions per users who transact	Quarterly	• Conversion rate • Retention rate	Declining trend over time

LOYALTY MARKETING

Referral rate	The percentage of current customers who refer your proposition to their network	Monthly using a moving average over time approach (MAT)	• Loyalty engagement	Declining trend over time
Review rate	The percentage of purchasers who leave a review	Monthly using a moving average over time approach (MAT)	• Purchases per purchaser • Reputation index • Referral response rate • Referral conversation rate	Declining trend over time
Review score	The average review score for the business and by product	Monthly	• Purchases per purchaser • Reputation index	<4/5 Declining trend over time
Loyalty engagement	This has two parts – the percentage of customers signing up for the loyalty scheme; the level of activity and engagement (including redemption, if appropriate) in the scheme	Monthly	• Purchases per purchaser • Reputation index	Declining trend over time

(Continued)

Table 8.1 (*Continued*)

Measure	Definition	Measurement interval	Interrelation	Warning-light trigger
Self-service effectiveness	The percentage of customers who set out to self-serve who do so successfully	Monthly	• Conversion rate effectiveness • Conversion rate	Declining trend over time
Customer churn	The churn rate, also known as the rate of attrition, is the percentage of customers who discontinue their engagement within a given time period	Monthly	• Self-service effectiveness • Review score	Increasing trend over time

SOURCE © Good Growth Ltd

Building this dashboard requires leaders to contract clearly with their e-commerce teams on the following:

- **Definition** – we have laid out generic definitions in Table 8.1. These will need clarifying and detailing for your business. The important thing is not to let third parties define the terms by which their performance is measured.

- **Targets** – target setting is an art not a science. Think of these as ranges rather than single data points. Think through any implications of setting targets and look out particularly for the law of unintended consequences.

- **Data source** – confirm where the data will be sourced from. Don't let your data be intermediated by the team or any third party. Ensure raw data come from a quality-assured source and are fed into reports transparently.

- **Presentation** – in our experience, digital data in particular can be presented in such a way that you can drown in numbers and be no wiser as to the state of your business. We have reduced the measures for leaders into this relatively limited dashboard but there are still a fair number we believe that leaders should track. Think about the hierarchy – we have presented them in ranked order for a reason: towards the bottom are activity measures; closer to the top process and end-goal ones. Broadly speaking, if the end goal is not where you want it, then move down and look for potential drivers of poor performance.

The most important point about measures is that they set the framework for how you will understand, review and recognize performance. Hence, the criticality of definition – everyone has to understand what is being measured and how the measure is created. We are not proponents of carrot-and-stick people management. Measures are there to encourage, warn and guide people to ensure that they keep their focus on the end goal, and act with good intent and in good time to keep the business on track. It is important, therefore, for leaders to contract clearly about:

- **Reviews** – ensure there are clear reporting and review processes, and an opportunity to discuss business performance in a considered and structured fashion. Knee-jerk responses to off-target numbers don't help you or the team. Discussions that occur only when things don't run smoothly don't build trust or a willingness to share concerns at an early stage that may avoid bigger issues later. Regular sessions where early concerns can get aired in a climate where blame is not allocated enable performance to be driven effectively.

- **Recognition** – it is important that whatever measures you apply to assess the effectiveness of the system play through into how people are recognized and rewarded. It's been our view for a while that, given the integrated nature of the system, whilst recognition should be aimed at individuals for effort and contribution, rewards in e-commerce should be determined at a team level. This encourages collaboration and the capability and effort to think through the consequences that actions in one part of the system have on the others. Vicious circles don't just arise when one element or process fails: they also arise when actions taken in one element impact adversely on the performance of another.

Core processes

We covered the four core activity processes that make up the e-commerce system in Chapter 7. What we haven't covered as yet is how to establish these as 'business as usual' in an organization. Broadly, this is approached in four stages:

1   Map current activity flows and decision points. Ensure you understand the order (or not) of the flow of activity, what gets done, who is involved, where and how decisions are made and what measures, if any, are in place to understand process performance.

2   Compare the 'as is' map to the process template (adjusted for any specific organizational circumstances), identify the gaps and establish the scale of investment and/or change required to close them.

3   Build a high-level plan with resources implications for change. Establish the additional value that could be created through implementation and the time it would take to establish an effective new way of working.

4   Get support to help those involved change their ways of working – facilitated meetings and reviews really help change bed-down and behaviours change. In our experience, facilitated change and structured capability built around the new process helps build organizational muscle and establish new ways of working.

It is not just these core e-commerce business processes that need review and change. They will only work if the management processes that support them (reporting, performance review and reward, business planning and so on) are adjusted to work with them. Business plans, for example, need to be built using the same KPIs and to factor in the cost and timings associated with test and learn. Conversely, e-commerce processes need to factor in the investment hurdle assumptions built into business planning when setting testing targets such that the cost of change is factored into the process, not added on afterwards.

Role definition

The trend in e-commerce teams is still to fragment into siloed and very narrow skillsets rather than think about the customer experience. As a result, a system-wide view is often held several layers away from the day-to-day management of activity. This is far less often the case in non-digital businesses where a P&L owner may be found several levels under the executive. As we argued in our previous book,[6] traditional scientific management models in organizations are increasingly less relevant given the pace of change. E-commerce structures are particularly vulnerable to rapid shifts in performance and inflexible, activity-based roles can make them far less agile and responsive than they need to be. Commercial roles therefore need to be more associated with delivering the best possible customer experience, rather than functional activity. This suggests to us that the shape of the commercial core of an e-commerce team needs to look like this (regardless of whether the resource is owned by the company or resides in an agency):

- **Team leader** – owns the whole system, holds the P&L for the channel, makes the trade-off between marketing and sales. Team leaders don't need to be accountable for the offer (but if they have marketplace in their mix then they need to own that offer as a complement to the core) but, like any retail director or channel director, they must be accountable and have direction over all the resources in the system. Here also resides accountability for culture and organization effectiveness.

- **Customer experience** – this person (or people) acts as the customer champion, builds the insight, keeps it refreshed, and owns the hypotheses that form the basis for testing in all four areas of activity.

- **Customer location and retention** – this person (or people) is accountable for establishing confidence in the brand online and sustaining it post initial transaction or lead engagement. If you like, they are the guardians of the 'Alpha and Omega', the beginning and end of the system and the point where the end meets the beginning. In our system model this is Locate and Retain.

- **Customer engagement and attraction** – this person (or people) is accountable for the processes that engage and respond to initial interest, and support this through to a successful completion. In our system model this is Acquire and Engage.

In this shape, the activity of test and learn sits in each of the two customer activity groups; the close synergy between paid advertising online and the optimization of 'owned' web estate is reflected in them being run together. We would put all data ownership in the customer experience area as this is where insight generation should reside. Our overall approach is to break down traditional functional silos and think about managing a system that needs integration and outstanding connectivity between activities to drive performance. The overriding principle is to organize around the customer, not the product and especially not the agency model. In these groups, it is also possible to drive commercial goal ownership right down the organization and allocate the KPIs in the dashboard in a way where the risks of unintended consequences are reduced as those that hold a tension are all under the same individual or team.

Customer-centric culture

At the heart of an effective e-commerce operation is a ruthless focus on the customer. This requires the development and sustenance of a culture that doesn't look inwards but looks and, much more importantly, listens, outwards. Classic consulting models and concepts such as the 'total operating model' talk about organization effectiveness in terms of the interplay between people, processes and technology. Indeed, the system we describe and the issues we have touched on to date very much reflect that relationship. But we think this approach risks a focus on skills and structures, as opposed to a more holistic approach that considers capacity and culture. We think the best way of scoping the breadth and depth of an operating model is to look rather differently at what drives effective operating models and consider them as defined in Figure 8.3 from the perspective of capabilities (encompasses the people, process and technology thinking), capacity (in reality, strategic workforce planning – now coming back into fashion) and culture.

Figure 8.3 The drivers of an effective operating model

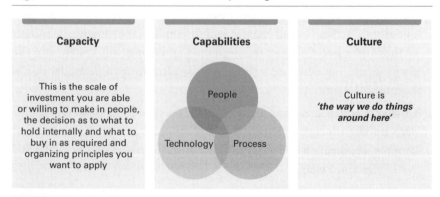

Capacity	Capabilities	Culture
This is the scale of investment you are able or willing to make in people, the decision as to what to hold internally and what to buy in as required and organizing principles you want to apply	People / Technology / Process	Culture is *'the way we do things around here'*

SOURCE © Good Growth Ltd

Organization culture is often seen as a subsection of leadership – after all, the theory goes, it is leaders who set the culture and effective leaders build great cultures that drive performance. In our view, it is much more nuanced than that. Yes, culture (often framed in terms of the setting of values) is a leadership accountability, but just because leaders subscribe to good values doesn't mean their organizations will. Positive cultures thrive where there are positive local climates; in other words, a healthy team, managed well, outwardly focused is far more likely to display more of the aspired values and behaviours than one in the next office that is disheartened, demotivated and poorly managed. Cultures are not consistent. They are 'the way we do things around here' and 'around here' can easily mean our micro-system, not the whole company.

Developing and sustaining healthy cultures in organizations is rather like gardening. Without active management and regular intervention, a garden can return to wilderness very quickly. Conversely, restoring a garden takes time and a great deal of work. Once the garden is established and controlled, you can't leave it alone for long. Something is too vigorous, other things die or fail to perform, plants reach the end of their natural life and get replaced: so it is for organization culture. For leaders to sustain a healthy culture means that every micro-system needs to be managed effectively and actively, not left to its own devices. As an ambition we believe active intervention needs to focus on getting three things right (Figure 8.4).

Customer-centric cultures seem to have three things in common. First and foremost, they are curious – particularly about customers, what they do, how they do it and why they do it. Second, they use bold experimentation to learn more and identify what they need to do to grow the business: they build insight, test it and then innovate with confidence. Finally, they are agile – they make quick decisions effectively, confident in their understanding of the customer and that, for significant decisions, they have proven the value through testing in advance. This requires a leadership that is willing to decentralize power, understanding and accepting of the validity of the insight and testing process, and willing to allocate resources behind the customer agenda.

Because culture is 'the way we do things around here' it is defined and sustained by far more than values and their resulting behaviours: core and management processes have to be designed and run in ways that reflect how leaders want the organization to be. Recruitment needs to reflect the culture and not focus on narrow criteria associated with experience or qualification. Attitudes become the defining criteria in identifying the best candidates for the future where organizations need people who can collaborate effectively, work across and around boundaries and act with the end goal in mind at all times.

Figure 8.4 Customer-centric culture

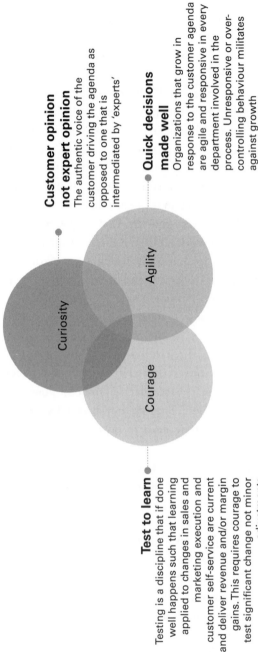

Customer opinion not expert opinion
The authentic voice of the customer driving the agenda as opposed to one that is intermediated by 'experts'

Quick decisions made well
Organizations that grow in response to the customer agenda are agile and responsive in every department involved in the process. Unresponsive or over-controlling behaviour militates against growth

Curiosity

Agility

Courage

Test to learn
Testing is a discipline that if done well happens such that learning applied to changes in sales and marketing execution and customer self-service are current and deliver revenue and/or margin gains. This requires courage to test significant change not minor adjustments

Benchmarking organizational effectiveness

To help our clients understand where they are and where they may have gaps we have developed the concept of e-commerce organization maturity. Figure 8.5 shows the framework we use in supporting leaders to identify what has to change in order to support transition to an integrated e-commerce system that delivers growth.

In our experience, the organization is the biggest barrier in digital transformation in any area. Which is really another way of stating the universal truth in business that people are generally difficult to get aligned to a new way of doing things. We deal with the leadership challenge at the end of this chapter. First, we want to focus on the different stages of organizational maturity and why understanding where you are helps find the lever to pull that will make the biggest difference to performance.

The differentiators in effective e-commerce organizations are fivefold:

- **Resource allocation** – effective digital businesses manage their system as a series of integrated processes and allocate their resources accordingly along a single, clearly codified customer-centric process. This doesn't mean necessarily that they all report into a single point of control; rather that the resources are aligned, measured and rewarded against performance of a coherent process. Doing this can reduce hand-offs, which in turn reduces the risk of performance issues and should reduce the level of resource needed to make the process work.

- **Agendas and targets** – one of the biggest barriers to performance is competing agendas and targets across teams involved in delivering desired outcomes. Given the tendency to fragment across activities that happens in e-commerce, this is a significant risk. The most effective teams are those where performance measures and goals are shared right along the system, encouraging alignment and collaboration.

- **Processes and KPIs** – these must be consistent and coherent if the system is not to spin into vicious circles. Those supporting each set of activities not only have to be fully understood and effectively managed but also they need to hand off effectively into the next set of activities and take what they need from the previous set. KPIs need to include those for process effectiveness as well as those that measure activity impact and overall outcome. They also need to be aligned and owned right along the value chain.

- **Performance software** – this is the set of software tools that wrap around a digital ecosystem. In our experience, there are three issues with less

Figure 8.5 Digital organization maturity model

Digital organization maturity model

BROWN

These organizations have resources distributed across several functions

There are competing functional agendas and targets

They do not work to common processes and aligned KPIs

They do not have complete performance software toolkits

The digital operation operates in a silo and its culture competes with that of the organization

BLUE

These organizations have the vast majority of resources in functional roles in one team

There is no direct alignment of strategic goals to team agendas and targets and no common culture

There are informal processes and a range of performance measures

They have complete performance software toolkits but these are not necessarily best in class nor are they used effectively

The digital operation is connected across some functions, but not all and its culture is different from that of the rest of the organization

PINK

These organizations have roles that support a clearly codified process

There is a single agenda for the channel and shared goals and KPIs for all involved and clear cultural standards

There are clear and codified processes but these do not include customer insight

They may have best-in-class performance software but it is not used effectively

There is a clear and coherent understanding of digital in every function and how they work to support its performance. There is a convergence of similar cultures but this isn't codified

BLACK

These organizations resource to support a codified single customer-led process

There is a single agenda, shared goals and a clearly defined and codified culture against which people are measured and assessed

There is a single codified process that prioritizes the customer agenda by demanding customer insight before instituting change and a single set of clear KPIs

They are using best-in-class performance software to build in-depth customer insight

There is a single joined-up and integrated approach to digital understood in each function and one codified culture for the organization that enables digital success

SOURCE © Good Growth Ltd

effective e-commerce teams: first, they don't have a full set of what we define as 'core' tools (web analytics, page analytics, survey and split testing); second, they make the wrong selection (not just perhaps a poorer tool, but quite often they buy what their IT department declares to be 'best in class', which turns out to be the proverbial sledgehammer to crack a nut); and third, even if they have an appropriate selection, they don't use them properly.

- **Disconnection** – organizations that have thought about how to integrate e-commerce into the wider business and that connect 'the dots' into a wider understanding of digital business and the opportunities it produces tend to be more effective. Understanding the wider context and linking the wider organization into digital are critical factors.

We have talked about the importance of codifying what is expected. In anything new, people quickly interpret for themselves to fill in the gaps of their understanding. That means there is a risk that what leaders want to happen may well not occur. In a relatively immature function where standards are highly variable, individual views on what is 'good' practice will vary significantly so the risk exists that practice will vary, and possibly at odds with how the organization wants to work. In these circumstances being clear, writing it down, reinforcing it through process and behaviour standards, establishing it as the norm through training and operating a 'rapid reaction' strategy towards any unwanted variation is important.

Unlike other maturity models, ours does not assume that every organization needs to become outstanding at everything. If you are leading a business that transacts entirely through digital then you will probably need to achieve this level to outperform competitors. If, however, you are in the majority of leaders and work in businesses for which digital is one of a number of channels or one through which it generates leads that are 'closed' elsewhere then, in our view, you need not aim to be 'best in class' at everything. Yes, you should be in the far right-hand column for use of performance software and insight-led processes but, at least in the early stages, you can operate effectively at lower levels in the rest.

Understanding where your organization sits in this model is best identified through a structured audit. This needs to look at the drivers of organizational effectiveness – there are many models available through which to look at organizations. We like to keep things simple so we review effectiveness through the three lenses of capacity, capability and culture, where:

Figure 8.6 The drivers of organization maturity

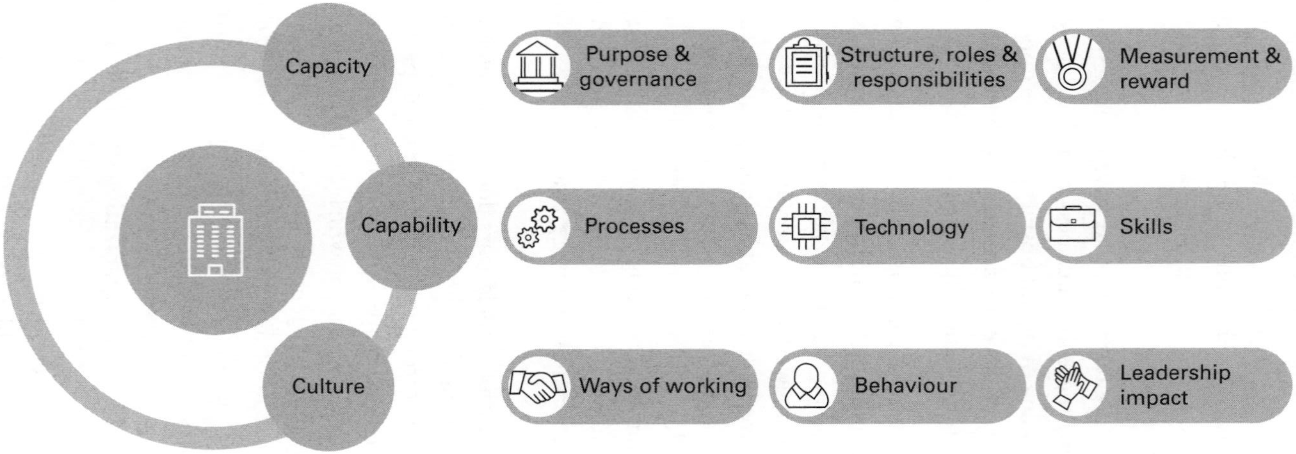

Capacity
Capability
Culture
Purpose & governance
Structure, roles & responsibilities
Measurement & reward
Processes
Technology
Skills
Ways of working
Behaviour
Leadership impact

SOURCE © Good Growth Ltd

capacity is the scale of investment you are able or willing to make in people, the decision as to what to hold internally and what to buy in as required, and organizing principles you want to apply; capability is the combination of processes, skills and technologies you need to bring to bear to ensure success; and culture is 'the way we do things around here' – the behaviours and ways of working that we see every day. Figure 8.6 shows the individual elements behind each lens.

To give some insight into each:

- **Capacity** – all organizations (and the key channels within them) need to be clear on why they exist and the business model(s) that they support. In e-commerce success comes from laser-like clarity that can help resource allocation decisions. Effective e-commerce structures are neither marketing nor IT. They focus on and are driven by customers and their stage of engagement with the proposition. The purpose and the structural framework should drive governance, measurement and reward and recognition – all need to be aligned with the processes, technology, skills and attitudes that you require to deliver the business model. This framework establishes clear accountabilities for digital success in every function.

- **Capability** – in e-commerce there are a set of skills that are required to deliver a successful outcome. These are not, as many believe, functional (for example, PPC expertise or an understanding of UX) but rather they are personal (such as data analysis, critical thinking and copywriting). Processes are the routines and disciplines by which you operate. They can be formal or informal and relate to internal management or to end-to-end delivery of product or service to the customer. In e-commerce the most effective start and finish with the customer. The exercise of these skills and the smooth running of processes are supported by technology. Getting these choices right is a key issue: getting the promised return is a significant organization challenge.

- **Culture** – 'the way we do things around here'. It is the sum of the attitudes and behaviours that leaders and managers tolerate, reward and encourage. It is also framed by senior leaders in decisions they make and the management systems they impose to control their business. Positive cultures that enable digital performance give permission, put the customer front and centre, and demand data and test everything. Negative cultures that undermine digital performance come in two forms: one where experts impose their agendas on the customer, internal and external; and one where there are rigid controls creating significant restrictions on agile and rapid responses to the customer in the market. Often negative cultures arise from the lack of strong and credible processes and the right capabilities.

To illustrate how these apply to the e-commerce system we have developed four pen-portraits, one for each of the activity groups.

Trust marketing

Personal relationships still play a huge part in effective selling, and where human interaction is lacking in the engagement stage of selling in e-commerce it plays an increasingly large role in early stage engagement. The most effective organizations look to maximize this through investing in activities that reinforce their status as a 'trusted' player in a very transparent market:

- Trust marketing is the process of establishing a powerful and authentic reputation for delivering:
  - on your proposition promise;
  - for all your customers;
  - and for wider stakeholders in the community.
- It is made up of three activities:
  - SEO;
  - social media marketing;
  - customer/third-party endorsements and referrals.
- It is delivered through these skills:
  - strategic thinking, customer insight creation;
  - critical thinking and analysis, test and learn;
  - copywriting;
  - creative judgement.
- And underpinned by a culture that is:
  - curious about the customer;
  - open to criticism;
  - data-driven;
  - authentic;
  - willing to learn.

Performance marketing

Increasingly, customer attention is acquired through payment in search, display and remarketing. The most effective organizations look to maximize their returns on this investment by focusing on efficiency and effectiveness. They understand the importance of judgement in this process and are moving away from automated programmatic solutions to a model where they can protect their brand as well as build their business:

- Performance marketing is the process of maximizing returns on:
  - paid search;
  - display advertising;
  - remarketing;
  - community.
- It is made up of four activities:
  - commercial modelling;
  - segmentation;
  - keyword strategy;
  - copy optimization.
- It is delivered through these skills:
  - commercial understanding;
  - critical thinking;
  - data analytics;
  - test and learn;
  - copywriting;
  - creative judgement.
- And underpinned by a culture that is:
  - curious about the customer;
  - willing to fail to learn;
  - agile and fast paced;
  - data driven.

Optimization

Driving performance of digital real estate sits at the heart of an effective e-commerce execution. The most effective companies treat this process as the underpinning of their product and promotion thinking, ensuring that they understand why customers do and do not act as invited (become a lead or buy a product or service):

- Optimization is the process of maximizing returns on:
  - landing pages;
  - the sales funnel;
  - the basket/transaction funnel.
- It is made up of four activities:
  - insight generation;
  - hypothesis creation;
  - segmentation;
  - test and learn.
- It is delivered through these skills:
  - commercial understanding;
  - critical thinking;
  - data analytics;
  - rich text analytics;
  - hypothesis creation;
  - test and learn;
  - design;
  - copywriting.
- And underpinned by a culture that is:
  - curious about the customer and the competition;
  - willing to fail to learn;
  - agile and fast paced;
  - data driven.

Loyalty marketing

Retaining customer loyalty and building long-term relationships delivers growth at the greatest margin. The most effective companies understand where lifetime value should drive the thinking and where to invest the effort to create value over time:

- Loyalty marketing is the process of maximizing returns on known customer data.
- It is made up of five activities:
  - direct e-communications (including LiveChat);
  - self-service;
  - personalization;
  - loyalty schemes;
  - referrals and recommendations.
- It is delivered through these skills:
  - proposition understanding;
  - critical thinking;
  - data analytics;
  - rich text analytics;
  - hypothesis creation;
  - test and learn;
  - design;
  - copywriting.
- And underpinned by a culture that is:
  - curious about the customer;
  - dedicated to customer retention;
  - willing to fail to learn;
  - agile and fast paced;
  - data driven.

As with all audits, this is best done externally. The key in commissioning it is to want to learn about where you sit today and what has to happen to move you up the curve to where you want to be. Effective plans are structured to enable you to improve in steps and focus on what delivers the best return in the shortest period. Organizations are untidy – there is rarely much value in investing merely to make them look good.

The leadership challenge

As we covered in Chapter 4, work done for our previous book looking at the leadership challenge in e-commerce introduced the importance of shifting the organization paradigm from leadership driven by theses to leadership driven by hypotheses.[7] We extended the thinking done by previous authors and argued that, in a world that is changing faster than we can learn where problems are adaptive rather than technical, organization leaders have to build the capability to understand the difference between a thesis and a hypothesis, and build the processes and skills to develop hypotheses collaboratively with their customers.

A thesis is a theory put forward as a premise to be maintained or proved; a hypothesis is a proposed explanation made on the basis of limited evidence as a starting point for further investigation. We continue to argue that the 'old world' model of arguing a thesis to justify investment is no longer tenable – given that there are no longer right answers that are clear and obvious. As we have laid out in this book: if test and learn is the best way forward, then organizations have to be able to test against hypotheses that are informed by 'deep data' about customers and the market. These can then be used to test solutions that can be rapidly 'mainstreamed' should they be successful. Organizations that continue to look for theses where all the data and thinking are aimed at justifying a single (and often costly) solution are far less likely to succeed.

We believe that the role of the leader has shifted significantly in a generation from one who knows the answer to one who knows how to put the right resources, financial and human, in the right place at the right time to reach the answer. The pace of change is such that we can no longer talk about being an effective leader *of* change but rather how to be an effective leader *in* change.

So what does this mean for leadership?

There is no one thing that has to change: as in our environment, there are many changes that need to be made. We believe these can be summarized in the framework shown in Figure 8.7.

Figure 8.7 Leadership in change

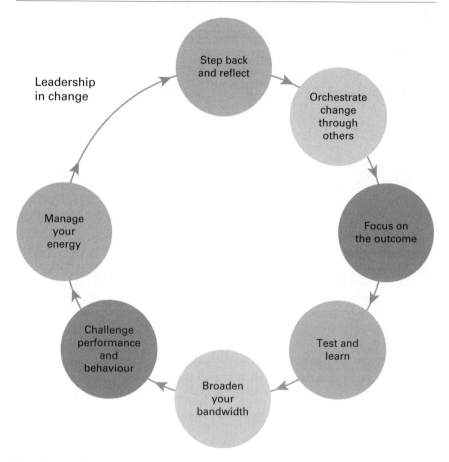

SOURCE © Good Growth Ltd

Briefly, this suggests that effective leadership in a changing world is built on the capabilities described in Table 8.2.

There are obvious implications from this framework for leaders in terms of individual skills and behaviours. To succeed will need strong communication skills, the ability to engage and mobilize people, and the courage to stand firm on values and address conflicts. There are also implications for being able to work across a diverse range of people (cultural, gender, ethnicity, sexual orientation and so on) and for understanding how to ensure the organization builds the capability to manage from hypotheses rather than theses. Finally, there are implications for

Table 8.2   Effective leadership capability

Step back and reflect	Reflects and identifies the key challenges; plans how to engage others before acting
Orchestrate change through others	Sets a compelling vision and collaborates to use everyone's talent and potential to deliver it
Focus on the outcome	Keeps the goal clear and can adapt to find new ways of achieving it using failure as positive learning
Test and learn	Uses hypotheses informed through deep customer/ market insight to experiment to find the best way forward
Broaden bandwidth	Champions the importance of a diversity of voices and ideas in looking for options that may resolve key issues
Challenge performance and behaviour	Stands firm on values as well as on performance outcomes and addresses the conflicts as they arise
Manage energy	Appreciates the time and energy it will take and has the stamina to see it through

SOURCE © Good Growth Ltd

self-management: finding time to think about the issues and yourself and being able to manage your well-being so that you keep healthy, mentally as well as physically.

Spotting adaptive challenges

If leaders have one key role in this new world it is to ensure that they spot adaptive challenges and guide their organizations into responding to them effectively. Table 8.3 is a quick checklist.

So, from a leadership perspective an adaptive challenge means that leaders have to:

- identify the challenge and frame the key questions and issues in such a way that people can understand the problem and how they might contribute to its solution;
- disclose to everyone any external threats that may exist if we cannot solve it;
- look to challenge 'group think' and the organization's current mindset through shifting roles and changing groups;

Table 8.3 Spotting adaptive challenges effectively

Technical challenge	Adaptive challenge
Easy to identify	Difficult to identify (and easy to deny)
Often lend themselves to quick and easy solutions	Require a change in organization values, beliefs or approach
Can often be solved by an authority or expert	People with the problem are needed in solving it
Require change in just one or a few places	Change required in many places often across boundaries
People generally receptive to technical solutions	People often resist even acknowledging the problems exist
Solutions can often be implemented quickly	Solutions require experiments and new discoveries

SOURCE © Good Growth Ltd

- make sure conflicts and disagreements are surfaced, exposed and then addressed;
- challenge organization norms and current practices.

Dialogue as a driver of success

At the heart of all the thinking is a proposition that collaboration and dialogue will drive better solutions than a top-down 'follow me' or a well-argued thesis from one particular perspective. This is as true externally as internally – dialogue with customers and suppliers is as important in today's business as dialogue with employees. We choose the word dialogue deliberately here. This isn't about 'selling' an idea or making a 'pitch'. It's about ensuring there is genuine exploration and the building of a shared understanding such that you can create greater insight from which to act; or greater certainty on how to respond.

At the heart of effective dialogue is a leadership understanding of both advocacy and inquiry. The importance of understanding the difference between advocacy and inquiry and how they can help leaders reframe 'mindsets' and mental models was developed by Peter Senge in his work on learning organizations.[8] Leaders need to be able to work effectively in both modes and, just as importantly, understand when to use them and be conscious of how they do so. In the past, the dominant element in

Table 8.4   The shift from thesis to hypothesis

Effective inquiry	Effective advocacy
Asking questions that are very open to start a conversation or are clearly linked to what you have just heard	Speak up for your beliefs and say what you think
Listen and show you are listening actively by summarizing and checking your understanding	Share assumptions that sit behind your analysis and opinions
Go and find new opinions – look for extremes and alternatives as well as for views closer to your own	Tell people what you feel as well as what you think – that helps them understand where you are coming from
Test assumptions by vocalizing them and getting others to challenge them	Give examples and use hypotheses as a way of sharing your view – that way, people will push back if they disagree and it stops you being defensive
Ask people to explain why they are saying what they say	Ask others for their opinions on what you are saying and remain open to challenge
Don't interrogate: explore and engage	Share where you are unsure or lack clarity: that helps others build and engage with what you are saying

SOURCE © Good Growth Ltd

communication in leadership was advocacy. Today, if we are to co-create and collaborate to find solutions in a fast-changing and uncertain world the dominant communication strategy needs to be inquiry.

Simply put, inquiry is the way we extract data, information and analysis from other people whilst advocacy is the proposition and defending of our analysis and opinion. Both play a key role in dialogue; but for a leader looking to ensure a real diversity of views and to build real and deep customer insight, spending time on inquiry early on and being careful about their own advocacy is critical to success. The checklist in Table 8.4 is a useful reminder about what to do to support organizations to shift from a thesis to a hypothesis mindset.

Orchestrating change through people

There is one other conclusion that we can draw from our analysis of leadership in a rapidly changing world and the importance of assuming that most challenges are best resolved through an 'adaptive' approach: leaders have to think carefully about how they choose to orchestrate solutions that require their organizations to change. The question then is how to co-create and collaborate effectively whilst avoiding either a breakdown into organizational fragments or a risk-averse stasis whilst more and more data is obtained?

Working with one of our clients, we developed a simple way of helping leaders engage with the key problem, when faced with uncertainty and disagreement, of where to start and why. We call this 'cutting through complexity'. This is illustrated in Figure 8.8.

Complexity within organizations is often also amplified by internal processes and a culture of risk aversion. What leaders need to do is to cut through this and find ways of continuing to move things forward – even if it isn't yet clear what the best approach may be. This dilemma lies at the heart of co-creation and collaborative responses. Our work suggests that by taking a leadership decision on whether to address the 'what' or the 'how' leaders can liberate their organizations and enable them to move forward.

Figure 8.8 Addressing uncertainty through insight and testing

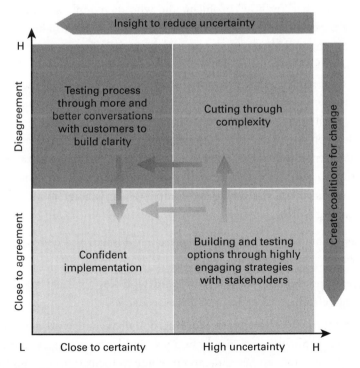

SOURCE © Good Growth Ltd

Addressing the 'what' requires insight. This is where the organization is uncertain about what has to happen to move forward. To make decisions it needs to dialogue with relevant stakeholders: normally, the most relevant are your customers or consumers, but sometimes the issues could be internal and then stakeholders are employees; or decisions could be about funding and further investment, in which case you are looking at engaging owners and other key sources of finance. Increasingly, digital channels are proving to be the most cost- and time-effective sources of customer insight across nearly all sectors. Insight generates understanding and provides the basis for resolving the 'how' through the creation of hypotheses.

Addressing the 'how' requires testing and learning from each test. This is where the organization understands what has to change but there is disagreement about what is the best way forward. Here leaders need to find ways of testing options, possibly through keeping several going at any one time in competition, or for a new product through prototyping or a small-scale investment. Again, in many circumstances digital channels are now able to provide leaders with cheap, quick and highly quantifiable outcomes before they look to mainstream and make significant investments.

Our experience suggests that leaders who identify correctly whether they have a 'what' or 'how' problem, and who then apply a structured and engaging process that is based on deep insight and a quantifiable process of testing, are more likely to engage their organizations in executing effectively in support of a clear vision. We have also learned that doing both at once is more than likely to sow the seeds of failure. It can enhance disagreement and create confusion, and will quite likely increase the costs of change without necessarily delivering enhanced benefits.

Whilst there are many factors that can influence the effectiveness of leadership in change and some key personal skills that will make a leader more likely to succeed, there are three things that leaders should ensure their organizations can do that will drive competitive advantage in an uncertain, fast-changing world:

- Differentiate between adaptive and technical issues and choose the right approach to resolve them.

- Engage and collaborate internally and with key external stakeholders through effective use of inquiry and advocacy.

- Make the right call between working on 'what' and working on 'how' and then apply effective insight and test and learn strategies that enable the right decisions to be made about where to focus resources and time.

Leadership actions

Organizations are the biggest barrier to successful optimization of digital strategy. The central challenge is how to get an organization aligned such that it enables strategy rather than diverts or obstructs. Alignment comes from a clearly articulated purpose, common goals and measures of success, clear processes that align activity to outcomes, aggregation of roles around the process not fragmented activity, and a positive culture that is managed actively by leaders to ensure congruent behaviours and ways of working. This can be benchmarked by looking through three lenses: capacity, capability and culture, and we have shared a framework in this chapter that can be used to judge commercial digital organization effectiveness. We have explored the importance of thinking through plans that change an organization in achievable steps, rather than quantum leaps. Delivering a digital strategy is a leadership challenge and we have suggested that it requires rather different leadership approaches from those perhaps more traditionally associated with success. At the heart of this is the concept of a collaborative dialogue with all key stakeholders including customers.

It shouldn't come as a surprise to see how this logic connects through with the development of the e-commerce system and the centrality of the insight-driven test and learn methodology to successful strategic optimization. Success comes from as close an alignment as it is possible to achieve between strategy and people, and the only way to do that is to create an organizational framework that defines what to do, how to do it and how success will be measured. Organizations that succeed are those that have been deliberately constructed.

This chapter has dealt with the deliberate organization choices that sit behind e-commerce and how these can be informed by defining an operating model and then establishing the existing gaps and developing clear plans to close them. It has also suggested a leadership approach that can underpin both internal change and external performance improvement. There are seven things that leaders might want to consider as they assess how to build an effective operating model:

- Make an initial assessment of where your organization is today against the benchmark framework; the further left you think you are, the more you should seriously consider commissioning a formal audit.

- Review your KPI frameworks and check relevance and focus against the model. To what degree are they shared by all those who play a role in delivering the end outcome online?

- How coherent are your processes? Do they cross functional boundaries seamlessly? Are they well understood widely? Are they written down anywhere and are people trained in them when they join the team?

- Have you the appropriate performance software? And, more importantly, are you using it effectively?

- Think about the behaviours you see around you from those involved in delivering your digital proposition. What goes on that is helpful? What goes on that is less helpful? Can you engage other stakeholders in how to address the 'less helpful'? Work out what you can do to address the unhelpful and take action with others if possible to drive change.

- Think about the way you have identified skills/capabilities for your team – are you focusing on those that will future proof the team or have you recruited skills that may stop you from learning, innovating and being commercially driven? Do you need to change the spec in your role profiles and job adverts going forward?

- Finally, think about yourself. How are you leading the part of the organization for which you have accountability? Are you driving a business approach that uses hypotheses and looks to test and learn? How much dialogue are you using in your approach? What capabilities do you need to build in yourself to help you manage the development of an effective organization?

References

1 http://www.efqm.org/the-efqm-excellence-model [accessed 4 May 2018]

2 https://www.nist.gov/sites/default/files/documents/2017/02/09/2017-2018-baldrige-excellence-builder.pdf [accessed 4 May 2018]

3 Bones, C and Hammersley, J (2015) *Leading Digital Strategy*, Kogan Page, London

4 Collins, J and Porras, JI (2002) *Built to Last,* Harper Business Essentials

5 http://www.jimcollins.com/article_topics/articles/good-to-great.html [accessed 1 July 2014]

6 Bones, C and Hammersley, J (2015), *Leading Digital Strategy*, Kogan Page, London

7 Bones, C and Hammersley, J (2015), *Leading Digital Strategy*, Kogan Page, London

8 Senge, P (1990) *The Fifth Discipline*, Doubleday, New York

Making digital choices that differentiate success from failure

09

Executive summary

The experience of leaders in optimizing digital strategies can be instructive for others facing similar choices. In this chapter, we hear from six leaders in a variety of industries with very different e-commerce frameworks who talk about their challenges, choices and where they think their next growth opportunities lie. Their businesses operate across the range of the emerging business models that we discussed in Chapter 6, and three of them are businesses with global coverage. Despite these differences, their experiences and what they highlight as the key choices that define success have many things in common. In talking with them, we identified some key themes and lessons learned that can help other leaders in developing their plans for change. Learning from peers direct, and not intermediated by their agencies, helps leaders understand the strategic and implementation processes that others have gone through.

Framing the challenge

Digital provides companies with both challenges and opportunities. The challenges are often the result of having to cope with the new problems that this fast-developing area of commerce throws up. The opportunities that digital offers relate to how we use it to address both longstanding and new business issues alike. One of the differentiators between success and failure is to ensure you are clear about the commercial challenge that you are addressing and how digital can provide the opportunity to find the right solution. For example, the long-established market leader for the supply of kitchens and joinery products to UK builders is Howdens. Kevin Barrett is their Commercial Director:

> Good product availability is key for any successful business. Our network of local depots has provided that for years, but there are new entrants using digital technologies as another way to achieve the same thing. We have therefore been thinking hard about the risks that the internet poses for our model; in the end, we actually see digital as a huge opportunity for us to improve our offer, rather than a risk we need to run away from.
>
> We already have an availability model that has delivered great commercial success. What we are doing now is thinking through what are the processes that could either be automated or sped up through digital.
>
> There is also a set of digital tools that we could develop that will help builders complete their everyday complex tasks, making it easier for them to do business in general, and enhancing our reputation by making it easier to do business in particular with us. These could include online planning tools that save time or reduce hassle, or improved information and access to expertise, or even ways of configuring quotes and products that suit their needs or specific jobs etc. (April 2018)

Consumer magazine publisher Time Inc. is also working through the changes digital is bringing to its legacy business and how it can use online to open up new markets. Time Inc. UK's Group Enterprise Director, Simon Whittaker, explained:

> Print circulations are under pressure everywhere, so it was no surprise that the new player acquisition rates for the online betting games related to our print titles were also in long-term structural decline. While there was a degree of acceptance of this, we challenged it by insisting that we should, somehow, be able to exploit digital to reach the audience we used to have in print.
>
> The goal was to take our online betting brands and to allow them to exist outside of their print constraints. Thankfully, through some clever thinking, we were able to find our audiences again. Our digital agency, Good Growth, helped us achieve that by overhauling our online paid search strategy. Since then we've seen continual growth in our online acquisition rates every single quarter. (April 2018)

Whilst Time Inc. has been using digital to reconnect with former offline customers, multinational lingerie and adult toy retailer Ann Summers regards its online presence like another store, just with added benefits. COO John Boyle explained the value that this thinking brings to its business model:

The web is effectively an elastic-walled store. I can put thousands of products into it without having to increase any physical space other than, possibly, my warehouse. It's quite easy to do.

There are differences between web shopping and traditional shopping. It's partly the amount of information you can make available to your customers about your products. Those web retailers that do well probably have great content, great instructions, information and reviews, which can convince people to buy. Our shop staff are really well trained, but it is still quite challenging to get across that same amount of information in a bricks-and-mortar store. That's one of the reasons why online can become the most profitable store you have. (April 2018)

Another company that is finding benefits from the shift to digital is Regus, the world's largest provider of flexible workspace. It has always found ways to engage well with its customers, but the growth of digital has brought a whole new set of cutting-edge tools to its marketing toolkit. As Nicholas Spitzman, former Digital Managing Director, puts it:

It's not just about optimizing your website. We have now got new ways to find out what the customer is actually looking for and what's the priority for him or her. It's quantifiable, it's scientific, it's immediate, and most of the time it's pretty defendable, even unquestionable.

Without digital conversion rate optimization (CRO) for example, it's hard to quantify some of these things. It would be hard to say what is the best way to present our product. Should it be location first or price first or sector first? Using CRO you can work out per segment, per country etc, which way works best.

Regus has seen such good results with this, we beefed up investment in this area to accommodate the new pace of change that digital offers. (April 2018)

Even e-commerce giant eBay is facing digitally induced challenges but, as you'd expect, it is meeting them head-on, with solutions that would simply be impossible offline. Vice-President Rob Hattrell explains:

The margin of error for customer service online is far smaller than offline, because you don't have the 'recovery' options that a physical store offers. Online customer journeys simply need to be as fault free as possible. So, fundamentally, online is simply the purest form of retailing when it comes to customer service. That's why we put so much effort into fine-tuning those customer journeys.

Also, we have a billion listings on eBay, so the challenge that brings for us is how to make them searchable and navigable. We are therefore developing new entry points to our listings using voice and image. Our technology investment in voice and image processing, powered by AI, and our continued investment to improve our core search algorithm, is our ongoing mission. (April 2018)

Getting the customer experience right for conversion

eBay is clearly at the cutting edge with many of its technology investments, but it still needs to get the basics right and for much of digital, that is about making sure the customer experience is as good as it can be. Rob Hattrell again:

> The only way you can prove your web design works – whether it's to simplify, complicate, put buttons in different places, move other things around, change images – is through a constant programme of A/B testing. We have thousands of these running at any one time. We are constantly statistically scoring behaviours and measures on each one. (April 2018)

A/B or 'split' testing is a key technique in improving the performance of every stage of the e-commerce system. It is a process of continuous improvement that in the best digital businesses doesn't stop, and circumstances and markets change so rapidly. So even with the huge numbers of tests that eBay performs, Rob doesn't regard a completed test as providing a forever result:

> Even something you undid a year ago can suddenly come back because consumers' habits and sense of what's important in what they see, is changing all the time. So, once you have done it once, it doesn't mean it's done forever. You need to constantly test. You need to constantly take things out, put things back in. You need to constantly revise your approach, always retrying and re-testing things. (April 2018)

One of the main developments in the customer experience over the last four years is a change to focus on making value propositions more digestible and easily understandable. This is critical, as we have explained earlier, as there is little or no human interaction on many websites. Earlier strategies like presenting complex FAQs (frequently asked questions) have not been that easy for all but the most informed customer and as design trends move to relying on fewer words so the challenge to explain becomes much more challenging. As more and more propositions become accessible online so their complexity and sophistication has to be communicated effectively. Nicholas Spitzman explains:

If Amazon is selling you a portable heater online, a basic description is good enough. However, if you are selling something like we were at Regus, you are going to have to explain a lot. A user may not know what Regus sells, or what way he or she can buy it and they might not even know that they can buy it online. When you bring someone to an e-commerce journey you have to explain all that. It's not easy, especially when there is no easy or obvious analogue in the real world. That, coupled with the fact that attention spans are generally smaller now, means we need to make everything online, especially our value propositions, very simple.

By using conversion rate optimization (CRO), we have got more sophisticated about how to make our propositions clearer. Every time we say something, we re-test and try to make it more nuanced. We want to know: Do people want to see what options are available? Do people want to see what ways to buy are available? Do they want to self-select? Previously we were just applying offline analogies to online. We were not doing a very sophisticated job at seeing what works best for the user. We are now though. (April 2018)

As Nicholas suggests, this requires a disciplined and structured process with a core principle of being driven by data rather than opinion. John Boyle agrees:

I think we are in danger of looking at data and making assumptions, rather than analysing it properly to come up with definite reasons why people do or don't shop with you. When you get a load of data and analyse it, and come up with some conclusions, without actually talking to any customers, how do you know if your conclusions are valid or not? It depends on how you cut that data. People often start with their own hypothesis, which is fine, but then some people just select the data that 'proves' they are right. That's cherry picking.

You also need to actually talk to customers, even if that is online as well. Our digital agency had conversations with our customers as they were leaving our site, having not purchased, and asked them why they were leaving. They came up with 35 different reasons. Two-thirds were about stock availability: didn't have my size, didn't have the colour I wanted, didn't have the matching knickers and bra. The other issues were things like, couldn't find the button to click through to payment etc. So, we then had sensible reasons why people had not transacted. That then drove us down a route of testing some of the hypotheses that were produced.

But rather than move a button to a new location, because someone said we should, we tested different options for button positions and adopted the one that maximized our click through rate. This technique helped us understand better about the construction of our website and the journeys through it. (April 2018)

For experienced practitioners, it is often not the improved results that comes from a disciplined and structured process of test and learn that are unexpected; it's the scale of the benefits that can sometimes take people by surprise. Here is Brett Moore, Digital Product Director at hotel and restaurant review and booking provider, TripAdvisor:

> We often have an idea that there's a problem here, or maybe there's an opportunity there, so we get our analytics people to go and look. We haven't had any huge surprises regarding the specific insights they come back with. It's more about quantifying them. For example, what impact will a change make on the number of sessions? How much is it then going to move people through that funnel and turn those sessions into bookings? And then what is it going to do to our overall revenue?
>
> We can have a hunch something is going to increase bookings, but quite often it can turn out to have a much more significant impact on revenues than we thought it would. We can then prioritize accordingly. (April 2018)

Nicholas Spitzman has had similar experiences:

> You might expect that a specific test would convert better, but sometimes when you see the size of the results, that can be surprising. (April 2018)

This scale comes from ensuring that you start by developing deep insight into the customer experience, regardless of the stage of the e-commerce system, use this to develop well-crafted hypotheses that don't leap to a solution, but provide a platform for testing many solutions any of which could drive growth. Understanding the real problem focuses creativity on solving that problem, not guessing what the problem is and building solutions that consume resources but don't deliver growth.

The customer acquisition story

One can think about some of the costs associated with acquiring customers to a digital channel as analogous to those for operating physical stores on a high street. It comes with its own complexities and resource decisions that require a ruthless focus on ensuring returns. Ann Summers' John Boyle puts it like this:

> You open your shop on the web, which can be relatively cheap, but then you have to pay to get traffic to land on your site. That's where Google acts like a landlord. The pay-per-click costs they levy are just the same as us occupying a

prime spot in a busy shopping centre or high street. Generally, the more you pay – if you are sensible and know what you are doing – the more people will come past your window and through your door. So, my view is that Google is both our newest and our most difficult landlord at the same time. (April 2018)

Using email campaigns to drive traffic to a digital channel is a well-tested approach. As with many aspects of digital commerce, proper testing and analysis is critical, otherwise the exercise can end up costing more than you make from it, as John points out:

Take our male customers who sometimes buy lingerie as birthday, valentines or Christmas presents. They know who we are and where we are online. They may only buy from us every 2, 3 or 4 years, but they are likely to come back to us, even if we spend nothing trying to re-activate them. So, if you are sending out re-activation emails, with discount incentives to shop, to seemingly loyal but very infrequent shoppers, you may end up giving away your margin needlessly to individuals who would have bought from you anyway. (April 2018)

Acquiring or reacquiring customers to an online channel doesn't have to be limited to using purely digital routes though, and this requires careful planning and a detailed understanding of attribution and resource optimization in order to ensure maximum value. Time Inc. builds multi-channel communication campaigns to drive traffic to its non-print websites. In their case, outdoor posters in specific locations, together with a coordinated adword campaign, are all aimed at driving traffic to its online betting sites, as Simon Whittaker explains:

We know which cities have the most bingo betting halls and equally, we know where our print media customers are. That means we can match those areas where people like bingo to those where our brands most resonate. It's the combination we need in order to identify in which specific cities to buy our outdoor advertising poster sites. We also understand our target audiences' shopping habits – if they like a particular supermarket brand, for example – so we can place our ads in exactly the right locations, both on- and offline. (April 2018)

As we discussed earlier, personalization, or at least segmentation for those you don't know, is a focus for leaders looking to maximize their returns in digital. The challenge is to work out how far you can go and how best you can respond to deliver an experience that is more engaging. Brett Moore talks about TripAdvisor's plans to progress further down this path:

We need to show our customers options that are even more relevant to them, so we've got an awful lot invested in projects to help us get more personalized than we are today.

We're looking to see where there are really clear differences in the profiles of our customers, to differentiate what they require from their purchase, and to try to create some specific experiences that will really maximize those opportunities for us. (April 2018)

Regus used Good Growth to help segment their audiences and show value propositions more directly to each segment. Nicholas Spitzman explains why:

This segmenting made it work better for the user and it converted more of them to more enquiries and more sales. Good Growth used small tests and complex tests and were able to show a lot of variety in the tools they use to get those answers, which is good. (April 2018)

Not every segmentation produces big differences, though. When it comes to behaviour in different countries, Regus found that there are far more similarities than differences. Nicholas again:

Different countries generally behave more similarly in terms of CRO than not. We will tweak rather than have drastic changes for different countries. We have found that, on the whole, if it's true for one large country, it's almost always true for every other country. (April 2018)

But Nicholas points out that where there are differences between segments, these are critical:

Some sources of traffic in some scenarios do work better with some propositions and not with others. The more advanced the nuances, the higher the impact will be on your sales. Don't assume that customers always want to look at it this way. There are important variations by traffic source, by the type of product being searched for. It's important to test for these and respond to those results. (April 2018)

There are a variety of ways you can respond to such findings to build campaigns with better returns, as Simon Whittaker from Time Inc. recalls:

We diverted more spend to desktop or mobile depending on the age of the player. Then we launched a paid social strategy, both to people who are interested in bingo and to geographical areas we felt were relevant. We used postcode data to map where we had the strongest print magazine circulations. In doing so, we discovered that for some titles, readers are older and more likely to be in the North East of England, while others have a younger customer base that can be more efficiently targeted via mobile devices. (April 2018)

Pricing through the digital channel

There are a number of price-related issues that arise in digital but the main one is transparency. As eBay's Rob Hattrell puts it:

> With digital, your price position is clear. It is laid bare and open for all to see. Within two or three clicks of a finger a user can find price comparisons elsewhere, and if you don't get it right people will just leave your online store. (April 2018)

The response, however, may not be to adjust your price. Simplistic comparisons often mask nuanced differences in the proposition that justify the difference – anyone who has been through an insurance or hotel comparison site can tell you that. The challenge for many businesses is to ensure that they have communicated the value of their proposition effectively. One of the leaders interviewed for this chapter operates in a business where the current engagement leaves price to its distribution channel. Howdens uses its website to communicate a significant amount of product information, but it has no prices at all on its website. This reflects its business model where its direct customers are installers and builders, who then set their own prices, including the cost of installation, for the final consumer. The website therefore has to work much harder than many competitors in persuading the end consumer to engage. In one aspect, kitchen appliances, this approach is coming under pressure from digital competition and this is causing a re-evaluation in how Howdens will go to market online in the future, as Keven Barrett explains:

> New online electrical appliance retailers have taken a lot of market share quite quickly. They haven't shown much profit yet, but what they have done is make product pricing very easy to compare and contrast. We need to respond to changes like that. So, it's safe to assume that we will be going to market in a very different way after we have reviewed our position and strategy. (April 2018)

Another pricing innovation that digital offers is dynamic pricing, whereby the cost of something changes depending on when you purchase it. The airline industry has used this for years, and there are particular reasons why they can and do, but others are now looking to go down the same route. Brett Moore from TripAdvisor:

> If you look at the vacation rental marketplace right now, I still think it's a little behind what you see in the airline industry, which I feel is the leader in this

field. I think there's a lot of people out there who want a good deal and who are flexible with when they can travel and that's something I don't think anybody in our industry is dealing with very well right now.

The difference is, there are far more accommodation options available than there are flights at a particular time. You might have a choice from 5, 10 or 15 flights to a particular city, compared to a few thousand homes or rooms. That's something we are trying to work around. And then we need to work out how to show that to our users, without putting across such a huge range that it becomes unhelpful for them. I don't think it will require any big technology change, it's more of a user experience process that we need to go through. (April 2018)

Getting the business basics right

As one delves deeper into the details of digital commerce, it is still important to remember the business basics. John Boyle makes the point that just because you are employing code as opposed to a physical store to merchandise and deliver your products, doesn't mean that the basic disciplines and standards are any different. In Ann Summers, he says, they need active management, just as in a bricks-and-mortar operation:

> I used to think of web retailing as a bit of a black art, with some very complex things going on. But what you actually have is an electronic shop and you have to have all the same disciplines in dealing with that shop as you have around the rest of your retail estate. As a basic, you still have to have desirable products people want to buy. So, your store stock choice is analogous to your online inventory. You have to have good landing pages, which is the same as having eye-catching window displays. And you have to have easy online checkout funnels, which is equivalent to keeping the queues short in your physical shops.
>
> Web retailing is no different from retailing out of a shop or a catalogue, in that the basics still apply. If you get them right, you can be a profitable retailer. (April 2018)

Of all the basics, customer service seems to be the one most people have mentioned to us as being critical. The absence of immediate human interaction can be an issue and where complex transactions are underway or where things go wrong, people want to engage with a human being to sort things out or deal with a highly individual issue. Even though Howdens doesn't deal directly with the end consumer, Kevin Barrett sees the integration of on- and offline customer service as key:

Even with a physical product like a kitchen, we see ourselves first and foremost as delivering a service, both to our customers (the builder), and their customers. With digital, we have ever more opportunities for interaction with customers and consumers, during the information-gathering, design and sales stages. But at all times, we need to make sure everyone has a true choice as to how they want to engage with us (in person, on the phone or digitally). What we do find is that, particularly when something goes wrong, that's when people need a human to talk to, to reassure them that we will be able to sort out their problems.

We want to achieve that combination of physical presence and human availability, while using digital to make it ever more engaging and efficient. (April 2018)

Company cultures

In talking to various industry leaders, we have noted a number of interesting differences in the cultures of digital native organizations compared to those that have had to make a transition to digital. At heart, these differences boil down to the three drivers of a successful digital culture we referenced in Chapter 8: a ruthless focus on the customer, pace and agility in decision-making, and execution. Many of the people we have spoken to have experienced both pure play digital businesses and those that established their success before the impact of digital. For example, TripAdvisor's Brett Moore used to be at American Express which, as a long-standing corporate, predates the existence of the internet:

> The mindsets at AmEx and TripAdvisor are massively different. At AmEx we would have to request funding for almost every change we wanted to make to our digital channel. I would have to get the money and effectively buy the technology resource to implement that. Therefore, you'd need really strong and robust justifications to get buy-in to get stakeholders to support you.
>
> At TripAdvisor I have a team making improvements all the time. That's what we do. It's digital. There's never any question about not having resource. Occasionally, we need to get some *more* resource for something as the task grows, but that's usually a quick calculation, to work out the size of the project.
>
> At TripAdvisor, we have a much bigger analytics team than there was at AmEx, a much bigger digital insights team. The actual management structure is all geared around that as well. (April 2018)

There are even differences between the approaches that companies have taken in their approach to digitizing their businesses. Here, John Boyle recalls where he was when the internet became a reality:

> I used to work at the department store group, Selfridges, and in the early days they just refused to engage with the internet. They argued it was all about the in-store experience and that was the most important thing for retail, especially in department stores. Having said that, in the year before I left, which is over 10 years ago now, they had come to the conclusion that they couldn't ignore digital, and I was on the programme to introduce a transactional website for the group. Despite their initial reluctance, their online presence is now very impressive.

> I'm now at Ann Summers and they embraced the web early on. With the internet, the customer has that guarantee of anonymity. You don't have to talk to someone or look anyone in the eye when you are buying (ie no embarrassing conversations). With all that privacy, you'd think the web would be great for Ann Summers, and it is. The culture at Ann Summers meant that they recognized that very quickly and were able to capitalize on what is a very important channel for us. (April 2018)

Kevin Barrett saw a number of companies through the transition to digital when he was at the consulting firm Accenture:

> During the first dot.com boom of the 1990s, we had to tell the insurance company Prudential that their door-to-door channel, the 'Man from the Pru', didn't have much of a shelf life now the internet was coming. It took a while, but that was the reality. And we had to tell Barclays Bank that their mass mailing of 'PC Banking' CD ROMs was probably an expensive mistake because they could have provided the same information better and cheaper, online. (April 2018)

Despite these teething problems both Barclays and The Prudential have turned themselves into very successful utilizers of the digital channel, partly thanks to major changes in their internal cultures, that have allowed them to thrive in this new era. These culture changes can be painful partly because companies who operate across both on- and offline channels still need to keep aspects of their established cultures because they retain large offline assets, for which these cultures have served them well over the years. That's not a problem for digital-only companies like eBay, but Rob Hattrell is still well aware of the differences:

Like many digital native companies, we have an open mindedness, a restless dissatisfaction. Even when you think you have got it right, you know you can get it better. This is a tech company trait.

It's different in the offline world. Opening a new bricks-and-mortar store is a big set piece investment. There are huge fixed costs, which are all spent before you even open the doors. You need to get it right or all that money is down the drain. It's therefore very important to avoid mistakes. Online it is different in that you are constantly organically investing in improving what you have. You almost welcome mistakes, because they don't cost that much if you test them well and they are actually a hugely positive part of your learning cycle. It's a very different cadence.

Online failure is therefore OK. This leads to a different culture. We are less governance heavy, much more open to risk, much more adventurous, much more consumer orientated, in every part of our anatomy. (April 2018)

Future trends

Predicting the future is challenging in such a fast-paced environment, but there were some emerging trends that our leaders are already engaging with. Overall, these focus on customer behaviour and how this is being changed by digital. These changes are focusing on both the continuation of how to digitize today's business but also on the need to build digital businesses that enable existing needs to be met in different ways, and different needs to be met that are only just emerging. Here, Time Inc.'s Simon Whittaker reflects on the future of print versus online media:

Print products provide a different consumption experience to online. The older generation, those in their 60s or 70s, will still be consuming print products for the next 20 or 30 years, so there is still plenty of life in the medium. The trick is to get the next generation to still want to consume paid media, whether that's in print or online. One answer to that? Our brands are still known and liked so, despite the fact that fewer magazines are being purchased, we can capitalize on the affinity people still have with their favourite brands to promote our online games – and so continue to generate income for us in years to come. (April 2018)

When it comes to the specific channel activity of conversion rate optimization testing, Nicholas Spitzman argues that no one can rest on their laurels:

What's coming down the road is a higher level of sophistication with testing; the depth and nuance of those tests will undoubtedly increase. I think we will all be re-testing a lot, partly because the interaction between all the variables on a website are changing constantly. For example, you might add something to a page that was an indirect part of a customer journey before, and at some point, if that page is changed, your entire customer journey is changed. Even if that specific test proved positive, you've got to look at it in the broader context and re-test the whole funnel. This is all good as it's an ROI positive activity. (April 2018)

Rob Hattrell finishes off this chapter with his views on the changing nature of consumer preferences, expectations and behaviours, and how he thinks the industry will respond:

The demands of consumers are accentuating. Even the disrupters are being disrupted, partly because of the speed that consumers are shifting their behaviour patterns, notably the speed at which they make decisions, consume information and then move on to something else. That means your execution needs to be sharper and faster down each of those core angles.

At the moment we are moving to cleaner pages, with lots of white, clarity, simple fonts etc, but we will continue to adapt to meet customer expectations. For example, the way the latest social media interfaces work, like Snapchat currently, may influence user preferences, so everyone needs to keep an eye on developments there.

Looking forward, eBay is going big on image search and image diagnostics. We are also placing our commerce into existing content, partnering with the people who produce that content, and using our AI to make the right connections. That's the next wave. Voice is another area we are working on. It's more real-time and immediate and questioning.

The data points for physical shops are more controlled but less voluminous, more simplistic, than with the digital channel. Online is more about data streams and people are working out new ways to utilize the huge amount of data flowing through those streams. The skills needed for that, both tech and human, are very different. Put simply, basic algorithms are way too simplistic now. I think the future is about combining qualitative and quantitative data by using AI. (April 2018)

Leadership actions

This chapter has shared practitioner experience and insights, and hopefully these have helped to explain why our response to them and many others like them has been to develop our thinking to create a framework that describes e-commerce as a dynamic system that is driven by a relentless curiosity to stay level with customers in whatever market leaders operate within. This curiosity is driven in every process by a determination to act from insight derived from analysing data, both quantitative and qualitative, and coupled with a structured and disciplined process of testing all the possible alternatives to find that which performs best. As our practitioners have indicated, as markets change so what performs best will change and this requires a continuous capability to test and learn. There are no right answers, merely answers that are 'right for now'.

As for actions that leaders might want to take as a result of reading this chapter, our thoughts focus more on what you are doing to step back, reflect and think about where you are going:

- Have you got a view of the potential developments in your market that may provide opportunities or challenges for which digital may enable a solution or contribute to a solution?

- What customer behaviour trends are you spotting now that might need to be considered as you develop your plans for the next two to three years?

- How consistent are you in standards and disciplines across different channels? Are you judging performance differently online and if so why?

- If you thought about your culture, particularly that in your e-commerce team and supporting or connected teams, how close are you to one that is relentlessly curious, agile and displays pace? What's the biggest gap?

- How much time do you and colleagues spend on thinking about the future and is this enough? If not, what can you do to find more time?

This is the business of transformation

10

Executive summary

This book has mapped out how leaders can optimize digital strategy. It has looked at why strategies fail and why they succeed and has explored emerging business models and why and when they might be appropriate. It has mapped out the e-commerce system and the organization challenges that make it difficult to succeed, and shared insights of what it is like to optimize strategy from leaders in a wide range of businesses. In addition, it has looked more widely at aspects that frame the environment in which digital leaders work: particularly the ethical dilemmas posed by some of the largest operators in the channel through which e-commerce is delivered. It hasn't shied away from pointing out the problems as well as the opportunities, but what we hope it has always done is argued from a position that is supported by data. This chapter pulls together the argument and establishes a framework through which leaders can evaluate performance and establish where to focus first as they look to optimize their own strategies.

What is digital strategy?

In our view, simply put, digital strategy is the resource allocation choices a business makes as to how it leverages digital technology in order to deliver the best possible returns to its shareholders. According to the authors of a 2017 article in the *Harvard Business Review*[1] these choices are focused on getting two challenges right: first, managing the impact of disruptive models. These put material pressure on revenue and profit growth both on legacy businesses and then on the insurgents as the legacy organizations fight back with their own digital strategies. The authors estimated that on average this competition has taken out half of the annual revenue growth and one third of the growth in earnings from those that failed to respond to digital. The second challenge is getting the promised returns. The authors suggest that the results of digital transformations are often underwhelming. Following a review of around 2,000 companies worldwide, the article suggests that the average return on digital initiatives in legacy organizations is below 10 per cent – barely above the cost of capital. This average masked a wide range of performance with the top-performing decile of companies achieving revenue growth 8 percentage points higher than the industry average and a return that is 10 times that of the bottom decile. This difference was driven, the research concluded, by how radical the decision to change their activity portfolio and how much they managed to change their position in their industry value chain.

This article, using its extensive research base, went on to describe six digital strategies as follows:

- **Platform play**: An attempt to redefine an industry's value chain so customers and/or suppliers can interact more directly and benefit from network effects. Marketplace is one example of this.

- **New marginal supply**: This is where a business offers an additional product or service not in the mainstream but where additional growth can be sourced – for example, offering assembly services for flat-packed furniture.

- **Digitally enabled products and services**: The use of digital technology to create new products or services – for example, in-car apps that record driving and can positively impact insurance premiums.

- **Re-bundling and customizing**: Thinking about product differently and presenting it bundled or repurposed to create additional income. An example would be a paywall for news content that offers personalization and a subscription opportunity.

- **Digital distribution channels**: The investment in digital distribution channels, in an attempt to make it easier for customers to access their products or services.

- **Cost efficiency**: This is the application of technology (including AI) to look for cost opportunities through automation or scale.

We believe these categories can form the basis of a useful leadership framework to think through digital transformation. The first five sit plumb in the middle of the focus of this book, which has concentrated on commercial digital transformation in search of growth, and whilst operating cost opportunities should not be ignored, as these tend to be defensive investments rather than game changing, we will set them aside from further consideration.

Defining choice

If digital strategy is the process of choosing where to allocate resources, and extensive research suggests that there are broadly five areas within which to make choices that can drive growth, then the next question is how best can leaders go about establishing the fact base that can help them understand which area(s) may offer them the best returns. Internally, all leaders will have some type of business plan process that establishes a required rate of return and, in our experience, in digital choices these have a tendency in hindsight to look more aspirational than realistic – a point echoed by the research published in the *HBR* article described above. There are, however, some key questions that should come ahead of any detailed business plan that may help leaders avoid negative or barely adequate returns:

- Is this 'me-too'?

In digital there is quite a lot of 'me-too' – you have to remember that neither Facebook nor Google were first movers; they learned from earlier entrants and found ways to make themselves more distinctive or more effective. So 'me-too' may not be a bad choice, but without these things it might not be the smartest:

  - an established brand that can move into the market and be seen as a credible, if not advantaged player;
  - an active and positive customer base that would respond quickly to give you momentum and external advocacy;
  - deep pockets that enable you to dominate share of voice in key channels (consideration and conversion) so that the majority of potential customers become quickly familiar with the proposition.

- Does this rely on things untested?

There are two known unknowns in digital choices – the efficacy of new technology and the quality of external partners. Both present larger risks than using technology that is relatively ubiquitous and relies on directly managed resources. Many successful digital propositions have done this well, but without these things, your risk profile will be significantly greater than it need be:

- internal expertise in the technology that you are planning to use and a rigorous process of user acceptance testing before moving into commercial operation;
- internal capabilities in contractor/partner management;
- the highest possible customer service and product quality controls, and effective processes for resolving issues and complaints;
- a rigorous process of merchant selection if you are looking at a marketplace or 'new marginal supply' offer and a strict contract process for dealing with failure.

- **Does this rely on research?**

Research-based propositions should all come with a health warning. Consumer research is about as reliable as political opinion polling: that is, it can be right and it can be spectacularly wrong. We have noticed that when it is wrong, the outcome is normally blamed on the execution, not the research. Yet in our experience, when the outcome isn't as predicted it is more often the case that the research is flawed. The great thing about digital is, as we discussed in Chapter 4, you can quickly and cheaply test your preferred choices before you invest significantly. However compelling the research case, your choice will be more robust if:

- you set up a proof of concept and let it run for sufficient time to learn about customers and the market;
- you establish a target set of commercials that have to be met to make the business case and measure the test against these;
- you use the test to build in-depth customer insight that allows you to confirm, amend or even scrap the proposition – whatever the outcome, you will have learned about the customer in the market and this is invaluable in understanding the opportunities for growth.

- **Can it be replicated?**

If you are innovating in your market or in a new market then this is the other side of the 'me-too' coin. You can't stop replication; indeed, as Oscar Wilde said, imitation is the sincerest form of flattery, but you can make it more difficult and more costly for others to follow. Making sure you have the following in place can reduce the risk of a rapid response that can squeeze margins under those required to add value:

- Protect any IP as much as you can. Don't just protect it in terms of a registered trademark; also protect it from threats such as it leaving through the door with departing employees. Even if you aren't using proprietary code, if how you are using third-party technology distinguishes your proposition from others then protect this as much as you can.

- Protect the talent you use to create and launch it. Many companies don't think through how they can use longer notice periods, long-term incentives and other mechanisms that make it more difficult for others to poach key people.
- Ensure all the marketing and sales execution highlights those aspects most difficult to replicate (for example, that could be your brand, your reach or scale, or the proprietary technology used to deliver the outcome).
- Ensure that you have built the whole e-commerce system to support it and have active plans in place to drive customer advocacy.

- **Do we understand the response?**

Newton's third law applies to commerce just as much as to the physical world: for every action there is an equal and opposite reaction. That is, it nearly applies: if you are smart, your choice will make it difficult, at least initially, for the opposition to react equally. The final question in looking at your options is: have we mapped the potential opposite reactions? You are more likely to succeed against your goals if you have:

- factored in the likely competitive responses and their impact on your own plans and goals;
- developed response options for your business and mapped out potential choices (for example, when and how do we decide to increase marketing spend to counter any reaction?);
- identified activities that are more difficult to respond to quickly or easily.

A simple 'ready-reckoner' as you think through your choices would be to use these questions as a checklist and mark your answers out of 5, where 1 is 'we haven't thought about this' and 5 is 'we have thought about it and I am confident that our thinking is robust and we can move forward to put together a detailed business and implementation plan'. Scores of 3 or under indicate areas where you or those proposing the solution need to do some more hard thinking. If a potential strategic choice is scoring 3 or under in the majority of these categories then it may well indicate that it is less attractive than others.

Think whole system, not expert solution

Digital strategy requires whole system thinking. Without this, choices will inevitably risk vicious circles as the customer experience fails to deliver. The whole system model we introduced in Chapter 7 can act as a template for any choices made in any of the five strategy categories above. At a strategic level they can be used to:

- map the customer journey through each quadrant:
  - Who are the target customers and how will you locate them? How big is the shopper market for what you are thinking of offering?
  - What wants and needs will the proposition meet and how is this different from other propositions already available? How will you communicate this?
  - Once engaged what does a customer in the market need to know in order to transact (become a lead or buy a product or service)?
  - How will you fulfil and how will this fulfilment help build customer loyalty?
  - Once you have a lead or a customer, what happens next?
  - Once you have a customer, how will you encourage endorsement and referral?
  - How will you communicate and engage with known customers such that you can retain their commitment and build loyalty?
  - How do you make sure you comply with local data protection and privacy requirements in your engagements with customers?
  - How does this fit into any wider digital transformation activity – will it conflict or complement? Can you use any aspect of this to help improve the potential impact?

- understand the organization requirements necessary to deliver successfully:
  - How will you resource this choice? What can you use from partners and what do you have to employ to be successful?
  - What processes will you need to introduce or amend in order to deliver this? How will they work together in an integrated way?
  - How will you measure success?
  - Do you have the right capability mix?
  - Do you have the right performance software and how well are you using it today?
  - How do you want people to work together to make this successful and what do you need to do to make sure this happens?

- build a test and learn programme to test early thinking:
  - How can you test this simply and quickly? (For example, can you use a micro site with limited offer and functionality to sense check your understanding of the market?)
  - How can you attract traffic from your target customer segment to engage with the test proposition?
  - How do you ensure you can build insight from every stage in this engagement?
  - What measures of success can you establish and for how long do you need to run a test to generate sufficient learning to improve the quality of your decision-making around this choice?

This approach will ensure that you are acting on an understanding of the insight on which the choice is being proposed, the full system solution that will be required to deliver successfully, the organization implications and what has to change to ensure the greatest chance of success, and the results of any testing that you can do in the market with real shoppers, shopping in real time. Doing this ensures that you have tested any 'expert' thinking and validated through data and insight any opinion, assertion or expertise that is often associated with digital strategy decisions. Putting this thinking through the process of the five choice questions above will help you establish how credible the choice is and the degree of challenge required to ensure that you are successful in generating a credible return on investment.

At the end, this is a leadership challenge

Digital strategy is the leadership of transformation. Strategy fails when leadership fails. Effective leadership doesn't just require you to make informed choices about where to allocate your resources to deliver growth: it requires you to lead the process of how to turn intention into action, ensure a data-driven and insight-informed implementation plan and then make sure you have an organization fit for purpose in terms of capability, capacity and culture. Even that is probably insufficient. You have to make sure that the plan happens – and it will never happen as planned so this is a constant process of engagement, review, adjustment and re-planning.

There is no easy route to deliver effective leadership. It is hard work. But it doesn't need to be an impossible undertaking. Having a clear framework through which you engage with a digital business helps you think strategically and, just as importantly, helps others in the team work in a coherent and collaborative manner on a shared understanding. Establishing standards for processes, behaviour, activity practice and measurement all help leaders be more effective in optimizing digital strategy. After all, the likeliest biggest barrier to success in digital isn't technology, it's the organization – and reducing the possibility of shooting yourself in the foot is an action completely within your own control.

Reference

1 https://hbr.org/2017/07/6-digital-strategies-and-why-some-work-better-than-others [accessed 8 May 2018]

INDEX

Note: Page numbers in *italics* indicate figures or tables. References are indexed as such.